Y0-BUU-667

THE BOOK SHOP
Leduc -- Ph. 986-8106
Used Books, Mags & Comics

# Temperature Conversion Table

TEMPERATURE

| American Oven Temperature Terms | Degrees Fahrenheit | Degrees Centigrade (Celsius) |
|---|---|---|
| | 160 | 71 |
| | 170 | 77 |
| | 200 | 93 |
| | 212 | 100 |
| Very Slow . . . . . . . . . . | 225 | 107 |
| | 230 | 110 |
| | 250 | 121 |
| Slow . . . . . . . . . . . . . | 275 | 135 |
| | 300 | 149 |
| | 302 | 150 |
| | 320 | 160 |
| Moderately Slow. . . . . | 325 | 163 |
| Moderate . . . . . . . . . . | 350 | 177 |
| | 356 | 180 |
| | 375 | 190 |
| | 390 | 200 |
| Hot . . . . . . . . . . . . . . | 400 | 205 |
| | 425 | 218 |
| | 428 | 220 |
| | 437 | 225 |
| | 450 | 232 |
| Very Hot . . . . . . . . . . . | 475 | 246 |
| | 500 | 260 |
| | 525 | 274 |
| Broil. . . . . . . . . . . . . . | 550 | 288 |

# WOMAN'S DAY ENCYCLOPEDIA OF COOKERY

**1979 Edition**
**For WOMAN'S DAY**

**JEANNE VOLTZ,** *Food Editor*

**For FUNK & WAGNALLS, INC.**

*Supervising Editor*—**NORMA H. DICKEY**
*Production Editor*—**KATHIE L. ATTLEE**
*Production Executive*—**EDWARD HAAS**
*Editorial Staff*—**DONNA L. AMOS, JUNE V. ROOK**
*Art Director*—**MURRAY KESHNER**
*Layout Artists*—**HERBERT ASCHER, MARTIN GORDON,
ERLA SIGURDARDOTTIR**

**Special Project Staff:**

*Contributing Editors*—**INEZ M. KRECH, JAMES W. TRAGER**

**Original Edition**

Prepared and edited by the Editors of WOMAN'S DAY
**GLENNA MCGINNIS,** *Food Editor*

**Special Project Staff:**

*Editor*—**NIKA STANDEN HAZELTON**
*Associates*—**L. GERALDINE MARSTELLER, HELEN FEINGOLD,
SUSAN J. KNOX**

**First Revised Edition**

**Special Project Staff:**
*Editor*—**MARIE ROBERSON HAMM**
*Associate Editor*—**ISABEL CORNELL**

*Copyright © 1966, 1973, 1979 by CBS Publications,
the Consumer Publishing Division of CBS, Inc.,
All Rights Reserved.
Distributed by Funk & Wagnalls, Inc.*

# Volume 1 Highlights

## Abalone–Avocado

Arranged alphabetically, the articles in this volume fall between
the two words listed above. Among the interesting and informative entries
found in this volume, several sections are worthy of special attention.
We have listed these below for your convenience.

# How to use the Woman's Day Encyclopedia of Cookery

The twenty-two volumes of the Woman's Day Encyclopedia contain a wealth of alphabetically arranged information. If you wish to prepare Apple Pie, look under Apple in volume 1. But to find all of the information in all of the volumes, you should use the twenty-third volume, the Index. Composed of five separate indexes, volume 23 includes: meal and menu planning; information on nutrition and diet; techniques of cookery and equipment use; a listing by author; and an alphabetical listing by ingredients.

This Encyclopedia contains many individual entries that supplement one another. Meal and Menu Planning, for instance, is treated throughout the Encyclopedia in many different entries. The first index in volume 23 collects these entries and lists volume and page numbers for such diverse items as Busy Day Dinners and Low Cost Meals. How to entertain or cook in different national styles will be simplified by consulting such items as Parties or Mexican Cookery. If you want to cook for a crowd or make up a Christmas menu, this index shows you where to find Quantity Cooking and three separate styles of Christmas meals.

If you are learning to cook or beginning to plan diets for a family, two other indexes offer assistance. The Encyclopedia entries that contain information on nutrition and diet are listed in one index, and techniques of cookery and equipment are listed in the other. If you want to know which foods are necessary in your child's diet or how to cut down on cholesterol, see the second index. If you want to find out which pan is appropriate for a layer cake, see Bake in the third index.

The fourth index in volume 23 is a listing by author of all the special articles in the Encyclopedia. Here you will find titles and location of articles by noted cookbook authors and food and health authorities.

A major part of volume 23 is the listing of all the recipes contained in the Encyclopedia, arranged alphabetically by main ingredient and by one or more menu categories. Thus, an Abalone Chowder recipe in volume 1 is listed in this Index under ABALONE and under SOUPS. A Crabmeat Dip recipe appears under CRABS, under DIPS, APPETIZER, and under APPETIZERS.

These volumes offer helpful advice on cooking, meal planning, food budgeting, and entertaining. Brimming with tempting recipes, mouthwatering photos, and interesting tid-bits about the origin and history of some of the ingredients, the Woman's Day Encyclopedia of Cookery is indeed a browsing library for food lovers.

**ABALONE**—This red or pink mollusk or shellfish is found in the Pacific Ocean off the coast of California. The beautiful, single, ear-shaped shell is about six to seven inches long and lined with mother-of-pearl which is used to make buttons. The muscle of the shell is the edible part of the abalone and has a delicious clamlike flavor. It is a great delicacy.

Fresh, canned, and dried abalone is widely used in Oriental cooking.

***Availability***—In the United States, the fresh shellfish is limited to California. The law prohibits its shipment fresh to other parts of the country.

***Purchasing Guide***—Plan about 3 servings per pound.

***Nutritive Food Values***—Good source of protein; fair source of iron and calcium.

***Caloric Values***—Fresh, 3½ ounces, raw = 98 calories. Canned, 3½ ounces = 80 calories.

***Basic Preparation***—Fresh abalone needs tenderizing before cooking. The meat should be cut into thin slices or strips and pounded with a mallet or rolling pin. Abalone must never be overcooked or it will become tough. Properly prepared, it makes an outstanding dish.

## ABALONE CHOWDER

  4  slices of bacon, diced
  6  slices of abalone, pounded thin and diced
  1  medium potato, peeled and diced
  1  medium onion, peeled and minced
1½  cups hot water
  3  cups milk or 2 cups milk and 1 cup light cream, heated
  1  tablespoon butter
     Salt and pepper

Cook bacon until golden in a 2-quart saucepan. Drain off all but 2 tablespoons of bacon fat from pan. Add abalone, potato, and onion. Sauté until golden brown. Add hot water and simmer until abalone and potato are tender. Add heated milk and butter and blend thoroughly. Season to taste. Serve very hot. Makes 4 to 6 servings.

## ABALONE SAUTÉ

Use abalone sliced thin and tenderized. Sauté in hot butter in skillet for about 1 minute, turning once. Season with salt and pepper to taste.

# ACORN SQUASH

**ACORN SQUASH**—A fall and winter vegetable that belongs to the gourd family. It has a dark-green rind, yellow-orange flesh, and many seeds. Acorn squash can grow as large as eight inches long and five inches across. Its flavor is on the sweet side.

Acorn squash is a native American vegetable, and was unknown in Europe. The first settlers found the Indians enjoying squash; in fact, the word squash comes from the Massachusetts Indian word *asquash* which means literally "eaten green."

**Availability**—Late summer through winter, but it is at its plentiful best in the late fall.

**Purchasing Guide**—It should seem heavy for its size and have a hard dark-green shiny rind, free from cuts and bruises, with distinct ridges. It may have some orange spots, but avoid those with large areas of orange; this usually indicates over-maturity.
3 pounds = 3½ cups mashed.

**Storage**—Cool, dry, well-ventilated place. If a large number is being stored, arrange squash so they do not touch and air can circulate between them. They can be stored for a few months, but they rapidly lose their quality.
Refrigerator shelf: 2 to 4 months.
Refrigerator frozen-food compartment, prepared for freezing: 1 year
Freezer, prepared for freezing: 2 years

**Nutritive Food Values**—Excellent source of vitamin A; fair source of vitamin C, riboflavin, and iron.
1 cup baked, mashed = 130 calories

**Basic Preparation**—Before cooking, wash well to remove wax coating. Cut into halves or quarters, lengthwise between ribs, using a heavy butcher knife or cleaver. Scrape out seeds and fiber. Allow one half or one quarter for each serving.
**To Bake**—Put halves, cut side down, in baking pan with ½ inch of boiling water. Bake in preheated hot oven (400°F.) for 40 to 50 minutes, or until tender. Turn halves cut side up and prick with fork; season with salt, pepper, and butter. Add a little brown sugar or a little minced onion, if desired. Or season with a pich of nutmeg, mace, or ginger. Continue baking until butter and sugar melt. To oven-steam, arrange quarters cut side up, add butter and seasonings and cover pan for baking.
**To Mash**—Prepare and bake as directed above. When tender cool slightly and scrape out pulp. Mash pulp, using a potato masher, electric mixer, or blender. Season to taste with salt, butter, and brown sugar if you wish, or add a little nutmeg, mace, or ginger to taste. Mashed cooked acorn squash may be seasoned and served like sweet potatoes. It may also be used in pie recipes calling for cooked mashed pumpkin.

Acorn squash may also be peeled and the pulp cubed and boiled. However, baking is the easier method since the rind is hard to cut away.
**To Freeze, Baked**—Bake as descirbed above, but for about 30 minutes only. Omit seasoning. Cool completely. Put halves or quarters in plastic bags, making sure pieces overlap to prevent air spaces, or freezer-wrap in foil. Seal tightly.

To use, defrost slightly, season, and bake until hot.
**To Freeze, Mashed**—Prepare as for mashed squash but omit the seasoning. Cool quickly and pack in freezer containers, leaving 1-inch headspace. To use, defrost slightly, heat in top part of double boiler, and season to taste.

Sausage—Stuffed Acorn Squash

Steamed Acorn Squash

## SAUSAGE-STUFFED ACORN SQUASH

2 acorn squash
1 pound bulk pork sausage
1 small onion, grated
1½ cups soft bread crumbs
1 teaspoon salt
⅛ teaspoon pepper

Cut acorn squash into halves and remove seeds. Oven-steam squash, cut side down, in covered baking pan with ½ inch of boiling water in preheated hot oven (400°F.) until tender. Meanwhile, mash sausage with fork and fry until cooked but not brown. Drain off fat. Add onion, bread crumbs, and salt and pepper to sausage. Fill centers of squash halves with mixture. Reduce oven heat to moderate (350°F.) and bake uncovered for about 30 minutes longer. Makes 4 servings.

## BAKED ACORN SQUASH SUPREME

2 acorn squash
  Melted butter
½ cup heavy cream
½ cup maple syrup

Cut acorn squash into halves, remove seeds, and put squash, cut side up, in greased baking dish. Prick with fork. Brush inside of each half with melted butter. Mix cream and maple syrup and fill each squash cavity about half full of the mixture. Bake uncovered, in preheated moderate oven (350°F.) 1 hour. Makes 4 servings.

## STEAMED ACORN SQUASH

Slice acorn squash about 1 inch thick. Put into large skillet with small amount of water. Steam, covered, until tender. Drain if water has not all evaporated. Pour melted butter over squash and sprinkle with brown sugar. Heat a few minutes longer to glaze squash.

# ADDITIVES—Substances added to foods either intentionally or unintentionally. Intentional additives serve four basic purposes: 1. to enhance nutritive values; 2. to maintain freshness and to preserve the food for later use; 3. to improve aroma, flavor, color and texture; and 4. to assist in processing the food. Unintentional additives may be residues of various chemicals or materials used in processing the food, ingredients of the packaging materials, and other unintended and accidental materials.

The use of additives is significant in the development of mankind's foods. Early man ate whatever he could find, subsisting on the seeds, fruit, and berries he gathered and on the animals or fish he could kill. Sometimes he feasted; at other periods he went hungry. As civilization progressed man learned to domesticate certain animals and to grow his own food: he evolved from a hunter and food-gatherer to a food-producer. Today's society demands what modern food technology makes possible, a year-round supply of all kinds of food, safe, wholesome, and consistent in quality and texture. In addition, the homemaker wants foods that are ready to serve or that require a minimum or preparation. This has led to many developments in food processing and preservation. Modern foods are preserved by dehydration, smoking, freezing, freeze-drying, canning, irradiation, and pickling, are packed in a variety of containers and materials, and are often precooked.

To maintain quality, stability, nutritive value, and consumer appeal, a number of chemical substances are used. These are food additives. They serve a variety of functions. As noted above, some are used as seasonings or to accentuate flavor; some preserve or improve color; others maintain the quality, texture, and keeping qualities and prevent staling and oxidation or the development of off-flavors. Other additives are used to increase the nutritive value by enriching bread and flour with vitamins (riboflavin, thiamine, and niacin) and minerals (iron) or by fortifying milk with vitamin D, margarine with vitamin A, salt with iodine, juices with vitamin C, and breakfast cereals with minerals and vitamins. The kind and amount of food additives used in the United States are regulated by the Food and Drug Administration of the United States Department of Health, Education, and Welfare. Regulations are based on federal laws and recommendations of such advisory bodies as the Food Protection Committee of the National Academy of Science-National Research Council. The control of food additives in Canada is the responsibility of the Food and Drug Directorate of the Department of National Health and Welfare, which enforces the appropriate provisions of the Canadian Food and Drugs Act.

**AGAPE**—This Greek word means "love." It was used to describe the charity feasts of the ancient Christians, when the rich contributed liberally to feeding the poor in the churches. During more recent times, religious sects such as the Wesleyans and Moravians have tried to revive this custom on a much simplified and almost symbolical basis.

**AGAR**—A vegetable gelatin made from various kinds of algae or seaweed. The algae are collected, bleached, and dried. Then the gelatin substance is extracted with water and made into flakes, granules, powder, or strips which are brittle when dry. It is also called Chinese or Japanese gelatin.

Agar was used as a jellying agent in home-cooking before commercial gelatin was widely available. It is still used in the Orient in the preparation of soups and jellies, and at home as a thickening agent; in the commercial manufacture of jams, jellies, ice creams, and mayonnaise. In medicine, it is essential in microbiology as a culture medium.

**AÏOLI or AÏLLOLI**—This French word comes from *ail*, meaning "garlic," and defines a sauce of the consistency of mayonnaise, but with plenty of garlic in it. *Aïoli* is usually served with boiled fish; it is also good with cold meats, cooked vegetables, and salads. *Aïoli* is a specialty of Provence, a southern province of France bordering on the Mediterranean, which is famous for its olive oil and well-seasoned hearty foods made with oil.

### AÏOLI

    4 large or 8 small garlic cloves
    1 egg yolk
    ¼ teaspoon salt
    1 cup olive oil
      Juice of 1 lemon

Peel garlic cloves. Mash in mortar or garlic press, or mince fine and then mash with tip of knife. Combine garlic with egg yolk and salt. Stir in, drop by drop, 3 tablespoons of olive oil. Stir in lemon juice, Stir in remaining oil, a little at a time, until sauce is thick. Makes about 1 cup.

**AKVAVIT or AQUAVIT**—The word comes from the Latin and means "water of life." *Akvavit* is its Scandinavian spelling. It is a colorless or light-yellow spirit. It is usually distilled from grains such as barley, or from potatoes, and is lightly flavored with caraway. The "water of life" is a favorite drink of the Scandinavians and northern Germans, who drink it in tiny glasses, followed by a beer chaser. In these countries, *akvavit* is always taken with food. The most famous *akvavit* comes from Aalborg in Denmark.

**À LA**—This French term means literally "in the manner of." It is usually followed by the name of the person who first created the dish (Waldorf Salad à la Oscar), or by the name of the person for whom it was created (Chicken à la King), or by the name of the place where the dish originated (Eggs à la Russe), or by one of the main ingredients in the dish (Macaroni à la Béchamel).

**À LA CARTE**—The literal translation of this French term is "in the manner of the bill of fare." *A la carte* is used to describe a meal in which each dish selected is paid for separately. The opposite term is *table d'hôte,* another French term, which means "the host's table." Here, one fixed price covers the cost of the whole meal.

**À LA GRECQUE**—This is a French culinary definition, meaning "in the Greek manner." The term describes vegetables cooked in a mixture of oil and vinegar, or lemon juice, with seasonings added. The vegetables are served cold or chilled. They make excellent appetizers or salads.

Artichokes, asparagus, celery hearts or stalks, cauliflowerets, cucumbers, mushroom caps, tiny white onions, whole spring onions, green and Lima beans, and zucchini squash can be cooked *à la grecque* with fine results. Vegetables are prepared for cooking in the usual manner and cut into bite-sized pieces. Frozen vegetables can be used and need not be defrosted before cooking.

### BASIC À LA GRECQUE RECIPE FOR VEGETABLES

    3 cups water
      Juice of 2 lemons or 2 tablespoons cider vinegar
    ½ cup olive oil
    ½ teaspoon salt
      Peppercorns
    1 celery stalk, minced
    ½ teaspoon crumbled dried thyme or 1 sprig fresh
      thyme
    1 bay leaf

Combine all ingredients in saucepan. Simmer, covered, for 5 minutes. Pour boiling mixture over vegetable that is to be cooked. Cook until vegetable is just tender. Cool in liquid. Drain reserving liquid and chill vegetable. Makes about 3½ cups liquid.

Although *à la grecque* vegetables may be served separately or in a mixed salad, it is essential to cook each vegetable by itself, since cooking times differ. The *à la grecque* liquid may be used several times for vegetables with a related flavor.

**À LA KING**—A plain or rich white sauce that should contain any one or combinations of these vegetables: sliced mushrooms, chopped green peppers, chopped or sliced pimientos. The sauce names the dish: chicken à la king, ham à la king, etc. A la king sauce is most frequently used for chicken cooked and diced, but it is equally well suited for turkey, tuna, ham, hard-cooked eggs, shrimp, or lobster. A la king sauce is an excellent food stretcher and it transforms leftovers into appetizing dishes.

A la king dishes may be served on toast, in patty shells, on rice, noodles, spaghetti or mashed potatoes, or on other foods that need a sauce or a dressing.

## HAM OR SHRIMP À LA KING

   3 tablespoons chopped green pepper
1½ tablespoons chopped pimiento
  ¼ cup butter
  ½ cup drained canned sliced mushrooms
1½ tablespoons all-purpose flour
1½ cups light cream
  2 cups diced cooked ham or cooked shelled deveined shrimps
  2 egg yolks
  ¼ to ½ teaspoon salt
    Dash of paprika
  2 tablespoons sherry (optional)

Sauté green pepper and pimiento in butter in a skillet over low heat for 5 minutes. Add mushrooms and sauté for 1 minute longer. Remove vegetables and reserve. Stir flour into pan liquid. Gradually stir in cream and cook until smooth and thick, stirring constantly. Stir reserved vegetables into cream sauce. Trim ham free of all fat before measuring. Add ham (or shrimps, chopped coarsely if very large) to skillet mixture. Cook over low heat for 2 minutes, stirring constantly. Beat egg yolks slightly; stir some of hot sauce into them. Blend well. Stir egg mixture into remaining hot sauce. Season to taste with salt and paprika. Cook for 1 minute longer over low heat, stirring constantly. Remove from heat and stir in sherry, if desired. Serve on rice, noodles, or in heated patty shells. Makes 4 to 6 servings.

**Variation**—Prepare recipe as above but substitute 4 quartered hard-cooked eggs, or one 1-pound can drained and flaked red salmon for the diced cooked ham.

# À LA MODE—In French, this means literally "in the fashion of." In cookery, à la mode has two completely different meanings. One is American, the other French. In American usage, à la mode describes cake, pie, pudding, or any other dessert topped with a scoop of ice cream, such as apple pie à la mode.

In French cooking, à la mode describes a beef pot roast larded with fat, braised with vegetables, and simmered in a sauce, such as *boeuf à la mode.*

## ICE CREAM À LA MODE

Blend together 1 cup heavy cream, 2 tablespoons powdered chocolate drink mix, 2 tablespoons confectioners' sugar and ½ teaspoon vanilla. Chill. Whip until stiff and serve over chocolate or vanilla ice cream. Enough for 8 servings.

## PEACH PIE À LA MODE

Combine 1 cup heavy cream with 3 tablespoons brown sugar. Chill thoroughly, whip until stiff. Spoon over wedges of peach pie. Softened vanilla or peach ice cream may also be used.

## STRAWBERRIES À LA MODE

Stud a large bowl of vanilla ice cream with whole fresh strawberries dipped into sugar. When ice cream has softened slightly, spoon into individual dishes. Also good with fresh raspberries or sliced peaches.

## MELON À LA MODE

For each serving, fill a chilled cantaloupe or honeydew half with two or more contrasting flavors of ice cream, or ice cream and sherbet or berries.

## BOEUF À LA MODE

    One 4-pound boneless beef round, chuck, or other cut suitable for a pot roast
  3 slices of bacon or salt pork
  1 tablespoon butter
  1 cup hot water
  2 cups dry white wine or hot beef bouillon (wine is preferable)
    Salt and pepper
  1 bay leaf
  1 parsley sprig
  ⅛ teaspoon crumbled dried thyme
  ⅛ teaspoon ground nutmeg
  1 cracked veal knuckle
    (ask butcher for this in advance)
  2 tablespoons brandy (optional)
  4 carrots, scraped and cut into pieces
  3 whole cloves
  6 small white onions, peeled

Trim beef to remove all fat. Cut bacon or salt pork into long thin strips. Push bacon strips through meat with larding needle, or with a thin knitting needle. Heat butter in heavy Dutch oven or deep casserole. Brown meat in it on all sides. Add hot water, wine, and seasonings and top with veal knuckle. Simmer, covered, over very low heat for about 2 hours. Add brandy and carrots. Stick cloves into one onion. Add onions to meat. Return to low heat. Simmer, covered, for another 1½ hours, or until meat is tender. Remove veal knuckle and discard cloves and bay leaf. The sauce should be brown and rich. If too liquid, remove meat to hot platter and keep hot. Heat sauce to boiling point and cook for 2 to 5 minutes, or until sauce has desired consistency, stirring constantly, add more salt and pepper if desired. Slice meat and strain sauce over it, or serve sauce separately. Serve with boiled potatoes, noodles, or plain rice, and a green salad. Serve it hot one day and cold the next. When cold, the sauce will have jellied. Makes about 8 servings.

# ALBACORE

**ALBACORE**— A fish which belongs to the tuna family. Albacore has the true white meat of all tuna and is used for the finest canned tuna and the most delicate dishes. Canned tuna labeled all white meat, solid pack, is albacore. Fresh albacore, found in some fish markets in areas where tuna is caught, makes for excellent eating.

**Availability**—Albacore is available fresh, or canned in oil or water pack. It can be used in all recipes calling for tuna.

**Purchasing Guide**—For fresh albacore steaks, allow 2 to 3 servings per pound. A 6 to 7 oz. can will make 2 to 3 servings.

**Storage**—Fresh, refrigerator shelf: 1 to 2 days
Fresh, refrigerator frozen-food compartment, prepared for freezing: 2 to 3 weeks
Fresh, freezer, prepared for freezing: 1 year
Canned, kitchen shelf: 2½ years
Canned, refrigerator shelf, opened but covered: 1 to 2 days

**Nutritive Food Values**—Excellent source of protein; small amounts of calcium, phosphorus, and iron.
Fresh, cooked, ½ cup = 66 calories
Canned and packed in water, 7 oz. can = 254 calories
Canned and packed in oil, 3 oz. drained solids = 170 calories

Albacore Divan

## ALBACORE DIVAN

2 packages (10 ounces each) frozen broccoli, cooked
2 cans (7 ounces each) albacore canned in oil
⅓ cup all-purpose flour
1 teaspoon salt
2 cups milk
⅓ cup grated Parmesan cheese
1 tablespoon fresh lemon juice
1 tablespoon fine dry bread crumbs

Put broccoli in greased shallow baking dish. Drain oil from fish into saucepan. Stir in flour and salt. Add milk and cook until thickened, stirring. Remove from heat and add cheese and lemon juice. Break tuna into chunks and arrange over broccoli. Cover with cheese sauce. Sprinkle with bread crumbs. Bake in preheated moderate oven (375°F.) for about 20 minutes, until hot and bubbly. Makes 6 servings.

## PICKLED ALBACORE

2 cans (7 ounces each) albacore
1 large red onion, thinly sliced
2 green peppers, sliced
2 oranges, halved and sliced
¼ cup olive oil
½ cup fresh lemon juice
1 cup fresh orange juice
2 bay leaves
½ teaspoon crumbled oregano
¼ teaspoon salt
   Salad greens

Break albacore into large pieces. Cover with slices of onion, green pepper, and orange. Combine remaining ingredients except greens, and pour over fish. Refrigerate for several hours. Garnish with greens. Makes 4 to 6 servings as a main dish, or 8 servings as a side salad.

Pickled Albacore

# ALCOHOL

**ALCOHOL**—Only the alcohol used in beverages needs to concern us here, although there are other varieties used in industry. Alcohol in its pure form is a transparent colorless strong liquid, volatile and very inflammable. It is distilled from a great variety of fruits and grains that contain either natural sugar or substances that can be transformed into sugar. By the addition of natural or artificial yeast strains and mineral compounds, the sugar is changed by the process of fermentation into alcohol and other by-products which are used commercially. This is ethyl alcohol, commonly known as grain or wine alcohol. It is found in beer, whiskies, wines, brandies, liqueurs, and rum. Alcohol must not be regarded as a single substance; failure to distinguish between the various alcohols can be fatal. Methyl or wood alcohol, which is very different from the grain or ethyl alcohol we drink, is the most frequently encountered poisonous alcohol. It should not be drunk or inhaled. The rule is: When in doubt about the origin of an alcohol or alcoholic drink, do not touch it.

# AL DENTE

**AL DENTE**—Literally, this Italian term means "to the tooth." It is used to describe foods cooked so that they are still firm to the bite and taste or, in other words, not overcooked. Pasta, rice, and some vegetables are cooked al dente.

# ALE

**ALE**—Ale is a fermented malt beverage; beer is its brother. Ale, like beer, is brewed from malt, cereals, and hops, but the method of brewing ale is different from that of brewing beer. Ale is "top fermented," that is, during fermentation at a higher temperature, its yeast rises to the top. The result is a brew with a more pronounced hop flavor than that found in beer.

Porter and stout are two well-known varieties of ale, both sweeter and darker than the others. Stout has a fuller hop flavor than porter and a slightly burnt taste. Both are more popular in Great Britain than in America.

The word "ale" comes from the Saxon *eale*. Since Saxon days, ale has been a household beverage in all northern European countries, where grapes for wine won't grow. It was drunk by old and young instead of water, which was then not safe. It has been brewed both at home and commercially. Throughout the ages, ale has inspired much splendid verse and prose. Shakespeare, in *The Winter's Tale,* says: "For a quart of ale is a dish for a king." The undergraduates of Vassar College in New York still acknowledge their debt to Matthew Vassar, founder of the college and a brewer, with:

> And so for you, old V.C.,
> our love shall never fail.
> Full well we know that all we owe
> to Matthew Vassar's ale!

Ale should be served cold, but not quite as cold as beer, at a temperature between 40° and 50°F. The glasses should be spotlessly clean and washed with a detergent so that not a trace of grease appears. Grease is the natural enemy of ale and beer, since it kills the foam.

Ale and beer are both used successfully in cooking. The recipes for ale and beer are interchangeable, but cheese and pork dishes taste better made with ale.

*Caloric Values*
About 1 cup = 100 calories

## KNACKWURST IN ALE

    4 knackwurst
    ½ cup ale
    1 tablespoon vinegar
    ½ teaspoon sugar

Simmer knackwurst in ale in covered saucepan over low heat for 15 minutes. Heat shallow heatproof serving dish and place knackwurst in it. Keep hot. Boil pan liquid and reduce it to ¼ cup. Stir in vinegar and sugar. Pour over hot knackwurst. Serve with mashed potatoes and red cabbage or hot sauerkraut sprinkled with caraway seeds. Makes 4 servings.

## WELSH RABBIT

    1 teaspoon Worcestershire
    ½ teaspoon powdered mustard
      Dash of paprika
    ½ cup ale
    1 pound natural sharp Cheddar cheese, shredded
      Hot toast

Combine Worcestershire, mustard, and paprika in a skillet. Add ale and let stand over very low heat until ale is heated through. Stir in cheese and continue to stir until cheese has melted. Do not overheat. Serve immediately over hot toast on heated plates. Makes 4 to 6 servings.

# ALEWIFE

**ALEWIFE**—This is an inexpensive edible fish belonging to the herring family. The origin of the name is obscure, although it may derive from the fact that alewife has a relatively big belly: The fish is a native of the Atlantic Ocean from Nova Scotia to the Carolinas, and a southern species called Blueback is found as far south as Florida. The fish runs in the spring. Alewives grow to about ten inches in length and to about a half pound in weight. The fish is rather bony, but the flavor is pleasant and less oily than that of shad.

Most alewives are salted down for home consumption and export. Some of the fish is smoked, and the roe is sometimes canned. Fresh alewives are limited to markets in localities where the fish is caught. They can be cooked like any fresh herring. Salted alewives can be used in place of salt herring or mackerel. They should be freshened in cold water before cooking. Be sure to wipe the fish dry before using.

*Caloric Values*
Fresh, 3½ ounces = 127 calories
Canned, 3½ ounces, fish and liquid = 141 calories

## ALEWIVES BAKED WITH LEMON

    4 alewives, salted in brine
    ¼ cup butter or margarine, melted
      Juice of 3 lemons

Soak alewives in cold water for at least 3 hours. Drain and wipe dry. Carefully split fish open. Place skin side down, in well-greased shallow baking dish. Combine butter and lemon juice. Spoon half of mixture evenly over fish. Bake fish in preheated moderate oven (350°F.) for 7 minutes. Spoon remaining butter-lemon mixture evenly over fish and bake for 5 minutes longer. Serve very hot with plain boiled potato, garnished with parsley. Makes 4 servings.

# ALLEMANDE—This is a classic French sauce, golden yellow in color, creamy in consistency, with excellent flavor. It is used with boiled or poached fish, meats, or vegetables. The main ingredient is *velouté* sauce (a sauce made with chicken, veal, or fish stock instead of milk or cream), to which egg yolks, cream and lemon juice are added. *Allemande* sauce is also known as *sauce blonde* or *sauce parisienne*. In spite of its name which means "German," it has nothing to do with Germany or things German.

## SAUCE ALLEMANDE

3 tablespoons butter
2 tablespoons flour
2 cups hot fish, veal, chicken, or clear vegetable stock
  Salt and pepper
¾ cup strong chicken stock, heated
2 egg yolks, slightly beaten
2 tablespoons heavy cream
1 tablespoon fresh lemon juice

Melt 2 tablespoons butter in top part of double boiler. Stir in flour and blend thoroughly. Gradually stir in hot stock. Cook, covered, over simmering, not boiling, water for 30 to 45 minutes, stirring occasionally. Season with salt and pepper to taste. Strain through a fine sieve into a saucepan. Stir additional hot chicken stock into sauce. Blend thoroughly. Over medium heat, let sauce cook down to two thirds of its original volume, stirring constantly. Remove from heat. Beat egg yolks with cream. Gradually stir hot sauce into egg yolk mixture. Return sauce to saucepan. Reheat over low heat, but do not boil. Just before serving stir in lemon juice and remaining 1 tablespoon butter, softened. Stir over low heat until butter is melted. Makes about 1⅔ cups sauce.

**Note:** ¼ cup sautéed thinly sliced mushrooms may be added to sauce.

# ALLSPICE (Pimenta dioica; often called Pimenta officinalis)—Jamaica pepper is another name for the dried unripe fruit of a twenty- to forty-foot tree *(Pimenta dioica)* that is related to the myrtle family. The tree is native to the West Indies and is grown in all of the American tropics, but it is so common to Jamaica that the island practically has a monopoly on the spice. The berries are picked green and dried in the sun. This wrinkles them, turns them a reddish brown, and intensifies their aroma.

In spite of the name, allspice is *not* a combination of spices but one spice only; it is so called because its flavor resembles a combination of clove, cinnamon, and nutmeg.

Allspice has a great many uses and can be bought both as dried whole berries or finely ground. It is frequently used in pickling and in the preparation of relishes and meats, especially pot roast; also in baking and in stewed and preserved fruits, mincemeat, and tomato-flavored dishes. It combines well with other spices.

## SPICY SWISS STEAK

1½ teaspoons salt
½ teaspoon ground allspice
¼ teaspoon pepper
2 pounds beef round steak about 1 inch thick
⅓ cup all-purpose flour
3 tablespoons shortening or salad oil
1 medium onion, minced
3 cups chopped peeled tomatoes, fresh or canned

Rub salt, allspice, and pepper well into steak. Dredge meat with flour. Pound in flour with edge of a plate or mallet. Heat shortening in heavy casserole. Brown meat quickly in hot fat on both sides. Add onion and tomatoes. Cover and bake in preheated moderate oven (350°F.) for about 1½ hours, or until meat is tender. Check occasionally for moisture. If necessary add a little hot water, or tomato to prevent sticking. Makes about 6 servings.

## SWEET POTATOES WITH ALLSPICE

1 can (1 pound, 7 ounces) syrup-packed sweet potatoes
¼ cup honey
1 teaspoon grated lemon rind
½ teaspoon ground allspice
2 tablespoons butter

Drain sweet potatoes and reserve liquid. Arrange pieces of sweet potato in greased shallow baking dish. Combine sweet potato liquid with honey, lemon rind, and allspice. Spoon mixture evenly over sweet potatoes. Dot with butter. Bake, uncovered, in preheated moderate oven (375°F.) for about 25 minutes, or until sweet potatoes are well glazed. Makes 4 servings.

## SPICY ORANGE SLICES

2 large oranges
2 tablespoons all-purpose flour
½ cup graham cracker crumbs
1 tablespoon sugar
½ teaspoon ground allspice
3 tablespoons butter or margarine

Cut oranges into slices about ¼ inch thick; remove seeds. Mix flour, crumbs, sugar, and allspice. Dip oranges into mixture, being sure they are well coated. Brown on both sides in butter. Makes 4 dessert servings or about 8 servings as garnish.

## QUICK ALLSPICE ORANGE-NUT BREAD

    2 cups sifted all-purpose flour
    1 cup sugar
    1 teaspoon baking powder
    ¾ teaspoon ground allspice
    ½ teaspoon salt
    ½ teaspoon baking soda
    1 egg
    2 tablespoons grated orange rind
    ⅔ cup orange juice
    3 tablespoons melted butter or margarine
    1 cup chopped nuts

Into large bowl sift flour with sugar, baking powder, allspice, salt, and baking soda. Beat egg thoroughly and combine with orange rind, juice, and melted butter. Add liquid to flour mixture all at once. Stir only until well blended. Stir in nuts. Bake in well-greased loaf pan (9 x 5 x 3 inches) in preheated moderate oven (350°F.) for about 50 minutes, or until loaf tests clean. Cool for 5 minutes before removing from pan. Cool completely before slicing. Makes 1 loaf.

# ALLUMETTE—This French word for match is used to describe foods cut into thin matchlike strips. The term *allumette* is applied in particular to an *hors d'eouvre* made with thin strips of puff paste spread with a savory filling and covered with more puff paste before baking; to potatoes cut into thin strips (called shoestring potatoes in America); and to a tea cake, also made from a strip of puff paste, frosted before baking.

# ALMOND—The word covers the tree and nut, the seed or kernel of *Prunus Amygdalus,* a subgenus which includes the peach tree. The almond closely resembles the peach in its blossom and young unripe fruit, although the almond tree grows larger.

The almond tree bears a leathery fruit which, upon maturing, splits open and exposes the nut in its shell. The pitted shell is light tan in color. The nut is covered with a medium-brown skin and is white inside.

Basically, there are two kinds of almonds, sweet and bitter, although there are many varieties of these. Sweet almonds are those we eat. Bitter almonds are a source of almond flavoring, but they must be processed first since they contain prussic acid, a poison.

Almonds have been cultivated since antiquity in Mediterranean countries and the Orient. In the United States, they are grown commercially in California. It is said that they were brought here by early Spanish missionaries, since almonds have long been a favorite in Spain. Almond trees are often grown for the beauty of their flowers. The loveliness of tree and blossom has inspired artists and poets through the ages; especially charming are the Chinese interpretations. The ancient Phrygians, seeing the tree blossom early in the season before any others, believed it to be the father of all life. To the ancient Greeks, the almond was a symbol of fertility, and to the Moslems, the mark of heavenly hope.

Almonds are mentioned in the Bible, since the wood of the almond tree, the blossom, and the fruit were part of the Hebraic ritual. When Israel sent gifts to Joseph, they were "a little balm, and a little honey, spices, and myrrh, nuts, and almonds" (Genesis 43:11).

In cookery, almonds are one of the pleasures of life. With little trouble and at low cost, they add flavor and texture to food and make many bland common-place dishes exciting. They are especially recommended for chicken, fish, seafood, curries, and as an ingredient of maindish sauces, but they can be added to almost any food, and used as a garnish for main dishes, salads, and vegetables. Whole, chopped, slivered, and toasted almonds are an ingredient of candies, ice creams, and dessert sauces. Almonds are greatly used in baking; most Scandinavian, Spanish, Greek and Near Eastern cakes are based on almonds. Shelled almonds are used unblanched, that is, with inner brown skin still on; and blanched, that is, with the skin removed to reveal the white kernel. Blanched or unblanched, whole almonds may be salted or sugared for eating out of hand.

Almond oil is used in some parts of Europe for cooking and eating. The best known almond confection is marzipan, almond paste molded into fruits, animals, and other fancy shapes, and tinted realistically or imaginatively. Germany and Denmark both make famous marzipan.

Almonds have also been used for thousands of years in powders, creams, and lotions to enhance the beauty of women. They are said to soften and whiten the skin.

*Availability*—Sold the year round in various forms. Almonds are picked in the fall, and the heaviest marketing occurs in November.

### Purchasing Guide
**Unshelled**—Look for nuts that are clean and free from scars, cracks, or holes, and well filled, so the kernel does not rattle. They are sold in bulk or in 1-pound plastic bags.

**Shelled**—Look for those that are plump and meaty, crisp and brittle. Limp shriveled nutmeats indicate staleness. Almonds are packaged in 5-pound boxes and 1- and 6-ounce plastic bags. You can also buy them in 6-ounce vacuum sealed cans in these forms:

**Unblanched**—Whole (also salted, roasted, buttered, and French-fried), Halved, Sliced, Coarsely Chopped, Finely Chopped, Meal, Diced.

**Blanched**—Whole (also salted), Broken, Sliced, Slivered (also toasted), Small Pieces
Unblanched or blanched whole, 1 pound = 3¾ cups
Unblanched or blanched, ground, 1 pound = 4 cups
Unblanched or blanched slivered, 1 pound = 5 cups

*Storage*—Shelled uncooked nuts will store well for almost a year if kept in an airtight container in a cool dry place, such as the refrigerator. They may be stored in a freezer in sealed containers for even longer periods. For oven-roasted nuts, allow not more than three months refrigerator storage, and even less for those cooked in oil.

*Nutritive Food Values*—Almonds provide some protein, iron, calcium, phosphorus, and B vitamins. They are also high in fat.
1 cup whole = 850 calories

### Basic Preparation

**To Blanch**—Cover with boiling water. Let stand for 3 minutes, then test to see if skins slip off easily. Remove almonds from water, slip off skins, and let dry on paper towels for several hours.

**To Sliver**—Cut into lengthwise strips with a very sharp knife while nuts are moist and warm.

**To Chop**—Use a long, straightedged knife and wooden board, or a chopping bowl and chopper. Almonds may also be chopped in a blender. Place ½ cup at a time in the blender container, cover, and whirl for 30 seconds at high speed.

**To Grind**—Use a special nut grinder, except for butters and pastes, when a food chopper or blender should be used. The easiest way to grind almonds is in the electric blender. Grind about ¼ cup at a time, at high speed. Do not overgrind or almonds will be pasty and oily, which is good for making almond paste, but not for general baking. For general baking purposes, almonds should be dry and fine, like meal.

## Almond Extract

Almond extract is prepared from the oil of bitter or sweet almonds. It is sold in 1¼- and 4-ounce bottles. Almond extract may be used to give almond flavor to cake or pastry, sauces, dessert puddings, gelatins, and other dishes.

## Almond Paste

Almond paste is a blend of ground almonds and sugar. It is available in specialty food stores in 8-ounce, 1-, 3-, and 5-pound cans. It should be kept in a cool place; stored in the refrigerator, it will keep indefinitely. Almond paste may be used to make marzipan, macaroons, and filling for Danish pastry or coffeecake.

## BURNT ALMONDS

Mix 1 cup sugar and ⅓ cup water in skillet; bring to boil; cook until mixture spins a thread (candy thermometer registers 230° to 234°F.). Add 1 package (6 ounces) unblanched almonds; cook for 2 minutes, or until syrup begins to sugar. Remove from heat; stir until mixture is dry and sugary. Return pan to low heat and continue cooking, stirring constantly, until sugar is melted and browned. Remove from heat; stir until nuts are well coated with syrup. Pour onto a buttered platter. With 2 forks, separate nuts quickly into single nuts. Put nuts separately on another buttered platter; let stand until cold. Makes 1½ cups.

## TOASTED ALMONDS

Spread blanched or unblanched almonds on ungreased shallow baking pan with sides. Bake in preheated slow oven (325°F.) until lightly browned, stirring occasionally. Almonds may be halved or cut into lengthwise slivers before toasting. Do not overbrown. Cool and pack in airtight container.

## SALTED ALMONDS

Spread blanched or unblanched almonds on ungreased shallow baking pan with sides. Dot with butter, using 1 teaspoon for each cup of nuts. Toast lightly in moderate oven (350°F.), stirring nuts frequently until golden brown. Remove from oven; sprinkle with salt, Cool and pack in airtight container.

## ALMOND SOUP

    1 cup blanched almonds, finely ground
    3 cups chicken broth
    1 small onion, stuck with 1 clove
    ½ bay leaf
    2 tablespoons butter
    2 tablespoons all-purpose flour
    ½ cup hot milk
    1 cup heavy cream
      Slivered toasted almonds

Combine almonds, broth, onion, and bay leaf in saucepan. Simmer, covered, for 30 minutes. Discard onion and bay leaf. Keep soup hot. Melt butter in another saucepan. Stir in flour. Gradually stir in milk. Cook over low heat, stirring constantly, until smooth and thickened. Stir mixture into chicken-almond soup. Cook over low heat, stirring constantly, for 5 minutes. Remove from heat and stir in heavy cream. Heat through once more, but do not let boil. Serve sprinkled with slivered toasted almonds. Good hot or cold. Makes 4 to 5 servings.

## TROUT WITH ALMONDS AND CREAM

    4 small trout, fresh or frozen
      All-purpose flour
    ½ cup butter
    ½ cup slivered blanched almonds
    ½ cup heavy cream
      Salt and pepper

Wash trout and dry well. Coat lightly with flour. Heat butter in skillet. Sauté trout in butter until browned on both sides. Remove fish to hot platter and keep hot. Sauté almonds in skillet until golden brown. Add cream and stir thoroughly to loosen all particles; the sauce will be brown. Season with salt and pepper to taste. Simmer gently for 2 minutes. Pour sauce over fish. Makes 2 to 3 servings. **NOTE:** This recipe may also be made with 1 pound of fish fillets, fresh or frozen.

## VEAL STEW WITH ALMONDS IN SOUR CREAM

3 pounds boneless veal shoulder, cut into 1½-inch cubes
   Seasoned all-purpose flour for dredging
½ cup shortening
3 medium onions, peeled and quartered
1 cup sliced celery
2 cups water
⅛ teaspoon crumbled dried thyme
12 small mushrooms, quartered, or ½ cup (one 4-ounce can) mushroom pieces, drained
1 cup slivered blanched almonds
¼ cup butter
1 cup dairy sour cream
¼ cup chopped parsley

Dredge veal with seasoned flour. Heat shortening in heavy pan and brown meat on all sides. Pour off pan drippings. Add onions, celery, water, and thyme to meat. Simmer, covered, over low heat for 1½ hours, stirring occasionally. Sauté mushrooms and almonds in hot butter until golden brown. Add to meat and simmer for 15 minutes longer. Stir in sour cream and reheat, but do not let boil. Sprinkle with parsley. Makes 6 to 8 servings.

## CHICKEN-ALMOND MOUSSE

1 envelope unflavored gelatin
1¼ cups chicken broth
3 egg yolks
1 cup ground cooked chicken
½ cup ground blanched almonds
2 tablespoons chopped parsley
1½ teaspoons lemon juice
½ teaspoon instant minced onion
½ teaspoon salt
¼ teaspoon white pepper
⅛ teaspoon hot pepper sauce
1 cup heavy cream, whipped

Soften gelatin in ½ cup of the chicken broth. In top part of double boiler, beat egg yolks and remaining broth. Cook over hot, not boiling, water until mixture thickens, stirring constantly. Remove from heat. Stir in softened gelatin. Blend until gelatin is dissolved. Add chicken, almonds, parsley, lemon juice, instant onion, salt, pepper, and pepper sauce. Chill until mixture begins to thicken to consistency of egg white. Fold in whipped cream. Brush a 1-quart salad mold with salad oil. Turn mixture into mold and chill until firm. Unmold and serve garnished with salad greens. Makes 4 servings.

## SAUCE AMANDINE

Sauté over low heat ¼ cup slivered blanched almonds in ½ cup butter or margarine until light golden brown, stirring constantly. Stir in 1 tablespoon lemon juice. Serve on chicken, sweetbreads, fish fillets, broccoli, green beans, asparagus, or other vegetables. Makes ¾ cup.

Sauce Amandine

## RICE PILAF WITH ALMONDS

¼ cup butter or margarine
¼ cup minced onion
½ cup chopped blanched almonds
1 cup raw rice
2 cups hot beef bouillon or chicken broth
   Salt and pepper to taste

Heat butter or margarine in heavy saucepan. Add onion and sauté until onion is transparent. Do not let brown. Add almonds and sauté for 1 to 2 minutes, or until barely golden. Add rice and sauté until rice is transparent, stirring constantly. Add hot bouillon all at once; mixture will sizzle. Cover tightly. Simmer over lowest possible heat for 15 to 20 minutes, or until rice is tender. Do not stir for first 10 minutes; then stir occasionally. Season. Makes 4 to 6 servings.

## ALMOND PASTE

1 pound blanched almonds
3 tablespoons juice
1 cup water
2 cups sugar

Force blanched almonds through fine blade of food chopper 4 times, or whirl in electric blender. Add lemon juice. Cook water and sugar until candy thermometer registers 240°F., or until a small amount of mixture dropped into cold water forms a soft ball. Add to ground almonds. Mix well. When cool enough to handle, knead until smooth. Cool. Pack in jar; cover, and store in refrigerator for at least 1 week to ripen. Makes about 2 pounds.

**Note:** If almond paste is too stiff to handle after storage, place in top part of double boiler and heat over hot, not boiling, water, until sufficiently soft to handle. Use in cookies, coffeecakes, or in other pastries and desserts.

## ALMOND-FILLED COFFEE RING

2 tablespoons very warm water*
1 package active dry yeast or 1 cake compressed
   yeast
¼ cup sugar
½ teaspoon salt
½ cup milk
1 egg, beaten
2 cups sifted all-purpose flour (about)
¾ cup butter or margarine
   Almond Filling
½ cup chopped candied cherries
   Confectioners' Sugar Frosting
   Whole candied cherries

* Use very warm water (105°F. to 115°F.) for dry yeast; use lukewarm (80°F. to 90°F.) for compressed. Sprinkle or crumble yeast into water. Let stand a few minutes, then stir until dissolved. Stir in sugar, salt, milk, and egg. Add 1½ cups sifted flour and beat until smooth. Stir in enough more flour (about ½ cup) to make a very stiff dough. Turn out on well-floured board. Roll to ¼-inch thickness. Spread ½ cup softened butter on upper ⅔ of dough and fold lower third over middle third. Fold top third over that. Turn and roll again to ¼-inch thickness. Fold in thirds. Put on cookie sheet and chill about 30 minutes. Repeat rolling, folding, and chilling three times.

Divide dough in half. Roll each into rectangle about 8 inches long; brush with remaining ¼ cup butter, melted, and spread with Almond Filling. Sprinkle with chopped cherries. Roll up like a jelly roll; form into ring. With scissors, cut through ring, almost to center, in slices about 1 inch thick. Turn each slice slightly. Put each ring on greased cookie sheet. Let rise in warm place until light (about 25 minutes). Bake in preheated moderate oven (350°F.) for about 30 minutes. Cool; frost with Confectioners' Sugar Frosting and decorate with whole cherries and angelica. Makes two 9-inch coffee rings.

Almond-Filled Coffee Ring, Glazed Almond Cookies

### Almond Filling

Force 1 cup blanched almonds through fine blade of food chopper. Blend in ½ cup fine dry bread crumbs, ¾ cup sugar, and 2 tablespoons melted butter. Add 1 well-beaten egg and mix thoroughly.

## Confectioners' Sugar Frosting

Combine ½ cup sifted confectioners' sugar with about 1 teaspoon milk or light cream, or enough to make a thick pouring consistency. Stir in a few drops vanilla.

## ALMOND TORTE

```
1 cup sugar, sifted
6 eggs, separated
  Grated rind and juice of 1 lemon
½ teaspoon almond extract
1 cup unblanched almonds, finely ground
½ cup toasted white bread crumbs
  Lemon-Orange Filling
1 cup heavy cream, whipped or confectioners' sugar,
  sifted
```

Beat sugar into egg yolks, a little at a time. Beat until very light and creamy. Add lemon rind and juice, almond extract, ground almonds, and bread crumbs. Blend well. Whip egg whites until stiff. Fold lightly into batter. Turn into two 8-inch layer-cake pans that have been greased and lined with wax paper. Preferably, use pans with removable rims. Bake in preheated moderate oven (350°F.) for about 40 minutes. Spread layers with Lemon-Orange Filling. Spread top and sides with whipped cream or sprinkle with confectioners' sugar. Makes 6 to 8 servings.

## Lemon-Orange Filling

```
  Grated rind of 1 lemon
  Grated rind of 1 orange
2½ tablespoons lemon juice
6 tablespoons orange juice
⅓ cup water
½ cup sugar
2 tablespoons all-purpose flour
⅛ teaspoon salt
1 whole egg
1 egg yolk
```

Combine all ingredients in top part of double boiler. Cook over hot, not boiling, water until smooth and thick, stirring constantly. Cool thoroughly before using. Makes about 1½ cups.

## ALMOND MACAROONS

```
½ pound almond paste
1 cup granulated sugar
3 egg whites, unbeaten
⅓ cup confectioners' sugar
2 tablespoons cake flour
⅛ teaspoon salt
```

Cover cookie sheet with unglazed paper. Work almond paste (homemade or purchased) thoroughly with hands. Add granulated sugar and egg whites, a small amount at a time, mixing thoroughly. Add remaining ingredients and mix well. Put teaspoons of mixture on prepared cookie sheets and flatten with fingers dipped into cold water. Cover and let stand for 2 or more hours. Bake in preheated slow oven (300°F.) for about 30 minutes. Lift unglazed paper from cookie sheet onto a damp cloth and remove macaroons. Makes about 2½ dozen.

## NONSWEET ALMOND HEARTS

```
½ cup sifted confectioners' sugar
1 cup butter (must be butter)
2 egg yolks
1 teaspoon vanilla, or almond extract, or rosewater, or
  lemon extract
2½ cups sifted all-purpose flour
1½ cups finely ground blanched almonds (Must be al-
  monds)
  Chopped nuts
```

Beat together sugar and butter. Stir in 1 egg yolk and extract. Add flour and almonds. Knead to a smooth dough. Chill for 2 to 3 hours. Roll out between sheets of wax paper to ¼-inch thickness. Cut with heart-shape cutter. Put on ungreased cookie sheet. Brush with 1 beaten egg yolk and sprinkle with chopped nuts. Bake in preheated moderate oven (350°F.) for 10 to 12 minutes, or until barely golden. Makes about 10 dozen 1½-inch hearts. A bland cookie that appeals to those not fond of sweets.

## GLAZED ALMOND COOKIES

```
1 cup soft butter or margarine
1 cup sugar
½ teaspoon each of almond and vanilla extracts
2 eggs, separated
¾ cup chopped blanched almonds
2⅔ cups sifted cake flour
½ teaspoon salt
48 unblanched whole almonds
```

Cream butter and sugar until light. Beat in extracts and egg yolks. Add chopped nuts, flour, and salt; mix well. Roll into 1-inch balls, dip into unbeaten egg whites (this provides the glaze), and put 2 inches apart on greased cookie sheets. Put a whole almond in center of each ball, and push down to flatten cookie. Bake in preheated moderate oven (350°F.) for about 10 minutes. Makes about 4 dozen cookies, which keep well and can be successfully shipped.

## FIGS STUFFED WITH ALMONDS

With a sharp pointed knife, cut a slit into dried figs. Insert a toasted blanched almond into each fig. Or fill pitted dates instead of figs for a Mediterranean confection.

## ALMOND BRITTLE

Caramelize ½ cup granulated sugar in heavy iron skillet over low heat. Stir constantly, if possible with a long-handled wooden spoon. When sugar is melted and free from lumps (they will appear at first, but just keep stirring over low heat), add ¼ cup unblanched almonds. Pour candy at once onto greased marble slab, enamel kitchen table, or greased china platter. Cool candy; break into pieces and put through food chopper, using coarsest blade. If you do not own a chopper, put candy in clean kitchen towel or napkin and pound with kitchen mallet or wooden potato masher until candy is finely crushed. Use to sprinkle on cakes after frosting and on puddings and ice cream.

**Note:** Almond, pecan, or peanut brittle can be purchased and crushed, if desired.

# ALSACE—This easternmost province of France is famous for its food and wines. Its two gastronomic masterpieces are *foie gras* (goose liver, usually made into pâtés) with truffles, one of the world's most prized delicacies, and *choucroute garnie,* a robust dish of sauerkraut, pork products, and boiled potatoes, cooked with white wine and juniper berries, which can be made at home.

The two best known wines are the classic Riesling and the flowery Gewürztraminer, and the best known spirit is kirsch, a colorless brandy distilled from cherries. Strasbourg, one of Europe's most beautiful ancient cities and site of a splendid cathedral, is the chief town of Alsace.

## CHOUCROUTE GARNIE

      4  pounds sauerkraut
      1  tablespoon lard
     ¾  pound bacon, diced
      1  large onion, studded with 3 cloves
      1  Polish sausage, cut into 2-inch pieces
      1  pound smoked pork shoulder
     ¼  cup brandy (optional)
      1  carrot, sliced
    10  juniper berries and 6 peppercorns, tied in a cheese-cloth bag
      2  bay leaves
     ¼  teaspoon crumbled dried thyme
         Salt to taste
      2  cups dry Alsatian or other white wine
      2  cups water
    12  medium-size potatoes, peeled and boiled
    12  frankfurters

Place sauerkraut in deep bowl. Loosen shreds. Fill bowl with cold water and let stand for 15 minutes. Drain and press out all water. Melt lard in Dutch oven. Add bacon and onion and cook until browned. Add sausage and pork shoulder and cook until meat is browned. Remove meats and reserve. Add sauerkraut to pan and cook, stirring constantly, until browned. Add brandy and cook for a few minutes longer. Add carrot, juniper berries and peppercorns, bay leaves, thyme, salt, wine, and water. Bring to a boil. Return pork shoulder to pan. Simmer, covered, over low heat for 3 hours. Return sausage to pan. Simmer, covered, for another 45 minutes. Add potatoes and frankfurters and continue simmering for 15 minutes more. Makes 6 to 8 servings.

## ALSATIAN NOODLES

      2  tablespoons butter
      4  cups (8 ounces) medium noodles, cooked and drained
         Salt and pepper
      3  tablespoons grated cheese
     ¼  cup salad oil

Heat butter in saucepan. Add about two-thirds of noodles. Season with salt and pepper. Cook over low heat for 5 minutes, stirring constantly. Add cheese and blend thoroughly. Turn into heated serving dish. and keep hot. Chop remaining noodles very coarsely. Heat salad oil in skillet. Add chopped noodles and cook until browned, stirring occasionally. Toss with noodles in dish. Serve hot. Makes 4 servings.

# ALTITUDE COOKING—High altitudes affect the cooking and baking of foods so special methods have to be worked out to give homemakers successful recipes. Recipes which are foolproof at sea level and generally speaking, at altitudes up to 2,500 feet, can fail completely at higher altitudes because of the different atmospheric pressure. Foods that need baking or boiling or that are rich in sugar are most affected by high altitudes. Some foods, such as cake mixes, are made especially for high-altitude cooking.

When a homemaker moves to a new home at a higher altitude than her previous one, it is suggested that she contact the local utility company or the State Extension Service for information on special high-altitude recipes.

# ALUM—The astringent effect of this chemical makes it useful in home-pickling to give crispness to cucumbers, melon rinds, onions, green beans, and other foods. Commercially, alum is used as an ingredient in some baking powders as well as in pickling. Alum can be bought in drugstores.

# AMBROSIA—This Greek word goes back to Greek mythology and designated the substance which, with nectar, constituted the food and drink of the Greek gods, giving immortality to those who partook of it.

The word is also used to define anything very pleasing in the way of scent or taste. In cookery, ambrosia is a dessert of orange slices or fruits, sprinkled with sugar and shredded coconut. Ambrosia is particularly popular as a dessert in the American South.

# AMERICAN

# COOKERY

# WESTERN COOKERY

## RED CAVIAR IN CREAM [Wash.]

½ cup dairy sour cream
1 package (3 ounces) cream cheese
2 slices of onion, chopped
Dash of salt
Pepper to taste
1 jar (6 ounces) red salmon caviar

Put all ingredients except caviar in blender. Whirl for a few seconds. Add caviar. Mix lightly and chill. Makes about 1½ cups. Spread on toast rounds and garnish with dill or chives for a first course. Or use as a dip for potato chips, scallions, and carrot and celery strips.

## CREAM OF CAULIFLOWER SOUP [Nev.]

1 large head cauliflower
Juice of 1 lemon
2 tablespoons minced onion
2 celery stalks, minced
¼ cup butter or margarine
¼ cup all-purpose flour
4 cups chicken broth or bouillon
2 cups light cream, scalded
Dash of nutmeg
Salt to taste
Grated Parmesan cheese (optional)

Wash cauliflower and break in flowerets. Cook with lemon juice in small amount of boiling water until tender. Drain and whirl cauliflower in blender until puréed, or force through food mill. Sauté onion and celery in the butter 2 or 3 minutes. Blend in flour and stir in broth. Cook, stirring, until slightly thickened. Stir in cauliflower, cream, nutmeg, and salt. Garnish with cheese. Makes about 1¾ quarts, or 6 servings.

## SOPA DE ALBONDIGAS
### [Meat Ball Soup]

4 cups (two 1-pound cans) tomatoes
2 cups beef bouillon
1½ teaspoons chili powder
2 teaspoons salt
2½ cups boiling water
1 pound ground beef
½ pound ground lean pork
1 slice of dry bread
1 egg, beaten
1 garlic clove, minced
¼ teaspoon each of crumbled dried mint, ground sage, and pepper
1 medium onion, chopped
2 tablespoons cooking oil

Force tomatoes through a sieve. Add bouillon, chili powder, 1 teaspoon salt, and the water. Bring to boil and boil until about one fourth of the liquid is evaporated. Combine meats. Dip bread into cold water, squeeze dry, and add to meat. Add remaining salt and other ingredients except onion and oil. Mix lightly but thoroughly. Brown onion in the oil; discard onion. Shape meat mixture into ¾-inch balls and brown in the hot oil. Add to soup mixture, cover and simmer 1 hour. Makes 6 servings.

## NEW MEXICO TAMALE PIE

1 onion, chopped
1 garlic clove, minced
½ green pepper, chopped
2 tablespoons olive oil
1 pound ground round
3½ cups (one 1-pound, 12-ounce can) tomatoes
Salt
1 dozen ripe olives, pitted
1 teaspoon ground coriander
1 or 2 tablespoons chili powder
1 cup yellow cornmeal
1 cup cold water
1 quart well-seasoned beef or chicken broth
Butter

Sauté onion, garlic, and pepper in hot olive oil in a skillet. Add beef and sauté until meat loses red color, stirring with a fork to crumble meat. Add tomatoes, 1 teaspoon salt, olives, coriander, and chili powder. Cook slowly for 20 minutes. Meanwhile, mix cornmeal and cold water in top part of double boiler. Add hot broth slowly and cook over boiling water until thickened, stirring occasionally. Line an oiled 2-quart casserole with half the mush mixture. Add meat mixture and top with remaining mush. Let cool slightly and crisscross top with knife. Dot generously with butter. Bake in preheated moderate oven (350°F.) for 45 minutes. Makes 6 servings.

## BEEFSTEAK AND OYSTERS

Broil a steak almost to desired degree of doneness. Cover with drained oysters. Season with salt and pepper and dot with butter. Bake in preheated moderate oven (375°F.) until oysters are plump (about 15 minutes) and begin to curl at the edges. Garnish with chopped parsley and lemon wedges.

26

## WYOMING BOILED LEG OF MUTTON WITH CAPER SAUCE

    1 leg of mutton, shank end removed
    ¼ cup shortening
    2 onions, cut in quarters
    1 bay leaf
    ½ teaspoon peppercorns
    2 teaspoons salt
    6 cups boiling water
    ¼ cup all-purpose flour
    1 teaspoon cider vinegar
    ⅓ cup light cream
    ½ cup drained capers

Brown meat in hot fat in large heavy Dutch oven. Pour off excess shortening. Add onions, bay leaf, peppercorns, and 2 teaspoons salt. Add boiling water. Cover and bring to a boil. Reduce heat and simmer until tender, about 3 hours. Remove meat to large platter and keep warm. Skim off fat from liquid. In small saucepan, mix flour with ¼ cup of the fat. Gradually stir in 3 cups of the liquid, stir over low heat, and cook until thickened. Add vinegar, cream, and capers. Reheat but do not boil. Serve at once. Makes 10 servings.

## TART MUTTON

    2 tart apples
    2 cups cubed cold mutton
    2 cups cooked rice
    3 tablespoons butter or margarine

Slice apples but do not peel. Use apples to line a greased 1½-quart casserole. Mix mutton with rice and pack mixture into apple-lined pan. Dot top with butter and bake in preheated moderate oven (350°F.) for 30 minutes, or until top is golden brown and apples are tender. Makes 4 servings.

## MONTANA LAMB ON SKEWERS

    2 pounds boneless shoulder of lamb
    ¾ cup French dressing
    1 garlic clove, minced
      Small mushroom caps
    6 slices of bacon, cut into squares
      Seasoned salt

Cut meat into 1-inch cubes. Put into bowl with French dressing and garlic. Refrigerate for at least 3 hours; turn meat occasionally. Arrange alternate pieces of lamb, mushroom, and bacon on skewers. Sprinkle with seasoned salt to taste. Broil until fork-tender over coals heated to turn gray. Turn occasionally to cook evenly. Serve with buttered brown or wild rice. Makes 4 to 6 servings.

**Note:** The broiling may be done in a range broiler.

## IDAHO LAMB HASH

    ½ small onion, minced
    1 tablespoon butter
    1 tablespoon all-purpose flour
    1 cup lamb, beef, or chicken stock
    ½ cup chopped celery
    1 tablespoon chopped parsley
    2 cups cubed cold roast lamb, cut into ½-inch cubes
    1 cup cubed boiled potatoes, cut into ½-inch cubes
      Salt and pepper

Sauté onion in butter. Stir in flour and cook slowly over low heat for 3 minutes, until light golden brown. Gradually stir in stock. Add celery and parsley and simmer, covered, for 15 minutes. Make sure that lamb is free of gristle. Add lamb and potatoes. Season with salt and pepper. Heat to just below the boiling point. Serve with Pickled Idaho Prune Plums. Make 4 servings.

## PORK WITH PEAS

    3 tablespoons soy sauce
    2 tablespoons cornstarch
    ½ teaspoon salt
    ¼ teaspoon monosodium glutamate
    1 tablespoon salad oil
    1 pound lean pork, cut into ½-inch cubes
    1 package (10 ounces) frozen peas
    1 teaspoon sugar
    ¾ cup water or chicken broth
    ½ cup fried blanched walnut meats

Mix 2 tablespoons soy sauce with 1 tablespoon cornstarch, salt, and monosodium glutamate. Marinate pork in it for 15 minutes. Heat oil and brown pork in it, turning occasionally to brown evenly. Add peas and sugar, cover, and simmer until peas are done, 4 to 5 minutes, separating peas with a fork as they begin to defrost. Mix remaining soy sauce and cornstarch. Add water and mix well. Pour over pork and peas and cook, stirring constantly, until clear and thickened. To blanch walnuts, boil for ½ minute, plunge into cold water, and scrub with a vegetable brush, getting off as much of the skin as possible. Heat enough oil to barely cover nuts and cook, stirring constantly, until golden brown. Sprinkle nuts on top of pork and peas and serve with rice. Makes 4 servings.

## CHINESE SWEET-AND-SOUR PORK

    ½ cup soy sauce
    ½ teaspoon ground ginger
    ¼ teaspoon each of salt and monosodium glutamate
    1 garlic clove, minced or mashed
    2 pounds lean pork butt, cut into thin strips, then into 1-inch pieces
      About ½ cup cornstarch
      Cooking oil for deep frying
    1 cup pineapple juice
    ½ cup white vinegar
    ¼ cup catsup
    ¾ cup firmly packed light brown sugar
    1 tablespoon Worcestershire
      Dash of red pepper sauce

2 large green peppers, seeded and cut into 1-inch squares
2 tablespoons sliced green onions
2 large tomatoes, cut into small wedges
2 cups pineapple chunks, drained
¼ cup water
Chinese parsley (optional)

Combine soy, ginger, salt, monosodium glutamate, and garlic. Pour over pork and allow to stand for 30 minutes; stir occasionally. Dredge pork pieces with 6 tablespoons cornstarch. Cook meat, a few pieces at a time, in hot deep fat (380°F. on frying thermometer) for 8 to 10 minutes, or until crisp and brown. Drain on absorbent paper; keep warm. In a skillet combine pineapple juice, vinegar, catsup, brown sugar, Worcestershire, and pepper sauce. Bring to a boil. Add green pepper and onion and cook for 1 minute over high heat. Add tomato, pineapple, and cooked meat. Mix 2 tablespoons cornstarch and water, and add. Stir and cook for 1 minute, or until sauce is thickened and hot. Turn onto heated serving platter. Garnish with Chinese parsley if you wish. This recipe makes 6 generous main-dish servings. If the dish is to be served Chinese style, as one of several other main-course dishes, it will serve 8 or more.

## SOONER-STATE BEANS WITH SPARERIBS

1 pound dried pinto beans, washed and drained
3 pounds fresh pork spareribs
Salt, pepper, chili powder
2 green peppers, cut into quarters
2 onions, sliced
3½ cups (one 1-pound, 12-ounce can) tomatoes

Cover beans with cold water, bring to boil, and boil for 2 minutes. Cover pan and let stand for 1 hour. Do not drain. Meanwhile, cut spareribs into serving pieces. Brown lightly in heavy skillet. Cover with water. Simmer, covered, until tender. Drain beans and pour into roasting pan. Arrange spareribs on top of beans. Add water in which spareribs were cooked. Season with salt, pepper, and chili powder. Put peppers and onions on top of pork; tomatoes over all. Cover and bake in preheated slow oven (325°F.) 1 hour. Makes 6 servings.

## COLORADO GAME MULLIGAN

1 piece boneless shoulder or rump of venison (about 2 pounds)
¾ cup wine vinegar
¼ cup olive oil
3 or 4 juniper berries
1 yellow onion, sliced
8 to 10 whole cloves
6 to 8 peppercorns
¼ cup butter or margarine
Water
1½ cups canned tomatoes
1 cup diced yellow turnips
¾ cup diced yellow onions
4 carrots, sliced
1 cup kernel corn
2 cups fresh sliced green beans
½ cup sliced celery

Wash meat and pat dry. Mix wine vinegar, oil, juniper berries, onion, cloves, and peppercorns. Marinate meat in mixture overnight or longer. Drain meat. Cube meat and brown on all sides in butter. Cover with cold water and bring to a boil. Reduce heat and simmer, covered, for 1½ to 2 hours, or until meat is tender. Add remaining ingredients and simmer, covered, until vegetables are tender. Makes 4 to 6 servings.

## UTAH SAND-PAIL PICNIC DINNER

For the cooked part of the meal, provide for each person a leg and a thigh of chicken, 2 ears of corn, and a large baking potato. Season chicken with salt and pepper, dredge with flour, brown well in hot fat. Cool, and refrigerate. Shuck corn, remove silk, spread with soft butter, season with salt. Wrap each ear of corn in aluminum foil. Scrub baking potatoes; grease skins with vegetable fat. Wrap each potato in foil. Now wrap each piece of chicken in foil. Into a large galvanized pail, put 2 inches of moist sand. Wrap each bundle of chicken, corn, and potato in a second piece of foil, using butcher wrap. Put a layer of chicken bundles on top of sand; fill with 2 more inches of sand. Add potato bundles, another layer of sand. Put corn bundles on top, cover with sand. Set pail on deep bed of coals, adding more charcoal as needed to keep fire going for 1½ hours. Then, wearing asbestos gloves, empty pail on the ground. Let each person fish for his bundle of chicken, corn, and potato. Discard outer layer of foil. Inner layer will be clean and free of sand.

## OKLAHOMA GRILLED CHICKEN

3 broilers, 2 to 2½ pounds each
2 cups cider vinegar
2 teaspoons salt
½ cup cooking oil
¼ teaspoon pepper

Have broilers split into halves. Mix the remaining ingredients and pour over the chicken. Let stand for 1 hour. Drain chicken, reserving marinade, and place chicken halves, skin side up, over charcoal or in a broiler about 8 inches from source of heat. Brush with marinade every 15 minutes during cooking. Broil for 20 to 25 minutes on each side, or until chicken is brown and tender. Makes 6 servings.

## HAWAIIAN CHICKEN

1 frying chicken (about 2½ pounds), cut up
2 tablespoons shortening
Salt and pepper
½ cup water
1½ pounds fresh spinach
1 cup coconut cream

Brown chicken pieces in shortening and sprinkle with salt and pepper. Add water, cover, and simmer until chicken is tender. Meanwhile, wash spinach and remove stems. Cut leaves into 1-inch pieces. Steam with a little water until spinach is tender. Drain spinach and chicken and combine. Add coconut cream and heat but do not boil. Makes 4 servings.

## TEXAS BARBECUED TURKEY

    1  turkey, 10 to 15 pounds
    ½  cup melted butter or margarine
    ½  cup cooking oil
    2  cups cider vinegar
    1  cup catsup
    ½  cup sugar
    2  medium onions, grated
    ¼  cup Worcestershire
    ⅓  cup fresh lemon juice
    2  tablespoons dry mustard
    3  tablespoons chili powder
    2  teaspoons pepper
    2  teaspoons salt
    2  garlic cloves, mashed

Defrost turkey if frozen by leaving at room temperature overnight. Remove giblets. Wash turkey; pat dry. To make sauce, simmer remaining ingredients for 10 minutes. Brush sides of turkey with barbecue sauce. Insert spit rod, running it through tail and diagonally through breast-bone. Fasten turkey with spit forks. Wings and legs should be tied closely to body. Rotate spit to make sure turkey is properly balanced and will turn evenly. To know exactly when turkey is ready, insert a meat thermometer into thickest part of the thigh. Heat charcoal until coals turn gray. Push coals to rear of firebox. Push spit into holders. Make a drip pan of foil to catch drippings and place under turkey. Brush turkey with barbecue sauce every 15 to 20 minutes while it rotates. Add charcoal as needed to keep temperature high. When thermometer registers 185°F., or the thickest part of the drumstick feels tender (about 20 minutes per pound), remove turkey. Allow to cool for 20 minutes before carving. Serve with any remaining barbecue sauce. Makes 10 to 15 servings.

## FISH BAKED IN A BLANKET

Clean a large whole fish weighing 4 to 5 pounds. Season fish inside and out with salt and pepper. Sprinkle with lemon juice and dot with butter. Make a thick paste of flour and water. Cover entire fish with paste; place on greased baking sheet. Bake in preheated very hot oven (450°F.) for 25 to 30 minutes. Remove from oven. Crack crust with mallet and remove fish carefully. Discard crust. Serve fish with lemon. Makes 6 servings.

## BARBECUED COLUMBIA RIVER SALMON

    4  slices of bacon, halved
    2–pound piece of fresh salmon
    1  teaspoon salt
    ¼  teaspoon pepper
    1  garlic clove, minced
    ½  cup chopped onion
    ½  cup chopped green pepper
    2  tablespoons cooking oil
    1½ cups canned tomatoes
    1½ teaspoons Worcestershire
    ½  bay leaf, crumbled

Place bacon in bottom of baking dish. Sprinkle salmon with salt and pepper. Lay on top of bacon. Sauté garlic,

onion, and green pepper together for 3 minutes in hot oil. Add remaining ingredients and simmer for 5 minutes. Pour over salmon. Bake in preheated hot oven (400°F.) for about 30 minutes, basting often. Makes 4 servings.

## ARKANSAS RIVER FRIED CATFISH

    4  pounds catfish
       Salt and pepper
    ¼  cup bacon drippings or lard
       Juice of 1 lemon
    ¼  cup chopped parsley

Clean and skin catfish and pat dry. Sprinkle with salt and pepper. Sauté in hot bacon drippings or lard over moderate heat until browned on both sides. Drain fish on paper towels and place on hot serving dish. Sprinkle with lemon juice and parsley. Serve with turnip greens. Makes 4 servings.

## FISHERMAN'S WHARF CIOPPINO

    1  onion, chopped
    1  green pepper, chopped
    ½  cup sliced green onion
    4  garlic cloves, minced
    3  tablespoons olive oil
    2⅓ cups (one 1-pound, 3-oz. can) tomatoes
    1⅓ cups tomato purée
       Pinch of dried thyme
    1  bay leaf
    1  teaspoon salt
    ¼  teaspoon pepper
    2  cups dry white wine
    12 small clams, in the shell
    12 small oysters, in the shell
    2  small lobsters or 4 lobster tails, quartered and cracked
    1  large or 2 small hard-shell crabs, split, with legs disjointed
    12 shelled and deveined shrimps

Cook onion, green pepper, green onion, and garlic in oil for 5 minutes. Add remaining ingredients except wine and fish. Bring to boil, cover, and simmer for 2 hours, stirring frequently. Add wine and cook for 10 minutes. Put scrubbed raw fish in large kettle. Pour sauce over all. Simmer, covered, for 20 minutes. Makes 4 generous servings.

## PIROK (Salmon Pie)

       Pastry for 2-crust 8-inch pie, unbaked
    2  cups cooked rice
    2  cups medium cream sauce
    2  medium onions, thinly sliced
    2  tablespoons butter
    1  pound fresh salmon or 1 can (1 pound) salmon
    2  hard-cooked eggs, finely chopped
    ½  cup grated Cheddar cheese
    ½  cup mayonnaise

Roll out half the pastry ⅛ inch thick and use to line an 8-inch square pan. Mix rice with ½ cup cream sauce.

Sauté onions in butter until golden. Place half of rice mixture in pastry. Add pieces of salmon. Distribute onions and eggs over salmon, then cover with remaining rice. Roll out second half of dough and place over rice. Moisten edges and seal to lower crust. Make a few slits in top crust for escape of steam. Bake in preheated moderate oven (350°F.) for 1 hour if raw salmon is used, or for 15 minutes in a very hot oven (450°F.) if canned salmon is used. Melt cheese in remaining cream sauce. Remove from heat and fold in mayonnaise. Cut Pirok into squares and serve with mayonnaise-cheese sauce. Makes 4 to 6 servings.

## LOMI LOMI SALMON

    1 pound salt salmon
    5 ripe tomatoes
    1 large onion
      Ice cubes

Soak salmon in water for 4 to 5 hours. Remove skin and bones and break or cut into pieces. Peel tomatoes and onion and chop. Squeeze all ingredients together through the fingers until all are in small pieces and well mixed. Add several ice cubes and chill thoroughly. Makes 4 to 6 servings.

## DUNGENESS CRAB LOUIS

    1 head lettuce, shredded
    3 green onions, diced
    5 or 6 radishes, sliced
    ½ medium cucumber, diced
    2 cups fresh crabmeat
      Salt and pepper
    2 tomatoes, quartered
    3 hard-cooked eggs, quartered
    ½ to 1 cup Thousand Island dressing
      Paprika for garnish

Combine lettuce, onions, radishes, cucumber, and crab-meat; season to taste. Garnish salad with tomatoes and eggs. Add dressing to lettuce mixture or spoon on top of each individual serving. Sprinkle with paprika. Makes 4 generous servings.

## BAKED LIMA-BEAN-AND-PEAR CASSEROLE

    1 pound Lima beans
    6 cups water
      Salt and pepper to taste
    ½ cup melted butter or margarine
    1 cup firmly packed light brown sugar
    2½ cups (one 1-pound, 13-ounce can) pear halves, cubed

Put beans in kettle, add water, and bring to a boil. Boil for 2 minutes; cover pan and let stand for 1 hour. Then simmer until tender; add more hot water if necessary. Drain, and season. Mix butter and brown sugar and a little syrup from pears. In a greased large casserole, alternate layers of beans and pears. Spread each layer with butter-sugar mixture. Top layer should be pears. Spread with remaining sugar mixture. Cover and bake in preheated slow oven (325°F.) for about 2 hours. Makes 6 servings.

## COWPUNCHER'S BEAN STEW

    1 pound pinto beans
    6 cups water
    ½ teaspoon ground cuminseed
    1 to 2 garlic cloves
    2 teaspoons salt
    2 tablespoons bacon fat or lard
    1 small red chili pepper, chopped fine (optional)

Bring beans and water to a boil. Remove from heat, cover, and let stand for 1 hour. Add cuminseed and garlic. Simmer, covered, over very low heat for 1½ hours, adding more water if necessary. Add salt and bacon fat. Continue cooking, stirring occasionally, until beans are tender. Top with chopped red chili pepper. Makes 6 servings.

## TEXAS RANCH-HOUSE BEANS

    4 cups dried pinto beans
    8 cups water
    ½ pound salt pork
    2 to 4 tablespoons chili powder, depending on taste
    ¼ to ½ teaspoon hot pepper sauce, depending on taste
      Salt to taste

Bring beans and water to a boil. Remove from heat, cover, and let stand for 1 hour. Add salt pork and simmer, covered, for 1½ to 2 hours, or until beans are tender and water is almost absorbed. While beans are cooking, remove scum from top and stir occasionally. Remove salt pork and stir in enough chili powder, hot pepper sauce, and salt to give beans a spicy flavor. Beans can be prepared ahead of time and reheated. Makes 10 to 12 servings.

## NEW MEXICAN RE-FRIED BEANS

Cover 1 cup California pink or pinto beans with 4 cups water. Bring to boil and boil for 2 minutes. Cover and let stand for 1 hour. Then cook until tender. Drain, reserving liquid. Heat 2 tablespoons bacon fat or lard, add beans, and cook over low heat for about 10 minutes, mashing beans with fork. Add bean liquid and cook until liquid has evaporated. Cook 1 minced small onion in 2 tablespoons bacon fat for 5 minutes; add ½ cup tomato purée. Add beans; season. Makes 4 servings.

## IDAHO CORN OYSTERS

    3 cups grated fresh corn
    3 eggs, well beaten
    1½ teaspoons baking powder
    ½ teaspoon salt
    ¼ teaspoon pepper
    3 tablespoons light cream
    ⅓ cup all-purpose flour
      Butter

Combine all ingredients and beat until well blended. Drop by tablespoons onto a hot buttered griddle and fry until golden brown on both sides. Makes 6 to 8 servings.

## ALASKA SOURDOUGH PANCAKES

      Water*
   2 packages active dry yeast or 2 cakes compressed
      yeast
   6 cups sifted all-purpose flour
   2 teaspoons salt
   1 teaspoon baking soda
   3 tablespoons molasses
   5 eggs, beaten
      Fat for frying

*Use very warm water (105°F. to 115°F.) for dry yeast; use lukewarm (80°F. to 90°F.) for compressed. Sprinkle dry yeast or crumble cakes into 4 cups water. Let stand for a few minutes; then stir until dissolved. Stir in flour. Cover and let stand for 24 hours at room temperature. Add salt, soda, molasses, and ½ cup hot water. Add eggs. Don't beat them in, but just mix them in. Let stand for 30 minutes. Cook on a lightly greased heated griddle in the usual manner. Makes about forty 5-inch pancakes.

## MONTANA SOURDOUGH DOUGHNUTS

   2 eggs
      Sugar
   1 cup sourdough starter
   ½ cup buttermilk
   1 tablespoon melted lard or cooking oil
   4½ cups sifted all-purpose flour
   1 teaspoon baking powder
   ½ teaspoon baking soda
   ½ teaspoon salt
   ½ teaspoon ground nutmeg
      Fat for frying

Beat eggs and 1 cup sugar together. Add starter, buttermilk, lard, and sifted dry ingredients. Mix well. Turn out dough and knead on a lightly floured board until smooth. Roll to ½-inch thickness and cut with 2¾-inch doughnut cutter. Put on greased cookie sheet and let rise for 30 minutes. Fry in hot deep fat (370°F. on a frying thermometer) until golden brown and done. Roll in sugar. Makes about 3 dozen.

## DENVER SANDWICHES

   ½ pound fresh ham, finely diced
   2 onions, chopped
   1 green pepper, chopped
      Butter
   8 eggs
      Salt and pepper
   8 slices of bread

Fry ham until crisp with onion and pepper in 1 tablespoon butter. Add eggs and seasonings, stir gently. When lightly browned, turn, cut into 4 wedges, and serve between slices of buttered bread. Makes 4 sandwiches.

## THOMPSON SEEDLESS GRAPES IN SOUR CREAM

   1 pound tart seedless grapes
   1 cup dairy sour cream
   ⅓ cup firmly packed dark brown sugar

Wash and stem grapes. Put in glass bowl. Top with sour cream and sprinkle with sugar. Chill for several hours before serving. Makes 4 servings.

## AVOCADO ICE CREAM

   3 egg yolks
   ¾ cup milk
   ¾ cup sugar
      Dash of salt
   1 cup heavy cream
   2 ripe medium avocados, peeled
      Few drops green food coloring

Beat first 4 ingredients together in top part of small double boiler. Put over simmering water and cook, stirring, until thickened and mixture coats a metal spoon. Cool. Whip cream until thick. Add avocado to cream, one slice at a time, beating until blended. Add coloring. Fold into first mixture. Pour into freezing tray and freeze until firm. Serve plain or with a sauce made from 1 box thawed frozen raspberries, whirled in blender. Makes 4 servings.

## LARAMIE APPLE-BUTTER PIE

      Pastry for 1-crust 9-inch pie, unbaked
   ½ cup sugar
   3 tablespoons all-purpose flour
   ½ cup apple butter
   2 tablespoons melted butter
   2 eggs, well beaten
   1½ cups milk
   1 cup light cream
   ½ teaspoon ground nutmeg

Use pastry to line a 9-inch pie pan, fluting a high edge. Mix sugar with flour. Gradually stir in apple butter and melted butter. Beat eggs with milk and cream. Beat into apple-butter mixture. Pour into pastry-lined pie pan. Sprinkle top with nutmeg. Bake in preheated moderate oven (350°F.) for 50 to 60 minutes, or until a knife inserted comes out clean. Cool on a rack. Makes 6 to 8 servings.

## OREGON PEACH CREAM ALMOND PIE

   3½ cups sliced fresh peaches
   ⅔ cup sugar
   ¼ cup all-purpose flour
   ¼ teaspoon ground nutmeg
      Pastry for 1-crust 9-inch pie, unbaked
   1 cup heavy cream
   ¼ cup sliced blanched almonds

Toss peaches gently with sugar, flour, and nutmeg. Turn into pastry-lined pan. Pour cream over peaches. Bake in pre-heated hot oven (400°F.) for 35 minutes. Remove pie from oven, sprinkle top with almonds. Return to oven and bake for 5 minutes more, or until cream is set and almonds are lightly browned. Cool. Makes 6 servings.

## FLAN SOL Y SOMBRA
### [Sun and Shadow Custard]

4 eggs
⅓ cup honey
½ teaspoon salt
1 teaspoon ground coriander
3 cups milk
1 teaspoon vanilla extract
2 tablespoons almond liqueur or rum
  Ground nutmeg

Blend eggs, honey, and salt. Add remaining ingredients except nutmeg. Blend well. Butter a 1½-quart baking dish; pour in mixture and sprinkle nutmeg over top. Set dish in a pan of warm water and bake in preheated very slow oven (250°F.) for 2 hours, or until firm. Cool; chill. Makes 4 to 6 servings.

## PICKLED IDAHO PRUNE PLUMS

4 pounds fresh prune plums
3 cups cider vinegar
4 cups sugar
2 cinnamon sticks
1 tablespoon whole cloves
  Piece of gingerroot
1 teaspoon whole allspice

Wash plums and prick each with fork. Combine vinegar and sugar in kettle and add spices, tied loosely in cheesecloth bag. Cook, covered, for 10 minutes. Reduce heat, add plums, and simmer gently for 10 minutes longer. Remove spice bag. Pack in hot sterilized jars, cover with boiling syrup, and seal. Makes about 4 pints.

# MIDWESTERN COOKERY

# STOCKYARD INN BEEF-VEGETABLE SOUP

  5 pounds beef shank with bone
    Salt
  2 quarts water
  1 garlic clove, minced
  ⅓ cup pearl barley
  ½ cup chopped celery tops
  2 cups chopped onion
  3½ cups (one 1-pound, 12-ounce can) tomatoes
  ½ cup butter or margarine
  1½ cups finely diced celery
  1 cup each, diced carrots and potatoes
  1 cup sliced green beans
  1 cup finely cut green cabbage
  2 cups fresh peas or 1 package (10 ounces) frozen
    peas
  1 cup finely cut fresh spinach
    Salt and pepper

Have beef shank cut into several pieces. Put in kettle with 1 tablespoon salt and next 5 ingredients. Bring to boil, cover, and simmer for 3 hours, or until meat is tender. Skim soup. Remove bones and meat and set meat aside. Add tomatoes to soup. Melt butter in skillet. Add vegetables, except peas and spinach. Sauté for 7 minutes, stirring frequently. Add to soup, cover, and simmer for 20 minutes. Add peas, spinach, and the meat, cut into bite-size pieces. Cover and simmer for 10 minutes longer. Add salt and pepper to taste. Makes about 5 quarts.

## IOWA CORN CHOWDER

  ½ cup chopped salt pork
  1 onion, chopped
  ½ cup sliced celery
  ½ green pepper, diced
  1½ cups diced raw potatoes
  2 cups water
  1 bay leaf
  1 teaspoon salt
  ¼ cup all-purpose flour
  2 cups milk
  ½ cup light cream
  2 cups fresh corn cut from cob

Brown salt pork in heavy saucepan. Add onion; cook for 2 minutes. Add next 6 ingredients. Simmer until potatoes are tender. Mix flour with a little milk; add with remaining milk to potato mixture. Heat until thickened. Add cream and corn. Heat gently. Makes 4 to 6 servings.

## TENDERLOIN STEAK
## WITH ROQUEFORT SPREAD [Ill.]

  8 club or tenderloin steaks, cut 1½ inches thick
    Salt and pepper
  ½ cup crumbled Roquefort cheese
  ¼ cup heavy cream
  1 teaspoon Worcestershire
  1 teaspoon grated onion
  ½ teaspoon fresh lemon juice
  ⅛ teaspoon salt
  2 drops hot pepper sauce
    Grated fresh horseradish

Cut fat edges of steaks to prevent curling during cooking. Broil steaks until desired doneness is reached. Sprinkle with salt and pepper. Blend remaining ingredients and spread mixture on steaks. Place steaks covered with cheese under broiler until cheese is melted and bubbly. Serve with grated fresh horseradish. Makes 8 servings.

## KANSAS CITY PICKLED BEEF
## [Mo.]

  2 cups cider vinegar
  4 pounds boneless round steak
  2 onions, sliced
  1 lemon, sliced
  1 teaspoon peppercorns
  1 teaspoon juniper berries
  2 bay leaves
  2 tablespoons shortening
  2 teaspoons salt
  1 cup red wine

Pour vinegar over meat in glass or stainless-steel pan or bowl. Add onions, lemon slices, peppercorns, berries, and bay leaves. Cover and let stand in refrigerator for 48 hours, turning meat occasionally. Remove from marinade. Wipe dry and brown slowly in hot shortening. Strain marinade and add 1 cup to meat. Add salt and wine, cover, and simmer slowly for 2 hours, or until tender. Thicken slightly with flour if desired. Pour juices over meat. Makes 8 servings.

## VEAL PARSLEY PIE
## WITH DUMPLINGS

  2 pounds cubed veal stew meat
  2 onions, chopped
  ½ cup chopped parsley
  1 teaspoon salt
  ¼ teaspoon pepper
    Dumplings
    Water

Put meat, onions, and parsley in a Dutch oven. Add salt and pepper. Add enough water just to cover. Cover and simmer for 1 to 1½ hours, or until meat is tender. Drop dumplings by tablespoons on top of simmering meat. Cover tightly and simmer for 10 minutes. Serve at once. Makes 4 servings.

### Dumplings

  2 cups sifted all-purpose flour
  2 teaspoons baking powder
  1 teaspoon salt
  1 cup milk

Sift flour with baking powder and salt. Add milk and beat well until dough is smooth. Drop on top of simmering stew.

## PORK, APPLESAUCE, AND KRAUT CASSEROLE [Ohio]

  2 onions, sliced
  ¼ cups butter or margarine
  2⅓ cups (one 1-pound, 3-ounce can) tomatoes
  2 teaspoons sugar
    Salt and pepper
    Dash of oregano
  1 cup soft bread crumbs
  2 cups (one 1-pound can) applesauce
  ¼ cup prepared horseradish
  2 cups (one 1-pound can) sauerkraut
  6 large lean pork chops
  1 tablespoon fat

Brown onions lightly in butter. Add tomatoes, sugar, 1 teaspoon salt, ¼ teaspoon pepper, and next 5 ingredients. Pour into large shallow baking dish. Brown chops on both sides in fat; sprinkle with salt and pepper. Put in baking dish with applesauce and kraut. Cover with foil and bake in preheated moderate oven (350°F.) for 1¾ hours. Makes 6 servings.

## HAM WITH MUSTARD CRUST

  2 pound slice of smoked ham, center cut
  ¼ cup prepared mustard
  ¼ cup all-purpose flour
  2 tablespoons dark molasses
  ⅓ cup seedless raisins
  15 whole cloves
  1 cup milk
  ½ cup light cream
    Raisin Gravy

Put ham in a shallow baking dish. Combine mustard, flour, and molasses and mix well. Spread mixture over the ham. Sprinkle top of ham with raisins and cloves. Mix milk with cream and pour over ham. Bake in preheated moderate oven (350°F.) for 1 hour. Remove ham from baking dish and place on a platter. Serve with Raisin Gravy. Makes 6 to 8 servings.

## LIVER PUDDING

  1½ cups raw rice
  2 cups water
  4 cups milk
  1 onion, chopped
  ¼ cup butter
  1 pound beef liver, chopped
  1 egg, well beaten
  1 tablespoon sugar
  1 tablespoon salt
  ⅛ teaspoon pepper

Pour rice into water mixed with milk. Cook over high heat, stirring occasionally, until mixture is very thick. Sauté onion in butter until golden brown. To make chopping easier, dip liver into boiling water for 1 minute or freeze partially. Add liver, egg, onion, sugar, salt, and pepper to rice mixture. Put mixture into well-buttered 2-quart casserole and bake in preheated moderate oven (350°F.) for 1 hour. Makes 6 to 8 servings.

## BOOYAW [Mich.]

  1 pound pickled pork, cubed
  5- pound chicken, rabbit, or any game, cut in pieces
  1 yellow turnip, cubed
  2 large onions, sliced
  6 carrots, cut into 1-inch pieces
  6 large potatoes, cubed
  2 celery stalks, chopped
    Salt and pepper

Cover meats with water and cook, covered, until meats are tender. Add vegetables, cover, and cook for 20 to 30 minutes, or until vegetables are tender. Season to taste with salt and pepper. Makes 8 servings.

## MANITOWISH WALLEYED PIKE

  2 pounds sliced filleted pike
    Salt and pepper to taste
  2 eggs, well beaten
    Yellow cornmeal
    Fat or vegetable oil for deep frying

Cut fish into small slices. Sprinkle slices with salt and pepper; dip into eggs; roll slices in cornmeal, coating well. Fry slices in deep fat (370°F. on a frying thermometer) for 3 to 4 minutes, or until fish is golden brown on all sides. Drain on absorbent paper and serve immediately. Makes 4 to 6 servings.

## PLATTE RIVER BAKED TROUT [Neb.]

  8 whole trout, cleaned
  2 tablespoons water
    Juice of 1 lemon
    Salt and pepper
  3 tablespoons chopped chives
  1 tablespoon butter
  3 tablespoons all-purpose flour
  2 cups heavy cream
  1 cup soft bread crumbs, tossed with 2 tablespoons melted butter

With a sharp knife bone the fish but do not remove the heads. (Bones may be left in if desired.) Put fish in a greased glass or earthenware baking dish in a single layer. Add water, lemon juice, and salt and pepper to taste. Sprinkle with chives. Bake in preheated moderate oven (375°F.) for 10 minutes. Melt butter and stir in flour. Gradually stir in cream. Add salt and pepper to taste. Cook over low heat, stirring constantly, until smooth and thick. Pour sauce over fish. Sprinkle top with bread crumbs. Continue baking for 10 to 15 minutes, or until top is lightly browned. Makes 8 servings.

## WISCONSIN CHEESE RABBIT

    2 tablespoons butter
    1 pound sharp Cheddar cheese, shredded
    ½ teaspoon dry mustard
      Dash of cayenne
    ½ teaspoon salt
    1 teaspoon Worcestershire
    ½ cup beer
    2 eggs, slightly beaten
    8 slices of toast
      Parsley

Melt butter in top pan of chafing dish over direct low heat. Add cheese and heat, stirring occasionally until cheese is melted. Put over boiling water, add seasonings, and pour in beer mixed with eggs. Cook until thick, stirring frequently. Serve on toast with garnish of parsley. Makes 4 servings.

## INDEPENDENCE BAKED CORN

    12 ears fresh corn
       Salt and pepper
    1 tablespoon sugar
    2 tablespoons water
    ¼ cup heavy cream

With a sharp knife cut down center of the kernels of corn. With back of the knife press out pulp without removing any of hull. Add salt and pepper to taste. Stir in sugar and water. Pour mixture into lightly greased shallow baking dish. Bake in preheated moderate oven (350°F.) for 30 minutes. Remove from oven and stir cream into corn. Serve at once. Makes 4 to 6 servings.

## SOUTH DAKOTA PARSNIP FRITTERS

Scrub parsnips and cook in boiling salted water until tender. Plunge into cold water and slip off skins. Mash. Season with butter, salt, pepper, and a dash of sugar. Flour hands. Shape into small flat cakes. Sauté in butter until delicately browned on each side.

## IOWA RAW FRIED POTATOES

    6 large raw potatoes
    ⅓ cup lard
      Salt

Peel potatoes and cut into ⅛-inch slices. Soak in cold water until slices are crisp. Drain and dry on paper toweling. Heat lard until very hot. Add potatoes, reduce heat, and fry slowly until crusty and brown. Turn occasionally with a pancake turner. Sprinkle with salt and serve immediately. Makes 6 servings.

## WILD RICE CASSEROLE [Minn.]

    1 cup wild rice
    ¼ cup butter
    3 tablespoons chopped onion

    3 tablespoons chopped green pepper
    ½ cup slivered blanched almonds
    3 cups hot chicken broth

Wash rice and drain well. Melt butter in skillet; add rice, onion, green pepper, and almonds. Sauté over low heat, stirring constantly, until rice begins to turn light yellow. Turn into a casserole; add hot chicken broth. Cover, and bake in preheated slow oven (325°F.) for 1½ hours, or until rice is tender and all liquid is absorbed. Makes 4 servings.

## WHOLE GLAZED SQUASH [N.D.]

    1 butternut squash, about 3 to 4 pounds
    ¾ cup firmly packed dark brown sugar
    ¼ cup butter or margarine
    1 tablespoon water

Bake squash in preheated moderate oven (350°F.) for 1 hour, or until squash is tender. Peel rind and leave squash whole. Mix brown sugar, butter, and water. Cook slowly for 3 to 4 minutes. Spoon thick syrup over all surfaces of the squash. Bake for 15 minutes longer, or until squash is glazed. Cut into serving pieces and serve with Canadian bacon or ham. Makes 4 to 6 servings.

## HOOSIER FRIED TOMATOES, CREAMY GRAVY

Slice firm ripe or green tomatoes. Remove stem end. Cut in ½-inch slices. Dip slices into pancake flour or cornmeal; season with salt and pepper. Fry in bacon fat until brown, turning once. Just before removing from skillet, sprinkle each slice with ½ to 1 teaspoon sugar. Keep in warm place. Make Creamy Gravy. Pour gravy around tomatoes and serve at once.
**Creamy Gravy**—Stir flour and milk into drippings in skillet, using 3 tablespoons flour for each 3 tablespoons drippings and 1½ cups milk. Stir and cook until thickened. Season with salt and pepper.

## POTATO-FLOUR MUFFINS À LA MARSHALL FIELD'S

    ⅛ teaspoon salt
    4 eggs, separated
    1 tablespoon sugar
    ½ cup potato flour
    1 teaspoon baking powder
    2 tablespoons ice water

Add salt to egg whites and beat until stiff. Beat yolks until thick; then beat in sugar. Fold yolks into whites. Add sifted flour and baking powder. Mix well and stir in water. Pour batter into greased muffin pans. Bake in preheated moderate oven (375°F.) for 15 to 20 minutes. Makes 12 muffins.

## BLACK WALNUT MERINGUE

4 egg whites
1 teaspoon cream of tartar
1 cup sugar
1 teaspoon vanilla extract
8 soda crackers, crushed fine
½ cup chopped black walnuts
  Ice cream
  Berries

Beat egg whites until almost stiff. Sift cream of tartar over whites and blend. Gradually add sugar and continue beating until mixture is very stiff. Add vanilla. Fold in cracker crumbs and nuts. Pile lightly in buttered 9-inch pie pan. Bake in slow oven (275°F.) 45 to 60 minutes. (Top should look dry.) Cut in wedges and serve with ice cream and berries. Makes 6 servings.

## PERSIMMON GRAHAM-CRACKER DESSERT [Ind.]

*The variety of persimmon grown in Indiana is not to be confused with the Japanese persimmon, grown and marketed from California. The Hoosier plumlike yellow persimmon probably came from Virginia; while green it is very astringent and puckers the mouth, but when ripe it is sweet and delicious in pies and puddings*

2 cups graham cracker crumbs
1 cup confectioners' sugar
1 cup puréed ripe persimmon pulp
½ cup coarsely chopped walnuts
¼ pound large marshmallows, cut into quarters
  Whipped cream

Mix all together. Cover and refrigerate overnight. Serve with whipped cream. Makes 4 to 6 servings.

## WISCONSIN WASPS' NESTS

1 cup granulated sugar
½ cup water
5 cups (1 pound) unblanched almonds, slivered
5 egg whites
⅛ teaspoon salt
1 teaspoon vanilla extract
3½ cups sifted (1 pound) confectioners' sugar
4 ounces (4 squares) unsweetened chocolate, melted

Cook granulated sugar and water until syrup spins a thread (234°F. on a candy thermometer). Add nuts slowly and continue stirring until all syrup is absorbed. Beat egg whites until frothy; add salt and vanilla; continue beating until whites are very stiff; gradually beat in confectioners' sugar. Fold in nuts and chocolate. Drop from teaspoon on well-buttered cookie sheets. Bake in preheated slow oven (300°F.) for 20 to 25 minutes. Makes 10 dozen.

## POLYNEES [Swedish Almond Tarts]

2 cups sifted all-purpose flour
½ teaspoon salt
1 tablespoon sugar
1 teaspoon baking powder
¾ cup butter or margarine
1 egg yolk
2 tablespoons brandy
  Raspberry jam
  Almond Filling

Sift flour, salt, sugar, and baking powder; cut in butter. Add egg yolk and brandy; blend well. Chill. Roll out dough ⅛ inch thick. Butter eight 4-inch fluted tart pans and line with rounds of dough. Roll remaining dough and cut into ½-inch strips. Place 2 teaspoons raspberry jam in each unbaked tart shell. Fill three-fourths full with Almond Filling. Arrange 2 strips of pastry on top to form a cross. Bake in preheated slow oven (325°F.) for about 30 minutes. Makes 8 servings.

### Almond Filling

Beat 4 egg whites until stiff but not dry. Gradually beat in ½ cup sugar and 1 cup ground blanched almonds.

## PRUNE KOLACHE

2 tablespoons water*
1 package active dry yeast or 1 cake compressed yeast
4 cups sifted all-purpose flour
¼ cup sugar
1 teaspoon salt
1 teaspoon grated lemon rind
¾ cup butter
3 egg yolks
1 cup heavy cream
  Prune Filling
  Confectioners' Icing

*Use very warm water (105°F. to 115°F.) for dry yeast; use lukewarm (80°F. to 90°F.) for compressed. Sprinkle dry yeast or crumble cake into water. Let stand for a few minutes; then stir until dissolved. Sift flour with sugar and salt. Add grated lemon rind and yeast; blend in butter. Beat egg yolks and add cream; combine with flour mixture. Blend well. Cover bowl tightly. Refrigerate overnight. Knead several times and roll on lightly floured board to ¼-thickness. Cut with 2-inch cutter and place rounds on ungreased cookie sheets. Cover, and let rise in warm place until double in bulk, about 1 hour. Using fingertips, make a depression in the center of each kolache. Fill with Prune Filling. Bake in preheated moderate oven (375°F.) for about 10 minutes. While warm, spread with Confectioners' Sugar Icing. Makes 4 to 5 dozen.

### Prune Filling

Soak 1½ cups prunes in water overnight. Simmer, covered, until tender; drain. Pit prunes and mash with fork. Add ¼ cup sugar and ½ teaspoon ground cinnamon.

### Confectioners' Sugar Icing

Mix 1½ cups sifted confectioners' sugar, 2 tablespoons boiling water, and 1 teaspoon lemon juice.

# SOUTHERN COOKERY

## CHARLESTON SHE-CRAB SOUP

¼ cup butter
1 pound crabmeat
2 cups light cream
2 cups milk
  Ground mace, salt, and pepper to taste
¼ cup cracker crumbs
2 tablespoons sherry

Melt butter, add crabmeat, and sauté for 1 to 2 minutes. Stir in cream, milk, and seasonings. Thicken with cracker crumbs and let stand over lowest possible heat for a few minutes, or until heated through. Do not boil. Add sherry just before serving soup. Makes 4 servings.

## BAKED SMITHFIELD HAM

Cover a Smithfield ham with water and soak for 12 hours. Change water and simmer over low heat for 4 to 5 hours, or until tender. Cool in liquid. When cold, remove skin. Put in roasting pan and make crisscross cuts in fat. Stud with whole cloves and sprinkle with a little sherry, if desired. Sprinkle with a mixture of 2 tablespoons fine cracker crumbs, 2 tablespoons brown sugar, and a little pepper. Bake in preheated hot oven (425°F.) for 25 minutes, or until lightly browned and hot. Slice ham paper-thin.

## TENNESSEE BAKED HAM

1 country ham (10 to 12 pounds)
4 cups yellow cornmeal
1 cup firmly packed dark brown sugar
1 tablespoon pepper
  Water
  Dry bread crumbs

Soak ham overnight in cold water. Drain, and wipe dry. Mix cornmeal with brown sugar and pepper. Add enough water to make a claylike paste. Put ham in a shallow baking pan. Cover ham with cornmeal paste, making shell about 1 inch thick. Roast in preheated moderate oven (350°F.) for 4 hours, or until meat thermometer registers 170°F. Add a little boiling water to the pan but do not baste. Remove from oven. Strip off paste and skin. Sprinkle ham with dry bread crumbs, replace in oven, and roast until brown. Makes about 24 servings.

## KENTUCKY BURGOO

1 fat stewing chicken (about 5 pounds)
2 pounds each of beef, lamb, pork, and veal shanks
  Cold water
3 tablespoons salt
6 each of potatoes, onions, and carrots, peeled and diced
2 cups each of diced celery, sliced okra, whole kernel corn, Lima beans, chopped green cabbage
2 green peppers, diced
  Dash each of cayenne, hot pepper sauce, steak sauce, and Worcestershire

Cover all meat with cold water and bring to boil in a 20-quart stock pot. Cover, reduce heat, and simmer for 3 to 4 hours, or until meat falls from bones. Remove meat from bones; discard bones. Cool meat and dice; return to stock. Add remaining ingredients. Simmer until thick, stirring frequently during first part of cooking and almost constantly toward the end. Makes 25 servings.

## MARYLAND FRIED CHICKEN

2 frying chickens (about 2½ pounds each), cut up
¾ cup all-purpose flour
1 teaspoon salt
¼ teaspoon pepper
½ cup butter or margarine
1 cup water
1½ cups light cream

Wash and dry chicken pieces. Shake in bag with flour, salt, and pepper. Heat butter in heavy skillet or chicken fryer. Put in chicken and brown quickly on all sides. Reduce heat, slowly add water, cover, and simmer gently until tender, about 30 minutes. Uncover and let chicken sauté slowly. Remove chicken to a hot platter. Blend 2 tablespoons flour into drippings in skillet. Gradually stir in cream and cook, stirring, until thickened. Season to taste and pour over chicken. If desired, garnish with corn oysters or small corn fritters, and broiled bacon. Makes 6 to eight servings.

## ROAST CROWN OF PORK, FLORIDA STYLE

1 crown roast of pork, made from 16 ribs
2 tablespoons butter
3 tablespoons chopped onion
3 tablespoons chopped celery
4 oranges, sectioned
1 large grapefruit, sectioned
1½ cups cooked rice
2 cups toasted bread cubes
1 tablespoon crumbled leaf sage
1 teaspoon salt
¼ teaspoon pepper
1 teaspoon grated orange rind

Preheat oven to hot (400°F.). Protect ends of rib bones with small pieces of aluminum foil. Place pork on a rack in a roasting pan. Place in the oven and immediately reduce oven temperature to moderately slow (325°F.). Roast for 40 minutes a pound to an internal temperature of 176°F. Melt butter and sauté onion and celery until tender. Cut orange and grapefruit sections into halves. Add sections and remaining ingredients to onions and celery and toss to mix. One hour before roast is done, fill center with the stuffing. Baste twice during the last hour with drippings in the pan. Garnish with additional orange and grapefruit sections, and preserved crabapples, if desired. Makes 6 to 8 servings.
**Note:** The stuffing may also be used for duck or chicken.

## CHICKEN-SHRIMP GUMBO FILE

  1 fowl (about 4 pounds), cut into pieces
    Water
  1 garlic clove
    Salt and pepper
  ¼ pound salt pork, diced
  1 sweet red pepper, chopped
  1 cup chopped onion
  ⅓ cup all-purpose flour
  2⅓ cups (one 1-pound, 3-ounce can) tomatoes
  1 package (10 ounces) frozen okra or 1 can (1 pound)
    cut okra, drained
  1 pound uncooked shrimps, shelled and deveined
    Hot pepper sauce
  2 teaspoons gumbo filé powder
    Hot cooked rice

Cook fowl with 5 cups water, garlic, 1 tablespoon salt, and ¼ teaspoon pepper for 3 hours, or until tender. Cool and remove meat from bones. Cut into pieces. Strain broth and reserve. Add enough water to make 6 cups. Cool and skim off fat. Cook salt pork until well browned and done. Remove pork from kettle and pour off all but ¼ cup fat. Sauté red pepper and onion in fat for 5 minutes. Add flour and brown. Gradually stir in broth. Add pork and tomatoes. Cover and simmer for 30 minutes. Add chicken, okra, and shrimps. Simmer, covered, until shrimps turn pink. Season with salt, pepper, and hot pepper sauce. Gradually add gumbo filé powder and stir until completely blended. Put a scoop of rice in center of each soup bowl before serving. Makes 6 servings.

## BRUNSWICK STEW

  1 stewing chicken (about 4 pounds), cut up
    Water
  4 slices of bacon
  ½ pound boneless beef chuck, cut into ¾-inch cubes
  1 small onion, minced
  1¼ teaspoons salt
  1 teaspoon paprika
  2 cups (1-pound can) tomatoes
  1 package (10 ounces) frozen Lima beans
  1½ cups (one 12-ounce can) whole kernel corn
  3 medium raw potatoes, diced
    Seasoned salt, and pepper
    All-purpose flour

Cover chicken with 4 cups water, bring to boil, and cook, covered, for 1 hour, or until tender. Cool chicken, remove meat from bones, reserving broth, and cut into bite-size pieces. Dice bacon and brown in kettle. Remove bacon and brown beef and onion in fat remaining in kettle. Add bacon, chicken broth, salt, paprika, and tomatoes. Bring to boil, cover, and simmer for 1½ hours. Add remaining vegetables and chicken and simmer for about 30 minutes longer. Season to taste and thicken slightly with a flour-and-water paste. Makes 6 servings.

## JAMBALAYA DE CANARD

  1 duckling, about 4 pounds, including giblets
    Salt and pepper
    Water
  1 cup long-grained raw rice
  ¾ cup chopped onion
  ½ cup chopped green pepper
  1 garlic clove, minced
  ½ pound bulk sausage
  1 bay leaf
  ½ teaspoon chili powder
  ½ teaspoon ground thyme
  1 tablespoon chopped parsley
  ½ cup diced cooked ham
  1 cup canned tomatoes

Bone duck, reserving bones and discarding excess fat. Sprinkle with 2 teaspoons salt and ½ teaspoon pepper. Brown duck in a skillet for 30 to 40 minutes, turning occasionally. Cook duck bones and giblets, except liver, in enough water to cover, with ½ teaspoon salt, for about 40 minutes, or until giblets are tender. Add liver 10 minutes before cooking time is over. Drain and reserve 2 cups broth; use remaining broth for soup or gravies. Chop giblets. After duck has been browned, drain off all excess fat from skillet and place duck pieces on absorbent paper to drain. Replace duck in skillet and add reserved broth. Cover and cook slowly for 1½ hours, or until duck is tender.

  Soak rice in enough water to cover for 30 minutes, then drain. Add onion, green pepper, and garlic to sausage and cook over low heat until vegetables are tender and sausage is cooked. Drain excess fat. Add soaked rice and stir over low heat until rice is dry. Add 1½ teaspoons salt, ¼ teaspoon pepper, bay leaf, chili powder, thyme, and parsley. Remove duck from pan and mix rice mixture into gravy. Cover and cook for 10 minutes, or until rice is almost tender. Add giblets, ham, and tomatoes. Mix carefully, taking care not to mash rice. Place duck pieces on top of rice. Cover and cook for 10 minutes longer. Serve rice topped with duck pieces. Makes 6 to 8 servings.

## FROGS' LEGS A LA CREOLE [La.]

  16 large frog legs
    Boiling water
    Juice of ½ lemon
    Salt and pepper
  2 eggs, well beaten
    Fine dry bread crumbs
    Fat for deep frying
    Onion Cream Sauce

Put frog legs in boiling water with lemon juice and salt and pepper. Scald for 4 minutes. Drain legs and pat dry. Dip legs into eggs and roll in bread crumbs. Fry in deep fat (370°F. on a frying thermometer) for 2 to 3 minutes, until legs are tender. Serve with Onion Cream Sauce. Makes 4 servings.

## Onion Cream Sauce

- 2 tablespoons butter or margarine
- 2 tablespoons all-purpose flour
- 1½ cups light cream
- ½ teaspoon salt
- 2 tablespoons minced onion
- 1 tablespoon minced parsley
- 1 egg, well beaten

Melt butter and stir in flour. Gradually stir in cream. Add salt, onion, and parsley. Cook over low heat, stirring constantly, until smooth and thickened. Beat some of sauce into egg. Add to remainder of sauce and cook for 2 minutes. Spoon sauce over frogs' legs.

## ANTOINE'S OYSTERS ROCKEFELLER

- ½ cup tightly packed parsley leaves
- 1 cup tightly packed spinach leaves
- 4 shallots or 1 small onion
- 1 tablespoon aniseed
- 1 cup water
- ¼ teaspoon hot pepper sauce
- ½ teaspoon salt
- ½ teaspoon ground thyme
- 1 tablespoon anchovy paste
- ½ cup butter or margarine
- ½ cup toasted bread crumbs
- 24 oysters
  Rock salt

Put parsley, spinach, and shallots through a food chopper. Simmer aniseed in water for 10 minutes. Strain out the seed. Add ground vegetables to anise-flavored liquid (this approximates the flavor of absinthe which was in the original formula). Simmer, covered, for 10 minutes. Season with hot pepper sauce, salt, thyme, and anchovy paste. Add butter and bread crumbs. If sauce is too thick to spread easily, thin it with a little of the oyster liquor. Open oysters with an oyster knife. Place oysters on a bed of rock salt in a shallow baking dish. Bake in preheated moderate oven (350°F.) for about 6 minutes *or* broil them for 5 minutes only, until the edges curl. Spread each oyster with a spoon of the prepared sauce and return to broiler for 5 minutes longer. Makes 4 servings.

## HOPPING JOHN

- 2 cups blackeye peas or beans
- 3 quarts water
- ½ pound sliced bacon
- 1 onion, minced
- 2 cups raw rice
- 1 tablespoon salt
- ¼ teaspoon pepper
- 1 hot red pepper

Bring peas and water to boil. Boil for 2 minutes. Cover pan and let stand for 1 hour. Cut up bacon and cook until brown; add onions and cook until golden. Pour bacon mixture into peas. Cover and simmer until peas are tender, about 1 hour. Stir in rice and seasonings. Cook, covered, without stirring until rice is tender. Makes 8 to 10 servings.

## GULF-BAKED RED SNAPPER

- 1 red snapper (3 pounds)
- 1 garlic clove
- 1 teaspoon salt
- ¼ teaspoon pepper
- ⅓ cup bacon fat, olive oil, melted butter, or margarine
- 1 tablespoon fresh lemon juice
- 2 onions, chopped
- 4 celery stalks, chopped
- ½ green pepper, chopped
- 2 tablespoons chopped parsley
- ½ teaspoon sugar
- 2 cups fresh or canned tomatoes
- ¼ teaspoon crumbled thyme
- 1 bay leaf
  Worcestershire

Put fish, cleaned, with head and tail removed, in buttered roasting pan. Crush or mince garlic. Add salt, pepper, melted fat, and lemon juice. Rub fish inside and out with this mixture. Let stand in cool place for 1 hour. Add remaining ingredients. Place in preheated moderate oven (350°F.). Bake for 40 to 60 minutes, or until fish flakes. Makes 6 servings.

## SHRIMP PILAU ST. AUGUSTINE

- ¼ cup diced fat salt pork
- 1 large onion, chopped
- 1 green pepper, chopped
- 1 pound deveined cooked shrimps
- 1 cup hot cooked rice
  Salt and pepper

Fry salt pork until well browned and crisp. Remove pork and cook onion and pepper in the fat. Add pork, shrimps and rice. Season to taste and simmer for about 10 minutes. Makes 4 to 6 servings.

**Variation**—Sliced okra may be added. Brown okra in a little butter; add 5 minutes before pilau is done.

## TURNIP GREENS WITH HOG JOWL

    1 pound mustard greens
    ½ pound salt pork, fresh hog jowl,
        or ham hock
        Water
    1 pound young tender turnip tops

Wash and drain mustard greens. Put in pot with meat. Add just enough water to cover. Simmer, covered, until meat is tender. Wash and drain turnip tops. Put in a pot with enough water to cover and simmer until tender. Add turnip greens with juice to mustard greens, meat and broth. Simmer, covered, for 10 minutes. Drain and reserve liquid. Slice meat and serve over greens. Juice drained from vegetables is called "pot likker" and is served in cups. Serve with corn bread. Makes 4 servings.

## FLORIDA FRUIT SALAD BOWL

        Juice of 1 lemon
    ¼ cup salad oil
    1 can (6 ounces) frozen concentrated orange juice
    2 grapefruits
    4 oranges
    1 avocado, sliced
        Salad greens

Put lemon juice, oil, and tangerine juice in blender. Whirl until well mixed. Section grapefruits and oranges, add avocado and salad greens. Pour dressing over salad and toss lightly. Makes 4 to 6 servings.

## VIRGINIA BATTER BREAD

    1 cup white water-ground cornmeal
    1 teaspoon salt
    1 teaspoon baking powder
    2 tablespoons butter
    4 cups milk, scalded
    4 eggs, separated

Combine dry ingredients. Add butter to milk. When melted, stir into cornmeal mixture. Blend thoroughly. Add well-beaten yolks. Fold in stiffly beaten whites. Pour batter into greased 2-quart casserole. Bake in preheated moderate oven (350°F.) for 45 to 50 minutes; stir twice before crust begins to set. Makes 4 to 6 servings.

## ANTEBELLUM SPICED NUT CORN BREAD

    ½ cup sifted all-purpose flour
    2 teaspoons baking powder
    ¼ teaspoon salt
    ¼ cup sugar
    ½ teaspoon ground cinnamon
    ¼ teaspoon each of ground allspice and nutmeg
    ½ cup white cornmeal

    ½ cup finely chopped pecans
    1 egg, beaten
    ½ cup milk
    2 tablespoons melted butter

Sift dry ingredients. Add nuts; stir well. Add egg, milk, and 1 tablespoon melted butter. Blend to make a batter. Put remaining 1 tablespoon butter in a 7-inch iron skillet. Heat skillet in preheated hot oven (400°F.), then brush heated butter on sides and bottom of pan. Add batter and return to oven at once. Bake for 30 minutes, or until corn bread tests done. Cut into 6 wedges and serve immediately. Makes 6 servings.

## SWEET-POTATO BISCUITS [N.C.]

    1 small sweet potato, baked
    2 tablespoons shortening
    1 cup sifted all-purpose flour
    1 teaspoon baking powder
    ¼ teaspoon salt
    2 to 3 tablespoons milk

Peel and dice sweet potato. Cut potato and shortening into flour sifted with baking powder and salt; add milk and stir until mixed. Turn onto floured board and knead gently. Roll to ½-inch thickness and cut into 2-inch rounds. Bake on greased cookie sheet in preheated hot oven (400°F.) for about 12 minutes. Makes ten to twelve 2-inch biscuits

## ALABAMA SOUR-MILK BISCUITS

    2 cups sifted all-purpose flour
    1 teaspoon baking powder
    ½ teaspoon baking soda
    1 teaspoon salt
    ¼ cup soft butter or margarine
    1 cup thick sour milk or buttermilk (use less if not thick)

Sift dry ingredients into bowl. Cut in butter with pastry blender. Add enough sour milk to make a soft dough, mixing lightly with fork. Turn out on floured board and knead about 20 turns. Roll out to ½ inch thickness and cut with floured 2-inch cutter. Bake in preheated very hot oven (450°F.) for 10 to 12 minutes. Makes 12 to 14.

## KENTUCKY LACE-EDGE CORN CAKES

    ½ teaspoon salt
    ½ teaspoon baking soda
    1 cup water-ground white cornmeal
    1 egg
    1¼ cups buttermilk

Mix salt and baking soda thoroughly with meal. Mix egg well with buttermilk. Combine both mixtures and beat until smooth. Drop by tablespoons of batter onto a hot greased griddle. Bake until underside is brown (lift edge gently and peek). Then turn, but only once. Never pat or flatten the cakes with a turner. Stir batter well before dipping out each batch. Makes 4 servings.

## SWEET POTATO PONE

    4 cups grated peeled raw sweet potatoes
    1 egg, well beaten
    ¼ cup melted butter
    1 cup milk
    ¾ cup dark corn syrup
    ½ cup all-purpose flour
    ½ teaspoon each of ground nutmeg and cinnamon
    ½ teaspoon salt

Mix sweet potatoes with egg, melted butter, and milk. Stir in corn syrup. Beat in remaining ingredients. Pour mixture into 1½-quart baking dish. Bake in preheated slow oven (325°F.) for 2½ hours. Stir occasionally during the first hour. Serve hot or cold. When cold, it can be sliced and served with milk or cream. Makes 6 servings.

## LEMON VELVET PUDDING

    3 eggs, separated
      Grated rind of 1 large lemon
    ⅓ cup fresh lemon juice
    ¼ teaspoon salt
    1 cup sugar
    ⅓ cup cornstarch
    1 cup water
    1 tablespoon butter
    1 cup heavy cream, whipped
    1 dozen ladyfingers

Beat egg whites until stiff; beat yolks until thick. Add lemon rind and juice to yolks. Mix dry ingredients. Gradually stir in water. Stir into egg yolks and cook over low heat, stirring constantly, until thick and smooth. Remove from heat, add butter, and stir until melted. Fold in egg whites. Let stand until cool. Fold in whipped cream. Pour into glass bowl lined with ladyfingers. Chill. Makes 6 servings.

## SWEET-POTATO PUDDING

    3 cups grated raw sweet potatoes
    ½ cup firmly packed light brown sugar
    ½ teaspoon salt
    1 teaspoon ground nutmeg
    ½ cup light corn syrup
    1 cup milk
    2 eggs, beaten
    ½ cup chopped pecans
    2 tablespoons butter, melted

Mix all ingredients in bowl. Blend well. Pour into buttered pan, 12 x 8 x 2 inches. Bake in preheated moderate oven (350°F.) for about 1 hour. Serve warm or cold with cream or ice cream. Makes 6 servings.

## TELEPHONE PUDDING

    6 eggs, separated
      Sugar
      Salt
    1½ teaspoons vanilla extract
    2 cups medium cream
    24 almond macaroons
    1 cup blackberry or black raspberry jam

Beat egg yolks with 6 tablespoons sugar and ⅛ teaspoon salt until thick. Add vanilla. Scald cream and beat gradually into egg-yolk mixture. Line a baking dish (13 x 9 x 2 inches) with macaroons, cut into halves. Pour custard over them. Set dish in pan of hot water. Bake in preheated moderate oven (350°F.) for 25 minutes, or until custard sets. Do not overcook. Remove from oven; dot custard with jam. Beat egg whites with ¼ teaspoon salt until foamy. Beat in 6 tablespoons sugar, 1 spoonful at a time, beating until stiff. Spread meringue over custard. Bake in preheated slow oven (325°F.) for 18 minutes. Serve warm or cold. Makes 8 servings.

## BENNE-SEED COOKIES

*Sesame seed is called benne in South Carolina*

    1 cup firmly packed light brown sugar
    1 cup benne seed
    ⅓ cup melted shortening
    1 egg, beaten
    ½ cup sifted all-purpose flour
    ⅛ teaspoon salt
    1 tablespoon hot water

Combine and blend all ingredients. Drop from teaspoon onto greased cookie sheets. Bake in preheated slow oven (325°F.) for about 10 minutes. Remove to rack. When cool, store in airtight containers. Makes about 2 dozen.

## GEORGIA PECAN PIE

      Pastry for 1-crust 9-inch pie, unbaked
    2 eggs
    1 cup dark corn syrup
      Dash of salt
    2 tablespoons melted butter
    1 tablespoon all-purpose flour
    1 teaspoon vanilla extract
    ½ cup sugar
    1 cup pecan halves
      Whipped cream

Line 9-inch pie pan with pastry. Beat eggs. Add remaining ingredients. Fill pastry-lined pan. Bake in preheated slow oven (300°F.) for 1 hour, or until barely set. Cool. Top with whipped cream. Makes 6 to 8 servings.

## LADY BALTIMORE CAKE

    ⅔ cup soft butter or margarine
    1½ cups sugar
    1 teaspoon vanilla extract
    ½ teaspoon almond extract
    2½ cups sifted cake flour
    2½ teaspoons baking powder
    ⅔ cup milk
    ½ teaspoon salt
    ½ teaspoon cream of tartar
    4 egg whites
      Fluffy White Frosting
    6 dried figs, chopped
    ½ cup each of chopped raisins and nuts

Cream butter. Add sugar gradually, beating until light. Add flavorings. Add sifted flour and baking powder alternately with milk, beating until smooth. Add salt and cream of tartar to egg whites. Beat until stiff, but not dry. Fold into first mixture. Pour into two 9-inch layer-cake pans, greased and lined on the bottom with wax paper. Bake in preheated moderate oven (375°F.) for 20 to 25 minutes. Cool. Make Fluffy White Frosting. To one third of frosting, add chopped dried figs, raisins, and nuts. Spread between layers. Use remaining frosting for top and sides of cake. Makes 8 to 10 servings.

### Fluffy White Frosting

In top part of double boiler, combine 2 egg whites, 1½ cups sugar, ⅛ teaspoon salt, ⅓ cup water, and 2 teaspoons light corn syrup. Put over boiling water and beat with rotary beater or electric mixer for 7 minutes, or until mixture will stand in stiff peaks. Fold in 1 teaspoon vanilla extract.

## BLUEGRASS SORGHUM CAKE

½ cup butter or margarine
1 cup sugar
1 egg
2 cups sifted all-purpose flour
½ teaspoon salt
1 teaspoon baking powder
½ teaspoon baking soda
½ teaspoon each of ground cinnamon and nutmeg
¾ cup sour milk or buttermilk
½ cup sorghum syrup

Cream butter. Add sugar gradually, beating until light. Add egg and beat thoroughly. Sift dry ingredients and add alternately with liquids to creamed mixture. Beat until smooth. Pour batter into greased pan (8 x 8 x 2 inches). Bake in preheated slow oven (325°F.) for 45 minutes. Makes 6 to 8 servings.

## GEORGIA PEACH LEATHER

Peel and pit freestone peaches and force pulp through sieve or food mill. To each 4 cups pulp add 1⅔ cups sugar. Mix, bring to boil, and boil for 2 minutes at high heat, stirring constantly. Spread thin layer on cookie sheets. Cover loosely with cheesecloth. Dry in sun for 3 to 4 days, or until candy can be rolled like leather. Sprinkle with sugar, cut into strips and roll. Store in an airtight container.

## SOUTH CAROLINA SYLLABUB

1 cup sweet sherry
1 cup Madeira
2 lemons
4 cups heavy cream
1 teaspoon ground mace
½ cup superfine sugar

Mix sherry with Madeira. Add juice from lemons. Peel outer rind from lemons and add peel to wine. Let stand for 30 minutes. Strain wine and add to heavy cream, along with mace and sugar. Beat ingredients with a rotary egg beater or electric mixer until very frothy. Spoon the froth into dessert dishes and serve. Makes 12 servings.

## FRIED CHICKEN WITH PUFFS AND GRAVY

    2  young broiling chickens (2½ to 3 pounds each)
        Salt and pepper
        All-purpose flour (about 2 cups)
        Lard (about 2 cups)
  1½  teaspoons baking powder
  3½  cups milk

Quarter chickens. Season with salt and pepper and roll each piece in flour. Use 2 iron frying pans. Add lard to depth of 2 inches or more. Heat lard, add chicken, cover and cook for a few minutes over low heat. Then sauté, uncovered, until nicely browned. Remove chicken to absorbent paper and keep in warm place. Reserve one pan and hot lard for cooking biscuits. Make biscuit dough using 1½ cups flour, ¼ cup lard, 1 teaspoon salt, baking powder, and ½ cup milk. Pat out on board to ½-inch thickness and cut into 2-inch rounds. Drop biscuits into hot lard, brown on both sides, drain on paper, and keep hot. To make gravy, pour off lard. Return ¼ cup lard to pan and blend in ¼ cup flour. Gradually stir in 3 cups milk. Cook over low heat, stirring constantly, until thickened. Season to taste. Serve chicken with biscuit puffs and gravy. Makes 4 servings.

# MID-ATLANTIC COOKERY

## CHEDDAR CHEESE SOUP [N.Y.]

1 onion, sliced
1 cup diced celery
¼ cup butter
¼ cup all-purpose flour
½ teaspoon dry mustard
1 teaspoon Worcestershire
½ teaspoon garlic salt
½ teaspoon monosodium glutamate
2 bouillon cubes
2 cups water
1 carrot, diced
4 cups milk
8 ounces sharp Cheddar cheese, shredded
Salt and pepper

In large saucepan, cook onion and celery in butter for about 5 minutes. Blend in next 5 ingredients. Add bouillon cubes, water, and carrot. Bring to boil and simmer, covered, for 15 minutes. Add milk and heat almost to boiling. Add cheese; stir until cheese is melted. Season to taste. Makes about 6 cups.

## HOLLANDSCHE BIEFSTUK
## [N.Y. Dutch Steak]

2½ pounds round steak or sirloin, about 1½ inches thick
3 tablespoons vinegar
¾ teaspoon salt
1 teaspoon pepper
½ cup butter or margarine
¾ cup water
Hot boiled potatoes

Cut meat into 2-inch pieces and pound with rolling pin. Mix vinegar, salt, and pepper and rub into both sides of meat. Set aside in cool place for thirty minutes. Heat butter in skillet. Brown meat quickly for 1 minute on each side for rare steak, a little longer for well done. Remove to a hot platter. Pour the water into hot skillet and bring to boil. Pour over steak and potatoes. Makes 6 servings.

## POT ROAST WITH APPLE CIDER

3½- to 4-pound eye round of beef
1 onion, sliced
6 whole cloves
Piece of gingerroot
Small piece of cinnamon stick
1½ teaspoons salt
2 cups apple cider
2 tablespoons shortening

Put beef with onion, seasonings, and cider in a large bowl in refrigerator. Let marinate overnight. Wipe meat; brown slowly in fat. Add marinade, cover, and simmer over low heat for about 2½ hours, or until meat is tender. Serve with pan juices. Makes 6 to 8 servings.

## PHILADELPHIA PEPPER POT SOUP

Veal bone
1 pound boneless stewing veal, cubed
½ pound tripe, cubed
½ bay leaf
Salt
½ teaspoon crushed peppercorns
3 onions, diced
1½ quarts water
2 raw potatoes, peeled and diced
2 carrots, diced
¼ cup diced celery
½ medium green pepper, chopped
2 tablespoons butter
Pepper
Minced parsley

Put bone, veal, tripe, bay leaf, 2 teaspoons salt, peppercorns, and one onion in large kettle. Add water. Bring to boil, cover, and simmer for 2 hours. Remove bone. Sauté remaining onion, potatoes, carrots, celery, and green pepper in butter for 10 minutes. Add to meat mixture and simmer for 30 minutes. Add salt and pepper to taste. Serve with parsley. Makes about 2 quarts.

## SCRAPPLE OR PANNHAAS
## [Pennsylvania Dutch]

1¼ cups yellow cornmeal
6 cups pork or ham broth
2 cups finely chopped cooked pork
1 teaspoon salt
¼ teaspoon white pepper
½ teaspoon rubbed sage
Fat for frying

Slowly sprinkle cornmeal into boiling broth. Cook until mush is thick. Blend in meat, salt, pepper, and sage. Pour mixture into a loaf pan (9 x 5 x 3 inches). Cool, and then chill. Unmold and cut into ¼-inch slices. Fry slices in hot fat until golden brown on both sides. Makes 8 servings.

## DELMARVA LEMON-FRIED CHICKEN

2 chickens (about 2½ pounds each), in pieces
¼ cup lemon juice
Cooking oil
¼ teaspoon garlic salt
½ teaspoon salt
¼ teaspoon crumbled thyme
¼ teaspoon crumbled marjoram
¼ teaspoon pepper
⅔ cup all-purpose flour
1 teaspoon grated lemon rind
1 teaspoon paprika

Wash chicken, pat dry and arrange in shallow dish. Mix lemon juice with ¼ cup oil, garlic salt, salt, thyme, marjoram, and pepper. Pour mixture over chicken and marinate in refrigerator for 1 to 2 hours. Remove from marinade and drain. Roll chicken in flour mixed with lemon rind and paprika. Heat ½ cup oil in large skillet and brown chicken on all sides. Place browned pieces in a baking dish in a single layer. Bake, uncovered, in preheated moderate oven (350°F.) for 45 to 50 minutes, or until chicken is tender. Makes 4 to 6 servings.

## ROAST LONG ISLAND DUCKLING

Allow 1 large or two small ducklings for 4 servings. Wash and dry ducks. Rub well with cut onion, salt, and pepper. Sprinkle with crumbled rosemary inside and out. Put ½ orange in each cavity. Place ducks, breast side up, on a rack in open roasting pan. Prick or score skin to allow fat to drain and help crisp skin. Roast in preheated slow oven (325°F.), allowing about 1¾ hours for small ducks and 2 to 2¼ hours for large duck. Drain drippings from pan every 30 minutes to get duckling crisp on all sides. Cut into halves or quarters for serving. Makes 4 servings.

## CHESAPEAKE DEVILED CRAB CAKES

    1 pound backfin crabmeat
      Butter
    2 tablespoons all-purpose flour
    ½ cup light cream
    ½ cup soft fresh bread crumbs (no crusts)
    ¼ cup minced green pepper
    2 tablespoons chopped green onion
    2 tablespoons prepared mustard
    1 teaspoon Worcestershire
    ⅛ teaspoon hot pepper sauce
    ½ teaspoon salt
    1 cup fine dry bread crumbs

Leave crabmeat in large lumps. Melt 1 tablespoon butter. Stir in flour. Gradually stir in cream. Cook over low heat, stirring constantly, until smooth and thick. Remove from heat. Add soft bread crumbs, green pepper, onion, and seasonings. Add crabmeat and mix lightly. Place dry bread crumbs in a shallow dish. Put a large spoonful of crab mixture on the crumbs, sprinkle dry crumbs on top, and shape into a cake. Do not pack. Heat 2 tablespoons butter in a large heavy skillet and sauté cakes lightly, adding more butter as needed. Carefully remove from skillet with broad spatula to individual hot plates. Makes 8 cakes (4 servings).

## SALT WATER TAFFY

    1 cup sugar
    2 tablespoons cornstarch
    ¾ cup light corn syrup
    ½ cup water
    ½ teaspoon salt
    2 tablespoons butter
    2 teaspoons vanilla extract

Mix sugar and cornstarch in saucepan. Stir in next 3 ingredients. Add butter and bring to a boil, stirring constantly until sugar is completely dissolved. Then cook without stirring until 260°F. registers on a candy thermometer, or until a small amount of syrup dropped into very cold water forms a hard ball. Remove from heat and stir in vanilla. Pour into well-greased 9-inch square pan and let stand until cool enough to handle. Then pull until white and satiny in appearance. Pull out in ½-inch strips and cut into 1-inch pieces with scissors. Wrap in wax paper. Makes ⅞ pound.

## SCHNITZ UN GNEPP
## [Dried Apples and Dumplings]

    2 cups dried sweet apples
      Water
    2 pound smoked ham butt, cubed
    2 tablespoons brown sugar
    2 cups sifted all-purpose flour
    3 teaspoons baking powder
    ½ teaspoon salt
    1 egg, beaten
    2 tablespoons butter, melted
    ½ cup milk

Cover dried apples with water and soak overnight. Put ham in a large kettle and cover with water. Simmer until ham is just tender. Add apples, water in which they were soaked, and brown sugar. Simmer for 1 hour. Drop double tablespoonsfuls of the dumpling mixture on top of simmering ham and apples. Cover and simmer for 20 minutes, or until dumplings are cooked.

**To prepare dumplings**—Sift flour with baking powder and salt. Mix egg with melted butter and milk. Add liquid to flour all at once and stir until just blended. Drop by double tablespoons on top of simmering mixture. Makes 8 servings.

## DELAWARE SPOON BREAD

    1 tablespoon shortening
    1½ cups milk
    ½ cup white water- or stone-ground cornmeal
    2 eggs
    2 teaspoons baking powder
    1 teaspoon salt

Turn oven to moderate (350°F.). Melt shortening in 1-quart casserole in oven. In a saucepan, scald 1 cup milk; stir in ground cornmeal. Cook until thick. Remove from stove and cool slightly. Beat in remaining ingredients. Pour the melted shortening into mixture in saucepan. Now pour the whole preparation back into casserole. Bake at 350°F. for 1 hour. Makes 4 servings.

## SHOOFLY PIE

    ¾ cup dark molasses
    ¾ cup boiling water
    ½ teaspoon baking soda
    ¼ teaspoon salt
    1½ cups sifted all-purpose flour
    ¼ cup butter or margarine
    ½ cup firmly packed brown sugar
      Pastry for 1-crust 9-inch pie, unbaked

Mix first 4 ingredients. With hands, mix next 3 ingredients. Pour about one third of molasses mixture into pastry-lined pie pan. Sprinkle with one third of flour mixture. Continue alternating layers, ending with flour mixture. Bake in preheated moderate oven (375°F.) for 35 minutes. Serve warm or cold. Makes 8 servings.

# NEW ENGLAND COOKERY

## MAINE SEAFOOD CHOWDER

6 slices salt pork, diced
1 onion, chopped
6 raw potatoes peeled and diced
2 cups water
1 teaspoon salt
2 pounds cod or haddock, skinned, boned, and cut into pieces
1 pound sea scallops, cut into halves
2 boiled lobsters (about 1 pound each) shelled and cubed
4 cups hot milk
2 cups light cream
¼ cup butter or margarine
Chopped parsley
Paprika

Cook salt pork until crisp. Add onion, potatoes, water, and salt. Simmer, covered, until almost tender. Add fish, scallops, lobsters, and hot milk. Simmer over very low heat for 10 minutes. Add cream and butter. Reheat but do not boil. Garnish with chopped parsley and sprinkle with paprika. Makes 6 servings.

## EGGS DROPPED IN CREAM

½ cup light cream
6 eggs
Salt and pepper to taste
Toast

Pour cream into a skillet large enough to hold 6 eggs. Heat cream, drop in eggs carefully and sprinkle eggs with salt and pepper. Cook slowly over low heat until eggs are set. Serve on toast. Makes 3 to 6 servings.

## PEACH SLUMP

6 cups sliced peeled ripe peaches
1 cup sugar
1½ teaspoons ground cinnamon
½ cup water
1 dozen or more uncooked baking-powder biscuits, about 1½-inch size

Combine first 4 ingredients in a heavy skillet. Heat to boiling point; reduce heat. Top with biscuits, cover and simmer about 30 minutes. Serve with cream. Makes 6 servings.

## FRIED APPLES WITH BACON

1 pound sliced bacon
6 large tart apples
½ cup all-purpose flour
½ cup sugar
1 teaspoon ground nutmeg
¼ teaspoon ground cloves

Fry bacon slices until crisp. Remove slices and drain on absorbent paper. Drain all fat but ¼ cup from frying pan. Cut apples, cored but not peeled, into ½-inch thick round slices. Mix flour with sugar and spices. Roll apple slices in flour mixture and fry in bacon fat until golden brown on both sides and apple is easily pierced and tender. Serve hot with crisp bacon slices. Makes 6 servings.

## SPOONED CODFISH CAKES [Mass.]

1 package (4 ounces) shredded salt codfish
4 cups cubed peeled raw potato
1 onion, minced
2 tablespoons all-purpose flour
Salt and Pepper
Fat for deep frying

Freshen salt codfish by soaking in cold water. Drain, Place codfish, potato, and onion in a saucepan and cook in boiling water to cover until potato is tender. Drain. Mash well. Add flour, and salt and pepper to taste. Blend well. Cool, then chill. Drop by tablespoons into hot deep fat (350°F. on a frying thermometer) and fry until brown, for 2 to 3 minutes. Serve with catsup or stewed tomatoes. Makes 4 servings.

## BAKED INDIAN PUDDING

4 cups milk
5 tablespoons yellow cornmeal
2 tablespoons butter
½ cup firmly packed brown sugar
½ cup molasses
1 teaspoon salt
½ teaspoon each of ground ginger, cinnamon, nutmeg, and mace
2 eggs, beaten
1 cup light cream
Cream or vanilla ice cream

In top part of double boiler over direct heat, bring to boil 3 cups milk. Mix 1 cup cold milk with cornmeal and stir slowly into hot milk. Put over boiling water and cook for 20 minutes, stirring occasionally. Add butter, sugar, and molasses. Remove from heat and add salt and spices. Stir in eggs and pour into greased 1½-quart baking dish. Bake in preheated slow oven (300°F.) for 2 to 2½ hours, stirring occasionally during first hour. Then pour light cream over top and finish baking without stirring. Serve warm topped with cream. Makes 6 to 8 servings.

## BOSTON BROWN BREAD

2 tablespoons shortening
¼ cup sugar
1 egg
¾ cup dark molasses
2¼ cups whole-wheat flour
1 teaspoon salt
¾ cup yellow cornmeal
1½ teaspoons each of baking powder and baking soda
1¾ cups buttermilk
⅔ cup seedless raisins

Cream shortening and sugar. Beat in egg and molasses. Beat in remaining ingredients. Spoon into 2 well-greased 1-quart molds, filling a little more than half full. Cover with greased lids or foil. Set molds on rack in deep kettle and add boiling water to come halfway up sides of molds. Cover and steam for 2½ hours. Replace boiling water to keep up level of liquid. Makes 2 loaves.

## BROILED CONNECTICUT RIVER SHAD

    3- or 4-pound shad
    Melted butter or margarine
    Salt and pepper to taste
    Parsley
¼ cup soft butter or margarine
 1 tablespoon fresh lemon juice

Have 3- or 4-pound shad cleaned and split. Put skin down on an oiled and preheated plank or ovenproof platter. Brush with melted butter and sprinkle with salt and pepper. Broil for 15 to 20 minutes, depending upon size and thickness of fish. Remove to a serving tray and garnish with parsley. Cream ¼ cup soft butter, add 1 tablespoon fresh lemon juice, and spread on fish. Serve at once. Makes 6 servings.

## WISCASSET LOBSTER STEW

Cook 2-pound lobster in salted water for 15 minutes. Drain; remove meat from shell and cut into pieces. Heat broken shells in 3 tablespoons butter in large saucepan. Add 2 slices onion and sauté for 5 minutes. Add 2 cups milk, 2 cups light cream, and salt and pepper. Simmer for 5 minutes more. Strain into another saucepan. Add lobster and mashed coral. Reheat and add 2 tablespoons butter. Makes about 1 quart.

## JOHNNYCAKE

 1 tablespoon sugar
 1 teaspoon salt
 1 tablespoon butter
 1 cup white water-ground cornmeal
 1 cup boiling water
¼ cup milk
    Bacon fat, butter, or margarine

Combine first 4 ingredients in a bowl. Cover with boiling water and stir vigorously until well mixed. Add milk and mix well. Drop batter by tablespoons onto hot griddle, well greased with bacon fat. Pat until ½-inch thick with greased pancake turner. Cook over medium heat until browned on one side. Put a little melted fat on the uncooked top of each cake, turn, and brown. Serve very hot with butter. Makes 9 or 10 cakes.
**To bake**—Melt 2 tablespoons fat in 8-inch square pan and grease sides of pan; heat in oven. Spread batter in pan and bake in preheated very hot oven (450°F.) for 30 minutes, or until cake is firm.

## SNICKERDOODLES

 6 tablespoons butter or margarine
 1 cup sugar
 1 egg
½ cup milk
 2 cups sifted all-purpose flour
 2 teaspoons baking powder
    Ground nutmeg
    Sugar

Cream butter until light and fluffy. Gradually beat in sugar. Beat in egg until well blended. Stir in milk. Sift flour with baking powder and 1 teaspoon nutmeg. Add to batter and stir until well blended and smooth. Drop by tablespoon onto a greased cookie sheet. Sprinkle top of cookies with sugar mixed with additional ground nutmeg. Bake in preheated hot oven (400°F.) for 8 to 10 minutes, or until cookies are golden brown. Remove from pan while warm; cool on a rack. Makes about 4 dozen.

## CONNECTICUT ELECTION CAKE

    Water*
 2 packages active dry yeast or 2 cakes compressed yeast
    Granulated sugar
½ cup firmly packed dark brown sugar
1¼ cups all-purpose flour
2¾ cups sifted cake flour
1¼ teaspoons salt
 1 teaspoon each of ground nutmeg and mace
 3 eggs
¾ cup shortening
½ teaspoon grated lemon rind
 1 teaspoon vanilla extract
½ cup milk
½ cup currants or seedless raisins
½ cup each of diced candied pineapple and citron
¼ cup diced candied orange peel
    Fruit frosting

* Use very warm water (105°F. to 115°F.) for dry yeast; use lukewarm water (80°F. to 90°F.) for compressed. Sprinkle dry yeast or crumble cakes into ¼ cup water. Let stand for a few minutes; then stir until dissolved. Add 1 teaspoon granulated sugar and let stand until frothy, 5 to 10 minutes. Pour ½ cup boiling water over brown sugar. Cool to lukewarm; add yeast and all-purpose flour. Beat until smooth. Cover and let rise for 30 minutes. Sift 1 cup granulated sugar, cake flour, salt, and spices into large bowl. Add all remaining ingredients except fruit and beat for 3 minutes. Add yeast mixture and beat for 1 minute. Add fruit. Let rise in greased 9-inch tube pan until light, about 1 hour. Bake in preheated moderate oven (375°F.) for 50 to 60 minutes. Cool for 20 minutes in pan. Invert on rack and cool. Spoon frosting over cake, letting it run down sides.
**Fruit Frosting**—Put 1 tablespoon each of light cream, pineapple juice, and butter in bowl; heat over hot water until melted. Add ¼ teaspoon each of grated orange and lemon rind and ½ cup sifted confectioners' sugar; beat until smooth. Add 2 tablespoons minced candied pineapple.

## GREEN MOUNTAIN RASPBERRY SHRUB

Mix 5 quarts red raspberries and 1 quart very mild vinegar. Let stand for 24 hours, then strain. Add 1 cup sugar to each quart juice. Bring to boil. Fill clean hot jars or bottles to overflowing. Seal and process for 5 minutes in boiling water bath. To serve, dilute with 3 parts cold water and pour over crushed ice in tall glasses. A refreshing summer drink, to be made when there are lots of raspberries. Makes about 3 quarts.

Anchovy and Potato Casserole

## ANCHOVY

**ANCHOVY**—This small fish belongs to the herring family. An anchovy is five to six inches long, narrow in shape, with a mouth that stretches almost to the gills. The best anchovies come from the Mediterranean, and they have been used as appetizers or as ingredients to flavor foods from the days of the ancient Romans.

Anchovies are used almost entirely in a preserved form, salted or pickled or packed in oil, and in fillets. Anchovy fillets come either flat or rolled around a caper. Anchovies are also made into a paste and into an extract. Used judiciously, and with a light hand, they add zest. If anchovies are too salty, soak in cold water or milk for about 15 minutes, drain, and pat dry.

Always keep a can or two of anchovies or a tube of anchovy paste at hand to make canapés for unexpected guests and to pep up leftover foods.

### ANCHOVY CANAPES

Spread crackers or toast rounds with butter. Top with slice of hard-cooked egg. Top this with an anchovy fillet rolled around a caper.

### ANCHOVY AND POTATO CASSEROLE

```
   Buttered crumbs
 6 raw medium potatoes, peeled
12 flat anchovy fillets, drained
 1 onion, minced
 2 cups light cream
¼ cup butter or margarine
   Pimiento
   Parsley
```

Sprinkle bottom and sides of greased casserole generously with buttered crumbs. Cut potatoes into paper-thin slices. Chop 10 anchovies. Place alternate layers of potato slices and anchovies in casserole, sprinkling each layer with minced onion; top layer should be potatoes. Pour cream over mixture and dot with butter. Bake in preheated moderate oven (350°F.) for 35 to 40 minutes, or until potatoes are tender and top delicately browned. Garnish with remaining anchovies, pimiento, and parsley. Makes 4 to 6 servings.

## ANGEL FOOD

**ANGEL FOOD**—A high, delicate, fluffy white cake which contains no fat and uses only the whites of eggs. Air, beaten into these, provides the leavening agent. Angel food is usually baked in a tube pan. It is one of the most glorious of American cakes. Few other cakes have inspired as much research to produce perfection. Women used to be judged as bakers on the quality of their angel food.

It is considered a true party cake and lends itself to many elegant desserts and variations. It can be decorated and frosted with fruits, icings, or whipped cream. It can be scooped out and filled with ice cream, custard, whipped cream, or fruit for a delicious dessert.

*Caloric Values*
Plain, 2-inch slice = 110 calories

### BASIC ANGEL FOOD CAKE

```
   1 cup sifted cake flour
1½ cups sugar
1½ cups egg whites (10 to 12 medium-size eggs)
  ¼ teaspoon salt
1½ teaspoons cream of tartar
  ½ teaspoon almond extract
1½ teaspoons vanilla extract
```

Sift flour and ¾ cup of the sugar together 3 times. Beat egg whites with salt and cream of tartar in large bowl at high speed of mixer until light and fluffy. Sprinkle remaining ¾ cup sugar over egg whites, 2 tablespoons at a time, beating thoroughly after each addition. Continue beating until stiff peaks form. Fold in extracts. Sift dry ingredients, 2 tablespoons at a time, over beaten egg whites. Fold in gently but thoroughly with a wire whip or rubber spatula. Pour batter into ungreased tube pan (10 × 4 inches). Make sure that there is not a trace of any fat or grease in pan, or cake won't rise. Cut gently through batter to remove large air bubbles. Bake in preheated moderate oven (350°F.) for 40 to 50 minutes, or until crust is golden brown and cracks are very dry. Invert pan immediately and place on funnel or bottle. Cool cake in upside-down pan for at least 1 hour. Cut cake out of pan with a sharp knife. Using two forks, separate cake into pieces or slice with a sawing motion using a knife with serrated edge. Makes 10 to 12 servings.

## ANGELICA

**ANGELICA** (Archangelica officinalis)— The name of this aromatic herb means "heavenly" in Latin. Angelica is a tall stout perennial with widespread leaves and greenish-white or bluish flowers shaped like umbrellas.

The plant is a native of northern Europe, but it is also found in Switzerland and the Pyrenees. Angelica was once considered a powerful protector against witches and fearsome creatures. In Elizabethan England it was used as an antidote for the plague.

All of its parts are aromatic. The dried roots and fruits flavor cakes, candies, beverages such as bitters, and liqueurs like Benedictine. The stems and leaf stalks are candied in sugar and used for decorating desserts because of their bright-green color and pleasant flavor. The oil is used for flavorings, perfumery, and in medicine.

It is not as readily available as other glacéed or candied fruits, but food specialty stores carry it. Since it has a tendency to dry out, it should be kept tightly wrapped in wax paper or aluminum foil.

## ANGELICA AS A GARNISH

Garnish a ham for Christmas with a poinsettia made of stem and leaves cut from angelica, petals cut from pimiento.

Trim a Bavarian cream dessert with tiny cubes of angelica and whole candied cherries.

Decorate frosting on *petits fours* with bits of angelica, candied pineapple, silver dragées, and candied cherries.

Frost a coffeecake with a white confectioners' sugar icing and sprinkle with tiny pieces of angelica and chopped nuts.

# ANISE [*Pimpinella Anisum*]—This culinary

herb belongs to the parsley family. It grows about two feet tall, and has feathery leaves and tiny grayish-brown fruits which are dried for use. The plants and fruits have a distinctive licorice flavor. The dried fruits are called aniseed.

Anise is of Mediterranean origin and is one of the earliest aromatic plants to be mentioned in history. The Hebrews, Greeks, and Romans valued anise for its reputed medicinal properties and the Emperor Charlemagne, who in the 8th century was interested in experimental farming, caused anise to be grown in his gardens in Germany. It has been popular ever since.

Anise is one of the best-liked flavorings in European cuisine. In Italy it is used in liqueurs; Germans and Scandinavians flavor their breads with aniseed. It goes into stews and seafood cocktails, and it enhances carrot, cauliflower, and beet dishes. Aniseed is also much used in baking and candy-making particularly in licorice confections. The aniseed is sold as whole seeds.

To release the full flavor of the seeds in cooking, place them between two sheets of wax paper and crush them with a rolling pin.

## SUGGESTED USES FOR ANISEED

**Appetizers, seafood-cocktail sauces**—Sprinkle top with ½ teaspoon crushed aniseed, or more to taste.

**Stews, pot roasts, baked pork chops, Chinese meat-and-vegetable combinations**—Cook ½ teaspoon whole aniseed, or more to taste, with other ingredients.

**Cream sauce**—Add ¼ teaspoon whole aniseed for each cup of sauce.

**Mild cheeses**—Blend whole aniseed to taste into cottage, cream cheese, grated Muenster, and other mild cheeses.

**In baking**—Substitute ½ to 1 teaspoon crushed aniseed or anise extract for other flavorings. Or sprinkle crushed aniseed on top of cookies before baking. Or use ¼ to ½ teaspoon of the whole aniseeds in fruit pies instead of cinnamon or nutmeg.

## SPRINGERLE

    4 eggs
    2 cups sugar
    2 teaspoons crushed aniseed
    3 to 3½ cups sifted all-purpose flour
    ½ teaspoon baking powder
      Whole aniseed (about 3 to 4 tablespoons)

Beat eggs until light. Gradually stir in sugar, beating well after each addition. Stir in crushed aniseed. Sift flour with baking powder. Add 3 cups of flour. Dough should be stiff enough to roll out to ¼-inch thickness. Add more flour if necessary. Flour springerle molds or decorated rolling pin. Press hard upon dough to get a good picture. Cut cookies apart. (These cookies are usually stamped with quaint wooden molds or rollers to make a picture. If you do not have a mold, cut the dough into ¾-inch by 2½-inch bars.) Grease cookie sheets and sprinkle each sheet with 1 tablespoon whole aniseed. Place cookies, picture side up, on cookie sheets. Let stand overnight in cool place to dry out. Bake in preheated slow oven (300°F.) for about 15 minutes, or until bottom of cookie is pale yellow. Makes about 5 dozen cookies.
NOTE: One teaspoon of anise extract may be added to egg mixture in place of crushed aniseed.

# ANNATTO—A yellowish-red vegetable dye made

from the pulp around the seeds of a small tropical tree, *Bixa orellana.* The tree is a native of the Caribbean and grows also in Central and South America. Annatto is widely used in coloring cheese, especially Cheddar, and, to a lesser extent, butter.

# ANTELOPE—The name of this ruminant mammal

comes from the Greek and means "a horned animal." It is related to the ox but is smaller and lighter and more gracefully built. There are zoologically no true antelopes in the United States, although a distinct group native to Oregon is known to Americans as antelope. For cooking, antelope is classified as game. The meat is on the lean side and is usually larded before cooking. Antelope meat may be roasted, broiled, or braised.

## ROAST SADDLE OF ANTELOPE

Wipe a saddle of antelope and lard it liberally with salt pork. Sprinkle with salt and pepper, rub with flour, and start in a hot preheated oven (450°F.) for 25 minutes. Reduce heat to 300°F. and cook for 1½ hours longer, or until the meat thermometer reaches 135°F., to 150°F. for rare meat.

# ANTIPASTO

**ANTIPASTO**—An Italian word meaning literally "before the meal," *antipasto* is one or several foods served in small quantities as a first course. It is essential that the foods be attractively arranged. Antipasto is the Italian equivalent of French *hors d'oeuvres* and American appetizers.

*Antipasto* can be very simple, such as slices of *prosciutto* rolled around melon wedges, or elaborate, as in fine restaurants, where dozens of foods are displayed in small dishes for the guest to choose from. For home use, *antipasto* can be arranged either on a big platter or on individual plates.

## ANTIPASTO VARIATO

Preferably, use a large round platter. In center of the plate, place the contents of a can of solid pack tuna fish, drained. Coat fish with mayonnaise and sprinkle with drained capers. Arrange around tuna, in alternating rows radiating from the center, any of these: thin slices of hard salami, finger-length rolls of *prosciutto* or boiled ham, drained fillets of flat or rolled anchovies, artichoke hearts in oil (drained), pimientos cut into strips, radishes, thinly sliced fennel or celery hearts, hard-cooked eggs cut into quarters lengthwise, each topped with an anchovy fillet, and green and black olives. Serve olive oil and wine vinegar on the side.

## CECI ALL' OLIO
### [Chick-Peas in Olive Oil]

Use canned or home-cooked chick-peas, well drained. Sauté them in a little hot olive oil and sprinkle with a little garlic powder. Season to taste with salt and pepper. Serve from a relish dish.

## MAIONESE DI SCAMPI E CAVOL FIORI
### [Shrimp and Cauliflower Salad]

On a serving plate, arrange alternate layers of cooked, shelled, and deveined shrimps and cooked, drained, cold cauliflowerets. Cover with mayonnaise that has been thinned with a little lemon juice. Sprinkle with chopped parsley.

## CAPONATINA

      2 medium eggplants
    ¾ cup olive oil
      2 onions, sliced
    ¼ cup tomato sauce
      2 celery stalks, diced
    ¼ cup drained capers
      6 green olives, pitted and cut into pieces
      1 tablespoon pine nuts
    ¼ cup vinegar, preferably wine vinegar
      2 tablespoons sugar
    ½ teaspoon salt
    ¼ teaspoon pepper

Peel and dice eggplant and fry in ½ cup of the olive oil until golden brown. Remove eggplant from skillet and reserve. Add remaining ¼ cup oil and onions and cook until onions are soft and golden. Add tomato sauce and celery. Cook until celery is tender, stirring occasionally. If necessary, add a little hot water to prevent sticking. Add capers, olives, pine nuts, and reserved eggplant. Heat vinegar and dissolve sugar in it. Add salt and pepper. Pour liquid over eggplant mixture. Simmer, covered, over very low heat for 20 minutes, stirring frequently. Cool before serving. This will keep for weeks in a covered jar in refrigerator. The recipe may easily be doubled and tripled. Makes 6 to 8 servings.

## PICKLED GREEN PEPPERS

Put 3 or 4 large sweet green bell peppers under broiler and turn often until they blister. The tough skin can be peeled off easily with a sharp knife when peppers are held under running water. Or bake in preheated moderate oven (375°F.) for 30 to 40 minutes and peel under running water. The first method is quicker. Cut peeled peppers into halves and remove cores and seeds. Then cut into strips about ½ inch wide. Place in a dish and pour over them a marinade made of 3 to 4 tablespoons fresh lemon or lime juice or wine vinegar, 3 to 4 tablespoons olive oil, and salt and freshly ground black pepper to taste. Cover and refrigerate for at least 2 hours before serving. These peppers will keep for 1 month, covered, in the refrigerator. Makes 6 to 8 servings.

## TOMATO AND MUSHROOM SALAD

      4 sliced chilled tomatoes
        Salt and pepper to taste
      2 tablespoons olive oil
    ½ teaspoon fresh or dry crumbled basil or oregano
      8 large mushrooms, sliced
      1 to 2 teaspoons fresh lemon juice

Arrange tomatoes in overlapping rows on serving dish. Sprinkle with salt and pepper, 1 tablespoon of the olive oil, and basil or oregano. Arrange mushroom slices on tomatoes. Sprinkle with remaining tablespoon of olive oil and lemon juice. Makes 4 to 5 servings.

# ANTIPASTO PARTY

## by GLENNA McGINNIS

An antipasto party is ideal for a club, where everyone brings something, or for a home party on which several hostesses collaborate. Many items are simply bought and arranged attractively. The cooked dishes are not difficult and can be made ahead. Nothing requires last-minute attention.

When I gave my antipasto bash, I invited fifty-six people and sixty-three came. Some had asked to bring house-guests, and I was sure there would be plenty of food. The menu and the marathon style of eating didn't call for seating guests and they spread out all over the house. I also spread the food about. This was an excellent idea because no serve-yourself lines ever formed.

On the dining room buffet I placed foods that would be appropriate with cocktails served from a bar set up in the living room on a table. Two men guests took turns as bartenders. If drinks are not served, the *first* things still should be grouped together for a starter. The more substantial dishes for the second "course" were placed on the big dining room table. The desserts, cheeses, fruits, nuts, candies and espresso were offered from a table in the family room.

The colors in the Italian flag gave the red, white and green color scheme. Guests helped themselves from raffia-wrapped bottles of Chianti placed in every room. Pitchers of ice water and cups were also available, since some of the food could make people thirsty.

I used colorful hot-pepper plants on the buffet, dining table and elsewhere and gave them as prizes for a get-acquainted game called "Who Am I?" As each guest arrived, a paper with the name of a famous Italian—fictional or real, living or dead—was pinned to his back. He then questioned other guests as to who he was, but the answers could only be yes or no. We used such names as Nero, Mussolini's horse, Caruso, Caesar, Michelangelo, Sinatra, DiMaggio. The five who guessed who they were first won prizes.

For favors, each departing guest was given a small colorful basket with a garlic bulb; a little red, white and green striped cotton bag of dried basil, tied with raffia; individually wrapped torrone (almond nougat); and an attractive little bottle of red-wine vinegar. A miniature bottle of an Italian cordial would cost more but be as suitable as the vinegar. I covered the little baskets with plastic wrap and tied on three bright red pepper pods with red, white and green rug yarn.

Here are lists of the items suitable for the three "courses." As few or as many as desired can be chosen. If very few, more of each item should be offered. The ones you buy ready to serve are indicated. Recipes are given for dishes to be prepared. There will very likely be leftovers to add zip to future family meals. They keep well in the refrigerator.

It is wise to shop several days ahead for all nonperishables and to prepare dishes ahead as directed in the recipes. Arrange foods (except greens and tomatoes) in serving dishes, garnish, wrap in plastic and refrigerate the day before the party so all cooking utensils are cleared away. It takes time to make an attractive display. Arrange in serving area at least an hour before guests arrive. Have a diagram drawn of where each dish goes. Choose serving utensils and have in place a day ahead. Provide a receptacle for disposal of paper plates, flatware, cups and glasses, if used. A bright plastic waste container can be tied in the party-color ribbons.

Our recipes are designed for serving 12.

## FIRST COURSE

*Foods to buy and arrange*

Radishes
Green onions
Tomato slices or wedges
Fennel or celery hearts
Stuffed green olives
Black ripe olives
Cured black olives
Roasted red peppers
Anchovy fillets
Sardines

Pickled eggplant
Pickled mild yellow and red banana peppers
Italian pickled garden salad
Thin and thick breadsticks
Italian bread
Genoa Toast, if available
Pure olive oil (to serve from a cruet)
Wine vinegar (to serve from a cruet)

*Dishes to make (recipes serve 12)*

Italian Tuna and Capers
Marinated Artichoke Hearts
Eggs Stuffed with Ricotta
Marinated Mushrooms

58

## ITALIAN TUNA AND CAPERS

4 cans (7 ounces each) Italian tuna, drained
   Crisp greens such as Boston lettuce, escarole or
   chicory
¼ cup drained capers
   Juice of 1 lemon

Spoon tuna gently on platter lined with greens. At serving time, sprinkle with capers and lemon juice. Makes 12 servings.

**Note:** American tuna can be used if Italian is not available.

## MARINATED ARTICHOKE HEARTS

¼ cup white-wine vinegar
¼ cup olive oil
½ teaspoon each oregano and basil
   Salt and pepper to taste
2 cans (15 ounces each) artichoke hearts, drained

Mix all ingredients, except artichokes, in saucepan. Bring to boil. Split artichokes and add to mixture. Bring again to boil, cover and simmer 10 minutes. Pour into storage dish and cool. Cover and refrigerate. Drain well before serving. Make several days ahead. Makes 12 servings.

## EGGS STUFFED WITH RICOTTA

1 dozen large eggs, hard-cooked
1 cup ricotta or creamed cottage cheese
   Seasoned salt
   Seasoned pepper
   Salt and pepper
   Finely minced green onion
   Dry mustard
   Italian parsley
   Pickled red pepper

Shell eggs carefully and slice lengthwise. Scoop out yolks and mash with fork. Mix with ricotta and add remaining ingredients, except last 2, to taste. Fill whites with mixtures cover lightly and refrigerate. Garnish with parsley and sliver of red pepper.

Can be made the day before party. Makes 12 servings.

## MARINATED MUSHROOMS

⅔ cup olive oil
   Juice of 2 lemons
1 bay leaf
2 garlic cloves, crushed
6 whole peppercorns
½ teaspoon salt
1 pound small whole fresh mushrooms, washed and trimmed

Put all ingredients, except mushrooms, in skillet. Add ½ cup water, bring to boil, cover and simmer 15 minutes. Strain and return to skillet. Add mushrooms and simmer 5 minutes, turning several times. Cool in the liquid, cover then chill. Makes about 2 cups. Can be prepared several days ahead. To serve, lift out of liquid with slotted spoon. Makes 12 servings.

**Note:** Substitute 3 jars (2½ ounces each) whole mushrooms, drained, for the fresh. Proceed as directed.

## MAIN COURSE

*Foods to buy and arrange*

Melon wedges
Prosciutto (pro-SHOOT-o)
Sliced capocollo (kahpo-KOH-lo)
Sliced pepperoni (peppe-ROH-nee)
Sliced salami
Pickled hot peppers

*Dishes to be made and served at room temperature (recipes serve 12). Remove dishes from refrigerator 1 hour before serving.*

Cold Braised Stuffed Breast of Veal
Baked Rice-stuffed Tomatoes
Sausage-stuffed Onions
Marinated Chick-peas

## COLD BRAISED STUFFED BREAST OF VEAL

3 slices firm-type white bread, crusts trimmed
⅔ cup milk
1 medium onion, minced
2 tablespoons butter or margarine
½ pound each boneless pork and veal, ground twice
¼ pound fresh-pork fat, ground twice
⅓ cup grated Parmesan cheese
1 package (10 ounces) frozen chopped spinach, thawed and well drained
¼ teaspoon each ground marjoram and thyme
3 teaspoons salt
1 egg, slightly beaten
½ cup shelled pistachio nuts
1 cup fresh or thawed frozen peas
   4- to 5-pound breast of veal, boned with pocket for stuffing
   Bones and trimmings from breast of veal
1 onion, halved
3 garlic cloves
1 carrot
1 bay leaf
2 sprigs parsley
2 to 3 quarts chicken broth, or half broth and half water
   Freshly ground black pepper

Prepare this dish 2 days ahead of time. Crumble bread into milk and let stand 10 minutes. Sauté minced onion in the butter, 7 to 8 minutes, stirring frequently, or until tender but not browned. Put in bowl and add ground meats and fat, cheese, spinach, herbs, salt and egg. Knead with hands or beat with wooden spoon until well mixed and fluffy. Squeeze bread dry and add to mixture. Gently fold in nuts and peas. Spread evenly in veal pocket and sew up opening with strong kitchen thread. Put bones and trimmings and next 5 ingredients in large soup pot or kettle and lay stuffed veal on top. Add broth to cover meat completely and grind in a little black pepper. Bring to boil, reduce heat, cover and simmer 1¼ hours, or until veal is tender. Transfer veal to large, heavy shallow dish and cool to room temperature, then refrigerate, covered. Makes about 24 thin slices. Broth makes a fine base for soup and can be frozen, if desired.

## SAUSAGE-STUFFED ONIONS

 16 (about 2 pounds) yellow onions, about 2″ in diameter
  1 pound Italian sweet-sausage links
  1 garlic clove minced
  1 tablespoon olive oil
 ¼ cup chopped parsley

Peel onions and simmer, covered, in small amount of boiling water 15 minutes. Drain and cool slightly. Hollow out centers by pushing hard on bottom, or pull out with small sharp knife or grapefruit knife. Chop centers fine. Remove sausage meat from casing, put meat in skillet with garlic and olive oil and sauté, breaking up with fork, until lightly browned. Add chopped onion and remaining ingredients and cook, stirring, about 10 minutes. Drain off excess fat and, with small spoon, carefully fill shells. Arrange in shallow baking dish with 1″ hot water, cover with foil and bake in preheated moderate oven (375°F.) about 30 minutes. Cool and refrigerate, Remove 1 hour before serving. Makes 12 servings.

## BAKED RICE-STUFFED TOMATOES

 12 to 16 small tomatoes
   Salt and pepper
  1 medium onion, minced
 ½ cup finely chopped green pepper
 ¼ cup finely chopped celery
  4 tablespoons butter or margarine
  2 cups cooked rice
   Few sprigs parsley, chopped
 ¼ teaspoon ground cinnamon
 ½ teaspoon sugar
 ¼ cup pine nuts or finely chopped pecans
  1 cup fine soft bread crumbs

Cut tops off tomatoes and scoop out pulp with small spoon. Sprinkle insides of tomatoes generously with salt and pepper and set aside. Force pulp through sieve or food mill. Sauté vegetables in 2 tablespoons butter until onion is translucent. Add to pulp with next 5 ingredients. Mix well and spoon into tomato shells, using 2 rounded tablespoons for each. Melt remaining 2 tablespoons butter and mix with crumbs. Sprinkle on tomatoes. Arrange in shallow baking dish and add about 1″ of hot water. Bake in preheated moderate oven (375°F.) about 30 minutes. Cool and refrigerate until 1 hour before serving. Makes 12 servings.

## MARINATED CHICK-PEAS

  4 cans (1 pound each) chick-peas, drained
  1 red onion, thinly sliced

 ⅔ cup olive or other salad oil
  6 tablespoons wine vinegar
 ¼ cup finely chopped parsley
   Salt and freshly ground pepper to taste

Toss all ingredients together. Prepare a day or two ahead of time and refrigerate, covered. Remove 1 hour before serving.

## THIRD COURSE

*Foods to buy and arrange*

Cheeses: Gorgonzola, provolone, Bel Paese, fontiña, ricotta or other Italian types
Whole fresh fruits in season
Torrone (almond nougat)
Jordan almonds (wrap 3 in rounds of bright-colored tissue paper and twist)

*Dishes to make (recipes serve 12)*

Zuppa Inglese (TSOOP-pah een-GLAY-zay)
Espresso (from instant coffee made according to directions on label—strong black regular coffee can be substituted)

## ZUPPA INGLESE

  4 cups milk
  3 tablespoons butter or margarine
   Sugar
 ¼ cup cornstarch
 ½ teaspoon salt
  3 eggs, slightly beaten
 1½ teaspoons vanilla extract
  3 packages (12 ounces each) sponge layers, 6″ in diameter
 ½ cup light rum
 1½ cups diced candied mixed fruit
  2 cups heavy cream
   Red and green candied-pineapple slices

Scald milk with butter in top part of double boiler over simmering water. Mix ¾ cup sugar, the cornstarch and salt in bowl and stir in some of hot milk. Stir back into milk in double boiler and cook, stirring until thickened. Cover and cook, stirring occasionally about 10 minutes. Stir small amount of mixture into eggs, then put back in double boiler, stirring. Cook, stirring about 5 minutes longer. Remove from heat, add vanilla and cool. Spread small amount of custard in thin layer in 10″ x 4″ loose-bottomed tube pan. Tear off 2″ chunks of cake and arrange in a layer on custard. Sprinkle with about 2 tablespoons rum and small amount of candied fruit. Repeat until pan is full and all ingredients are used, pressing each layer down with spatula to avoid empty spaces. Chill overnight, then loosen sides with spatula and unmold on large cake plate. (Patch or smooth out any uneven spots.) Whip cream and sweeten with ½ cup sugar. Swirl on top and sides of cake and decorate with flowers made of strips of candied pineapple. **Note:** Swirl on whipped cream and decorate a few hours ahead. Refrigerate until serving time.

# APÉRITIF by James A. Beard

*Apéritif* is a French word describing an alcoholic beverage taken before a meal to stimulate the appetite. In France and Italy an *apéritif* is usually a wine or a drink with a wine base, but elsewhere the word is often broadened to include such spirits as aquavit, or *akvavit,* to use the Scandinavian spelling of this Northern European favorite.

Most Europeans drink wine-based *apéritifs* at room temperature. Sometimes they dilute them with sparkling water. A popular American custom among those who prefer chilled *apéritifs* is to cool the wine in the refrigerator so that it need not be diluted with ice when served. *Apéritif* wines should never be shaken. If they must be iced quickly, they should be stirred over ice as one does a martini. The result is an *apéritif* frappé.

The French and Italian *apéritifs* are best known and usually ordered by their trade names. They can be described in four general classifications depending upon the predominant flavor or ingredient:

1. The Vermouth group
2. The Quinquina or quinine group
3. The Bitters group
4. The Absinthe group

Probably the most popular of the *apéritif* vermouths is Cinzano. This is actually a trade name that is becoming a generic word by usage; it is popularly used to include sweet vermouths made by a number of manufacturers. Europeans drink sweet vermouth straight without chilling it. Iced Cinzano is the American version.

Dry vermouth (an essential in the martini cocktail) is rarely served straight as an *apéritif,* but it is one of the ingredients of the Vermouth Cassis. This is a frappé composed of dry vermouth, *Crème de Cassis,* a strip of lemon peel, and a splash of sparkling water.

Among the quinquina *apéritifs,* the best known in the United States is Dubonnet. There is a subtle difference in the Dubonnet made in th is country and that produced in Europe, and each has its own following. The blond variety of Dubonnet is an American specialty not found in France. St. Raphael is another well known quinquina drink, made from white wine, that is now produced in the United States. Both *apéritifs* are popularly drunk chilled or on-the-rocks, with a strip of lemon peel.

There are many other lesser known quinquinas. Some are heavily aromatized. Some are overly sweet by American standards. Among the most popular in Europe is a delicious light-bodied Bordeaux wine, Lillet, which is usually served chilled, on-the-rocks, or with a splash of sparkling water. Amer Picon is an *apéritif* liqueur generally consumed straight. Kina-Roc is similar to Dubonnet. Suze and Gentiane are highly flavored with gentian. Byrrh (not to be confused with beer) is a sweet *apéritif* with a red-wine base.

The family of *apéritif* bitters is perhaps best exemplified by Campari. This is usually drunk straight or with soda. Fernet Branca has a very low alcoholic content, and is usually combined with vermouth, orange juice, or lemonade, or drunk straight to soothe a ruffled stomach.

Probably the most famous of all *apéritifs* is absinthe, a green liqueur with an aromatic licorice flavor. Absinthe made by the original formula contained the herb artemisia, or wormwood, and it is now banned in most countries because of its pernicious effects. Pernod is a popular French substitute, and there are also Spanish and Greek versions. Anisette is similar in flavor to absinthe but is somewhat sweeter. Several of the substitutes for absinthe are known by trade names, such as Oxygenée. *Apéritifs* in the absinthe family are customarily mixed with water and, even in Europe, ice is sometimes added.

Although *akvavit,* the high-proof national drink of Scandinavian countries, is generally taken with food, it is also regarded as a preprandial drink and is always served ice cold. The principal flavor is that of the caraway seed. Like *akvavit,* vodka as an appetizer is drunk straight and cold. It has no dominant flavor, tasting only of alcohol. Zubrowka, which is vodka flavored with aromatic grass, has a slightly bitter flavor. While vodka is generally regarded as a Russian drink, it is made throughout Northern Europe and also in the United States.

Apéritif:
Champagne
Cassis

# APICIUS

**APICIUS**—The author of the one and only Latin cookbook of antiquity, *The Roman Cookery Book,* that has come down to us. The book is extremely important, and also very entertaining, in telling us about the foods of the ancient Romans and how they were prepared, thus opening a window on the daily life of the ancient world. Apicius lived during the reign of Tiberius (B.C. 42-37 A.D.), at a time of the most incredible culinary extravagances, such as stews made entirely from songbirds' tongues. Apicius apparently also ran a cooking school. He committed suicide because he got into debt for spending too much money on food. Apparently he felt that the equivalent of several hundred thousand dollars which he had left would not be enough for him to live on. He was very highly regarded by his contemporaries.

## A POINT

**A POINT**—A French term meaning literally "to the point." In cooking, it refers to the perfect state of readiness of food as it is brought to the table.

## APPETIZER

**APPETIZER**—A small portion of food served before, or as the first course of, a meal. Appetizers should be attractive in shape, color, and garnish, and have interesting flavor and texture combinations. Above all, they should not be too filling, since they are meant to stimulate, not to dull, the appetite for the meal that is to follow. Serve them always in small portions.

Apparently, appetizers have a basic appeal to human nature since every national cuisine features them. The Scandinavians have their *smörgåsbord* and open-faced sandwiches, the Slavs their *zakuska,* the Italians their *antipasto,* and the French their *hors d'oeuvre.*

Appetizers provide the creative cook a first-class opportunity to produce food that is pretty. They can vary from simple canapés spread with a canapé butter and garnished with a sprig of parsley to elaborate hot creations. The garnishes should all be edible.

### CANAPÉ

A French word meaning literally "a couch." In cookery, canapés are small hot or cold appetizers served on bread, crackers, or a pastry base so that they can be picked up with the fingers. Unlike hors d'oeuvre which are served alone, canapés must have this base.

Canapés should be dainty and pleasing to look at. They must be served crisp and fresh, and most of them should be prepared just before serving. Canapés may be very simple, consisting of a cracker spread with a canapé butter and decorated with a little meat, fish, egg, or cheese, or a sprig of parsley or watercress, or a slice of pimiento, pickle, radish, olive, or lemon.

For canapés, use firm-textured bread or bread one day old. If not available, quickly partially freeze bread before cutting. White, rye, whole wheat, pumpernickel, and any breads trimmed free of crust are suitable for canapés, provided that bread and filling complement each other. Delicate crabmeat, for instance, is best served on white bread, a tangy cheese on dark bread. The breads can be cut into any fancy shapes with cookie cutters, or more simply into rounds, squares, diamonds, or fingers. Melba toast and plain or fancy crackers also make excellent bases for canapés. Allow about 4 to 6 canapés for each person.

### COCKTAILS

Cocktails are appetizers that are served at the table with a sauce or dressing, and they are not to be confused with the potable alcoholic or nonalcoholic kinds. Seafood and fruit as well as vegetables are the ingredients most frequently used. Shrimp cocktail, with a tangy sauce, is probably the favorite cocktail, especially before a steak dinner. Cocktails are always cold; most of them should be well chilled.

### DIPS OR DUNKS

These savory mixtures are soft enough to be scooped up with crackers, potato chips, or vegetables without the aid of a spoon or knife. They are the quickest and easiest of appetizers. Dips are better suited to small groups than to large ones. They are typically American and not known in European entertaining.

Dips can be hot or cold. They should be firm enough so that they will not drip on clothes and carpets. Napkins should be available when dips are served.

Among the foods to be dipped are crackers, potato chips, narrow toast strips, corn chips, cooked shrimps, cocktail frankfurters, iced cucumber strips, mushrooms, Belgian endive blades, iced green-pepper sticks, cauliflowerets, carrot sticks, radishes, celery sticks, and pretzels. All should be crisp and firm.

Dips may be very attractively served in big scooped-out apples, scooped-out eggplant, avocado, or red or green cabbages, or in a scooped-out pineapple.

### HORS D'OEUVRES

These words mean literally "outside the work. "Hors d'oeuvres are cold or hot appetizers that, unlike canapés, do not have bread or crackers as the base for other foods. Hors d'oeuvres are usually eaten at the table, with a knife and fork, before the main part of the meal.

The hors d'oeuvres should not repeat the ingredients of the main dish, or be too similar to it. If you're serving fish, avoid seafood hors d'oeuvres; if you're having pork, do not serve bacon hors d'oeuvres.

Hors d'oeuvres can be served singly, or they can be varied. It is essential that they should be attractively arranged. It is easier to arrange hors d'oeuvres prettily in several small dishes than on one large one. The small dishes can be grouped on a tray or a lazy susan. Hors d'oeuvres can also be arranged on individual plates. Parsley sprigs, watercress, radish slices, thin lemon twists, and pickles are good garnishes. The food should look pleasing, but should not be tortured into fancy shapes.

An immense variety of foods is suited for hors d'oeuvres, provided the selections are served in small quantities. Among these are aspics, salads, caviar, pâtés, eggs, small skewered foods, mayonnaise-dressed eggs, fish, or meats, chicken livers, artichokes, asparagus, vegetables *à la grecque,* and salads that are not sweet.

## NIBBLES OR TIDBITS

These colloquial expressions are often used to name appetizers that can be picked up with the fingers or with a cocktail fork or toothpick. Almonds and other nuts, some of the relishes, bits of cheese, are often referred to in this way.

An attractive way of serving nibbles is to stud a pineapple, grapefruit, or red cabbage with tidbits on toothpicks.

## RELISHES

Relishes include cold and crisp vegetables and other foods such as cottage cheese and preserves. They are usually served from a platter, and often on a bed of crushed ice to preserve crispness. Certain relishes, such as celery, carrots, scallions, pickles, and olives, may be left on the table during dinner.

In days past, relishes used to be more popular than now, especially with farm families. Old-timers relate the glory of a midwestern farm table set with a score of homemade relishes. Relishes are still the pride of Pennsylvania Dutch cooking. There they are colloquially called "the seven sweets and seven sours," although literalminded souls should not always expect to find fourteen relishes on the table.

## SPREADS

These are mixtures firmer than dips, and to be spread, as the name suggests, on crackers, bread, or toast with a knife or spoon.

# COLD CANAPÉS

## CANAPE BUTTERS

These savory butters add flavor to canapés and some of them may be used without additional spreads. Tightly covered, they keep well in the refrigerator. If the canapé butter is too hard to spread on the base, warm a little at room temperature and cream with spoon to desired consistency.

Cream ¼ cup butter with any of the following:
**Anchovy Butter**—Use 1 to 2 teaspoons anchovy paste or mashed anchovy fillets and ½ teaspoon fresh lemon juice. Good with a slice of hard-cooked egg.
**Caper Butter**—Use 1 tablespoon finely minced drained capers.
**Chili Butter**—Use 1 to 2 tablespoons chili sauce.
**Chive Butter**—Use 1 tablespoon finely minced chives or green onion tops and 1 teaspoon fresh lemon juice.

**Chutney Butter**—Use 1 tablespoon chutney. Good with ham and meats.
**Curry Butter**—Use ¼ to ½ teaspoon curry powder. Good with fish.
**Egg Butter**—Use 2 mashed hard-cooked eggs, a dash of hot pepper sauce, and salt and pepper to taste. Good with vegetables.
**Garlic Butter**—Use 1 small garlic clove, mashed.
**Horseradish Butter**—Use 1 to 2 tablespoons drained bottled horseradish. Good with meats and cheese.
**Onion Butter**—Use 1 teaspoon finely minced onion or onion juice.
**Parmesan Butter**—Use 2 tablespoons grated Parmesan or Romano cheese. Good with eggs and meat.
**Parsley Butter**—Use 2 tablespoons finely minced parsley.
**Pâté Butter**—Use 2 tablespoons mashed liverwurst or any canned pâté. Good by itself. Or decorate with watercress or radish slice.
**Pickle Butter**—Use 1 or 2 tablespoons minced pickle. Good with meats.
**Sardine Butter**—Use 2 tablespoons mashed sardines and ½ teaspoon each of fresh lemon juice and minced onion.
**Shrimp Butter**—Use 2 tablespoons minced or mashed cooked shrimp and ½ teaspoon fresh lemon juice. Serve with an additional shrimp or a slice of hardcooked egg.
**Tarragon Butter**—Use ½ teaspoon finely chopped dried or fresh tarragon and a few drops of tarragon vinegar (optional). Good with fish or chicken.
**Watercress Butter**—Use 2 tablespoons finely chopped watercress and 1 teaspoon fresh lemon juice. Serve as is, with a few additional sprigs of watercress.

These recipes make ¼ to ⅓ cup.

## CHEESE CANAPÉS

**Blue Cheese Spread**—Cream equal parts of blue cheese and unsalted butter. Spread on crisp crackers.
**Camembert Cheese Spread**—Cream equal parts of Camembert and unsalted butter. Spread on toast rounds. Sprinkle with chopped walnuts.
**Cottage-Cheese Spread**—Top toast rounds with cottage cheese mixed with chopped tongue or ham or crisp bacon. Garnish with slice of stuffed olive.
**Simple Cheese Spread**—Cream together 1 cup shredded cheese (Swiss, Cheddar, cheese food, etc.), and ½ cup butter. Spread on rye or other dark bread and place under broiler until slightly browned. Or serve as is, topped with a radish slice. Makes about ¾ cup.
**Tiny Cheese Sandwiches**—Spread crust-trimmed cracked-wheat bread with mayonnaise. Make sandwiches with bread and slices of cheese, sprinkled with pepper. Cut each sandwich into 4 squares. Dip ends of tiny pickled onions in paprika. Fasten onions on sandwiches with toothpicks.

## DANISH BEEF CANAPÉS

Butter thin slices of tiny rye-bread rounds. Top with thin slices of cold rare roast beef and paper-thin onions, fried crisp and dark brown.

## FRANKFURTER ROUNDS

Cut end from unsplit frankfurter roll. With fork, hollow out enough center to hold a frankfurter. Spread hollow generously with mustard. Insert cooked frankfurter. Wrap in wax paper and chill. Cut into slices; dot each slice with a bit of pickle relish.

## PEANUT-ONION CANAPÉS

Spread rounds of toast with peanut butter. Put a tiny white onion ring on each, a dot of catsup in the middle.

## SARDINE ROUNDS

Spread rounds of white bread with sardines mashed with lemon juice and mayonnaise. Garnish with cucumber slice, pimiento, and parsley.

## SALAMI-EGG CANAPÉS

Cut sandwich rolls into this crosswise slices. Butter. Cover each piece with slice of salami. Spread egg salad to within ½ inch of edge. Put 1 teaspoon caviar in center. Border egg with minced green onion. Cut into 6 wedges.

## TUNA ROLL-UPS

1 can (6½ ounces) tuna, drained and finely chopped
½ cup mayonnaise
1 teaspoon prepared mustard
¼ cup each minced celery and green onion
24 thin slices firm-type white bread, crusts trimmed
Finely chopped dill or parsley

Mix first 4 ingredients. Spread filling on each bread slice; roll up tightly, dip each roll in dill; wrap in wax paper; chill. To serve hot, omit dill and brush with mayonnaise or melted butter. Sprinkle lightly with onion salt and broil until heated and well browned.

## FRUITED CHICKEN PINWHEELS

2 cans (4¾ ounces each) chicken spread
2 packages (3 ounces each) cream cheese, softened
½ cup chopped walnuts
¼ cup crushed pineapple, drained
¼ cup chopped golden raisins
½ teaspoon ground ginger
1 loaf (1 pound) fresh unsliced firm-type white bread
Pimiento-stuffed olives

Mix all ingredients, except last 2. With knife, trim crusts from bread and cut loaf in six ¾-inch lengthwise slices. Flatten each slice with rolling pin until pliable enough to roll up loosely. Spread each slice with a rounded ⅓ cup chicken spread mixture. Put a row of olives at narrow end of bread; starting with this end, roll up and wrap each tightly in plastic wrap. Chill well or overnight. Cut each roll in five ½-inch-thick slices. Makes about 30.

# HOT CANAPES

## BAHAMIAN TOMATO CANAPES

3 or 4 small ripe tomatoes
12 to 16 bread rounds
Butter
Bahamian or other sharp mustard
¾ cup mayonnaise (about)

Slice tomatoes about ¼ inch thick. Cut bread rounds as nearly as possible to match size of tomato slices; sauté bread in butter until golden. Put tomato slice on each round and spread lightly with mustard. Spread generously with mayonnaise. Broil until mayonnaise puffs up and browns. Makes 12 to 16.

## CRAB CANAPES

2 cups crabmeat
Mayonnaise
¼ teaspoon Worcestershire
1 large cucumber
Salt and pepper
24 small bread rounds, sautéed in butter
Parsley, drained capers, and pimiento

Remove cartilage carefully and shred crabmeat fine. Mix with enough mayonnaise to hold it together. Season with Worcestershire. Peel cucumber and chop very fine. Season lightly with salt and pepper. Spread a thin layer of cucumber on each bread round. Cover with a mound of crabmeat. Place under the broiler to brown lightly. Decorate with parsley sprigs, drained capers, pimiento strips. Makes about 24.

## HOT CRAB TRIANGLES

1 package (8 ounces) cream cheese, softened
½ teaspoon dry mustard
1 tablespoon milk
¼ teaspoon salt
Dash of cayenne
1 can (6 ounces) white crab meat, drained
2 tablespoons minced chives or green onion
2 tablespoons finely chopped blanched almonds
12 slices firm-type white bread, crusts trimmed
Paprika

Beat cheese until fluffy. Combine mustard with milk and add to cheese with next 5 ingredients. Mix well and spread generously on bread slices. Sprinkle lightly with paprika. Cut each slice in 4 triangles, put on baking sheet and bake in preheated hot oven (400°F.) 10 to 12 minutes, or until well browned. Makes 48.

## HOT CHUTNEY AND BACON FINGERS

20 to 24 toast fingers
10 to 12 slices of bacon
1 cup well drained chutney, chopped fine

Cut toast fingers the width of a bacon slice and half the length. Cut bacon slices in half crosswise; fry over low heat until half done, but not brown. Spread chutney on toast fingers and top each with half slice of bacon. Broil 5 inches from heat until bacon is crisp. Serve hot. Makes 20 to 24.

# COLD APPETIZERS

### MILE-A-MINUTE APPETIZERS

1 loaf (1 pound) firm-type unsliced white bread
Butter or margarine, softened
Fillings

With knife, trim crusts from bread and cut loaf in 8 lengthwise slices. Spread with butter. Fill as directed below.

**Egg-Anchovy** Cover 2 slices bread with hard-cooked egg slices. Cut between egg slices to form squares and top each slice with a caper-stuffed rolled anchovy and a sprig of parsley. Insert toothpick in center of each square. If desired, trim off bread around egg slices.

**Deviled Ham** Spread 2 bread slices with canned deviled ham (or luncheon-meat spread). Cut slices in triangles or squares of desired size. Garnish each with a cucumber or pickle slice and a cherry-tomato wedge. Secure garnish with toothpick.

**Salami** Cover 2 slices bread with sliced salami. Cut bread in desired sizes and shapes and garnish each with a cocktail onion and ½ pimiento-stuffed olive. Secure with toothpick.

**Cheese** Spread remaining bread slices with cheese spread of your choice. Cut in desired sizes and shapes. Garnish each with a grape slice or radish slice and secure with toothpick.

**Note** Appetizers can be varied to suit taste and availability of ingredients.

### TOMATO CAVIAR

3½ cups (one 1-pound, 12-ounce can) tomatoes
1 package (3 ounces) cream cheese
1 tablespoon cream (about)
1 tablespoon onion juice
24 bread rounds, sautéed in butter
¼ cup mayonnaise (about)
1 small jar red caviar

Drain tomatoes for at least 2 hours; reserve juice for other purposes. Blend cheese with enough cream to make it spreadable; mix in onion juice. Spread each sautéed bread round with cheese. Mash tomatoes and spread a little over cheese on each round. Cover with mayonnaise. Put a few dots of red caviar in the center of each round. Makes 2 dozen.

## LAYERED CHEESE MOLD

2 packages (8 ounces each) cream cheese
2 teaspoons lemon juice
Grated Parmesan cheese
¾ cup chopped parsley
⅛ teaspoon garlic powder
Dash of onion salt
⅓ cup creamed cottage cheese
¼ teaspoon dried basil
2 tablespoons tomato paste

Divide cream cheese in 3 parts. Cream one part well with lemon juice and ⅓ cup Parmesan cheese, then stir in parsley. Put in bottom of lightly oiled 3-cup mold or bowl with straight sides. Chill while preparing second layer. Cream second part of cream cheese with garlic powder, onion salt and cottage cheese. Spread over first layer and chill. Cream third part of cream cheese with basil, tomato paste and 2 tablespoons Parmesan. Spread evenly over second layer. Cover with waxed paper or plastic wrap and chill overnight. To unmold, dip mold in warm water a few seconds, then turn out on serving plate. Serve with crackers. Makes 3 cups.

## CHEESE-BEEF LOG

1 package (8 ounces) cream cheese
½ cup finely shredded sharp Cheddar cheese
2 teaspoons well-drained horseradish
¼ cup finely chopped dried beef
2 tablespoons finely chopped parsley

Combine first 3 ingredients and beat until blended; chill. Mix beef and parsley and sprinkle on piece of waxed paper. Spoon cheese mixture on top and shape roll in 1 inch in diameter, rolling until coated with mixture. Wrap in paper and chill several hours. Cut in ¼-inch slices and serve on crackers or toast rounds. Makes about 40 slices.

## CHEESE-FILLED MEAT SLICES

1 package (8 ounces) cream cheese
1 tablespoon milk
1 package (8 ounces) sliced olive loaf
Chopped parsley

Beat cream cheese and milk until smooth and creamy; add more milk if necessary to make the cheese easy to spread. Spread cheese on all meat slices and stack them up together to make a striped package. Sprinkle the top layer of cheese with parsley. Chill. With a sharp knife cut from the top down in ¼-inch slices, then cut each slice, again from the top down, into 3 narrow slices. Makes about 4 dozen.

## SPICY BLUE-CHEESE-STUFFED CELERY

1½ ounces cream cheese
¼ cup crumbled blue cheese
1 teaspoon Worcestershire
　Celery stalks
　Chopped parsley

Mix first 3 ingredients. Cut celery in serving-size stalks and stuff with mixture. Sprinkle with parsley and chill until serving time. Makes about 12, depending on celery.

## DRIED-BEEF AND CANTALOUPE APPETIZERS

Wrap bite-size pieces of ripe cantaloupe in slices of dried beef. Secure each with a toothpick.

## RAW-VEGETABLE APPETIZERS

Radish roses
Carrot strips or curls
Cauliflower bouquets or slices
Celery strips
Cucumber strips
Cherry tomatoes (leave blossom end on)
Zucchini strips
Broccoli bouquets
Green-onion strips
Any preferred dip

Select 2 or more vegetables from list above, prepare ahead and keep crisp in bowl of ice water in refrigerator. Arrange in groups in large salad bowl or on deep serving platter. Sprinkle a few ice cubes around vegetables to keep them crisp. Serve with dip.

**Note:** For low-calorie appetizers, serve vegetables with shakers of seasoned salt and pepper.

# HOT APPETIZERS

## MEATBALLS IN CHERRY SAUCE

　Cherry Sauce
1 pound ground lean pork
½ cup soft bread crumbs
1 egg
2 tablespoons minced onion
¼ cup finely chopped water chestnuts
2 tablespoons milk
¾ teaspoon salt
⅛ teaspoon pepper
¼ teaspoon garlic salt
1 teaspoon Worcestershire

Prepare Sauce and set aside. Mix remaining ingredients well and shape into 3 dozen small balls. Brown slowly in skillet without added fat. Drain well, add to sauce and simmer gently about 10 minutes. Serve hot with cocktail picks.

### Cherry Sauce

1 can or jar (1 pound) pitted dark sweet cherries
¼ cup orange juice
3 tablespoons each brown sugar, vinegar and lemon juice
2 tablespoons soy sauce
¼ teaspoon each Worcestershire and grated orange rind
1 tablespoon cornstarch

Drain cherries and put syrup in large saucepan. Add remaining ingredients and mix well. Cut cherries in half and add to mixture. Cook, stirring, until clear and slightly thickened.

## GRILLED BEEF STRIPS

1 pound round steak, about 1 inch thick
1 clove garlic, thinly sliced
　Fresh ginger, about 1-inch piece, thinly sliced, or 1 teaspoon ground ginger
⅓ cup soy sauce
2 tablespoons sherry
1 teaspoon sugar

Remove fat from meat and slice meat very thin. Add remaining ingredients and mix well. Let stand about ½ hour. Thread on bamboo sticks or skewers and broil over hot coals or in broiler. Makes about 20, depending on number put on each stick.

## BACON-WRAPPED APPETIZERS

Using shears, cut partially cooked bacon slices in half crosswise or in other suitable length and wrap around any of the following foods. Secure with toothpick, arrange on rack in baking pan and bake in preheated very hot oven (450°F.) until bacon is crisp and food is heated or cooked, depending on ingredient used.

Fresh or canned pineapple cubes, well drained

Well-drained pimiento-stuffed olives

Ready-to-eat pitted prunes, soaked in sherry, if desired, and stuffed with a walnut half or piece of crystallized ginger

Peeled cleaned raw shrimps, sprinkled with lemon juice and salt and pepper

Raw scallops, sprinkled with lemon juice

Chicken livers, halved and sprinkled with crumbled sage and salt and pepper

## CHINESE-FRIED CHICKEN WINGS

    3 pounds (about 16) chicken wings
    2 eggs, slightly beaten
    ⅔ cup milk
    1 cup all-purpose flour
    2 tablespoons soy sauce
      Vegetable oil for deep-frying
      Salt

Using kitchen shears, cut off wing tips, cutting at the joint. Reserve tips for use at another time. Divide sections at joint. At center of each section, cut to the bone all the way around, then make 5 cuts lengthwise through chicken meat and skin from each center to each end. Mix next 4 ingredients until smooth and blended. Dip chicken in batter and fry in hot deep oil (350°F. on frying thermometer) until browned and crisp. Drain and sprinkle with salt. Makes about 32 pieces.

## POLYNESIAN FRIED SHRIMPS

    2 pounds jumbo shrimps (24 to 30)
  1½ cups pancake mix
    2 teaspoons curry powder
    1 cup milk
    1 egg
    1 tablespoon vegetable oil
  2⅔ cups packaged toasted coconut
      Fat for frying

Shell shrimp down to the tail segment; leave tail shell on. Devein if necessary. Cut each shrimp along the line of the vein, but do not cut through to the other side. Spread each shrimp flat. Mix next 5 ingredients until smooth (batter will be thick). Holding shrimps by tail, dip each in batter, draining off excess. Coat with coconut. Set aside about 30 minutes, then fry 2 to 3 minutes in 1 inch of hot fat in skillet (set at 325°F. if electric), turning once until golden brown. Drain on paper towel and keep warm in preheated 325°F. oven.

## ARTICHOKE-CLAM PUFFS

    2 packages frozen artichoke hearts
    1 package (8 ounces) cream cheese
    ¼ teaspoon hot pepper sauce
    2 tablespoons sherry
    1 can (about 6½ ounces) minced clams, drained
      Paprika

Cook artichokes according to package directions until just tender (do not overcook). Drain and put on greased broiler-proof serving plate. Beat cream cheese with pepper sauce and sherry, then stir in clams. Spoon mixture onto cut sides of artichokes and sprinkle with paprika. Broil until browned. Makes about 36.

## CHEESE BITES

    1 cup coarsely shredded sharp Cheddar cheese, at
      room temperature
    ½ cup butter, at room temperature
    1 cup crisp rice cereal
    1 cup all-purpose flour
    ⅛ teaspoon salt
    ½ teaspoon hot pepper sauce

Put all ingredients on board or in bowl and mix well. Pinch off marble-size pieces and put on lightly greased baking sheet. Bake in preheated moderate oven (350°F.) 10 to 15 minutes, or until lightly browned. Store airtight. Makes about 4 dozen.

## WATER-CHESTNUT AND PINEAPPLE ROLL-UPS

Cut bacon slices in thirds, slice water chestnuts and drain canned pineapple chunks. Wrap a bacon slice around a chunk of pineapple and a slice of water chestnut. Secure with a toothpick. Broil, turning once or twice, until bacon is crisp. Drain on paper towel. Put on rack in shallow baking pan and, just before serving, reheat in preheated moderate (350°F.) oven about 5 minutes.

## PASTRY-WRAPPED OLIVES

    1 cup all-purpose flour
    2 tablespoons grated Parmesan cheese
  2½ tablespoons heavy cream
    ¼ cup vegetable oil
   25 well-drained medium black or pimiento-stuffed green
      olives
    1 egg white, slightly beaten
      Poppy seed, finely chopped almonds or additional
      grated Parmesan cheese.

Combine first 4 ingredients and mix well. Shape dough in a strip and cut in 25 small pieces. Put an olive in center of each and cover completely with dough, rolling in hands. Brush with egg white and sprinkle with poppy seed. Put on ungreased cookie sheets and bake in preheated slow oven (300°F.) about 20 minutes. Serve warm. Makes 25.

**Note:** For crunchiness, stuff each black olive with an almond sliver

## CREAM-CHEESE PASTRY

1 cup butter
1 package (8 ounces) regular cream cheese
½ teaspoon salt
2 cups all-purpose flour
1 egg yolk
2 teaspoons cream or milk

Using electric mixer, beat first 3 ingredients together until smooth and blended. With fingertips, fork or rubber spatula, work in flour to form a smooth dough. Flatten dough in foil to form 8-inch x 6-inch rectangle; chill; (can be chilled several days before using, if desired). Remove from refrigerator and let stand 8 to 10 minutes. Divide dough in portions and keep unrolled portions in refrigerator until ready to use. Roll one portion on floured pastry cloth with floured rolling pin (first rub cloth and pin well with flour, then shake out excess) to thickness indicated in individual recipe. Shape as directed and chill before baking. Brush tops only of all pastries with egg yolk beaten with cream. Bake as indicated.

**Note:** Pastry can be reworked and rerolled to the last scrap. It still remains tender and flaky.

## MUSHROOM-FILLED TRIANGLES

Mushroom Filling
1 recipe Cream-cheese Pastry, above

Roll each in rectangle; fold over in thirds. Reroll, fold again, then roll in rectangle about 12 x 9 x ⅛ inch thick. Cut in 2-inch squares and put a small amount of filling in center of each square. Fold in triangle and crimp edges with floured fork. Put on ungreased cookie sheet and chill 1 hour. Bake in preheated moderate (350°F.) oven about 20 minutes. Makes about 4 dozen.

## MUSHROOM FILLING

½ pound mushrooms
2 tablespoons butter or margarine
1 medium onion, chopped
½ teaspoon salt
  Freshly ground pepper
  Dash of nutmeg
1 teaspoon lemon juice
2 teaspoons all-purpose flour
½ cup dairy sour cream
1 teaspoon dillweed

Trim off any tough stems and wipe mushrooms with damp paper towels. Chop fairly fine. Heat butter in skillet, add mushrooms and onion and cook briskly, stirring, about 4 minutes. Sprinkle with salt, a few grindings of pepper, nutmeg, lemon juice and flour. Cook 1 to 2 minutes longer. Remove from heat and add sour cream and dill.

## PARMESAN TWISTS

½ recipe Cream-Cheese Pastry.
  Finely grated Parmesan cheese (about ½ cup)
1 egg yolk beaten with 2 teaspoons milk or cream

Divide chilled dough in half and roll each half in rectangle a generous ¼ inch to ½ inch thick. Sprinkle heavily with cheese, pressing it lightly into dough with rolling pin. Fold dough over itself in thirds and roll again. Sprinkle with more cheese, press with pin and fold again. Roll 18 x 4 x ¼ inch thick. Brush with egg yolk mixture and sprinkle with cheese. Cut in strips about 4 x ¾ inches. Twist strips in spirals, put on ungreased cookie sheet and brush ends with remaining egg yolk mixture. Chill 1 hour, then bake in preheated moderate (350°F.) oven 15 to 20 minutes, or until crisp and golden. Carefully remove from sheet at once. Makes about 2 dozen.

**Note:** For a smaller appetizer, cut baked twists in half.

## FILLED PATTY SHELLS

1 recipe Cream-Cheese Pastry
  Choice of chicken, tuna, shellfish or other salad

Divide dough in 4 portions and roll each in rectangle ⅛" thick. Fold in thirds, then roll again. Cut with 1½" round cutter. Put half on cookie sheet and prick with fork. Cut out center of remaining rounds with small cutter or thimble. Moisten edges of bottom rounds and top with remaining rounds, pressing lightly. Chill 1 hour, then bake in preheated moderate (350°F.) oven 18 to 20 minutes. Fill with choice of salad just before serving. Makes 2 to 3 dozen.

# COCKTAILS

## CRABMEAT OR SHRIMP RÉMOULADE

1 pound cooked flaked crabmeat, or cooked, shelled, and deveined shrimps
6 lettuce cups
1 cup mayonnaise
1 tablespoon minced sweet pickle
1 tablespoon drained capers
1 tablespoon prepared mustard
1 tablespoon minced parsley
1 teaspoon minced onion
⅛ teaspoon each of salt and pepper

Place crabmeat or shrimps in lettuce cups. Combine all other ingredients and blend well. Spoon over seafood. Chill before serving. Makes 6 servings.

## SHRIMP COCKTAIL SAUCE WITH MUSTARD

2 tablespoons cider vinegar
6 tablespoons olive oil
3 tablespoons prepared mustard, such as Dijon mustard
1 small garlic clove, minced
3 anchovy fillets, minced
½ teaspoon salt
1 tablespoon minced chives or scallion tops
1 tablespoon minced parsley
1 hard-cooked egg, mashed

Combine all ingredients and blend well. Chill, and serve with cooked, shelled, deveined shrimps. Makes ¾ cup.

## DICED-CUCUMBER COCKTAIL

2 large cucumbers
¼ cup catsup
¼ cup chili sauce
1 teaspoon Worcestershire
  Juice of ½ lemon
1 teaspoon prepared white horseradish
  Dash of hot pepper sauce or cayenne
4 lettuce leaves

Chill cucumbers. Combine remaining ingredients, except lettuce, to make sauce; chill. Just before serving, peel cucumbers. Make lengthwise parallel grooves with tines of fork. Dice into ¼-inch pieces. Place on lettuce leaves in cocktail glasses. Top with sauce. Makes 4 servings.

## FRESH PEACH COCKTAIL

2½ cups diced peeled ripe fresh peaches
1 tablespoon fresh lemon juice
2 tablespoons sugar
  Chilled ginger ale
  Fresh mint

Combine peaches, lemon juice, and sugar. Fill sherbet glasses; add 1 to 2 tablespoons ginger ale to each glass. Garnish with sprig of mint. Makes 4 servings.

## WATERMELON COCKTAIL

Make watermelon balls with melon-ball scoop, or cut into 1-inch cubes, removing seeds. Sprinkle melon with lemon juice and superfine sugar, using ½ tablespoon lemon juice and 1 tablespoon superfine sugar for each portion. Cover and chill. Serve in cocktail glasses; garnish with fresh mint.

# DIPS

## CREAM-CHEESE AND CLAM DIP

1 package (8 ounces) cream cheese
1 can (10½ ounces) minced clams
½ small onion, grated
1 teaspoon Worcestershire
  Dash of garlic salt
1 teaspoon celery salt

Let cheese soften at room temperature. Drain clams, reserving liquid. Add cheese, remaining ingredients, and 2 tablespoons reserved clam liquid. Blend thoroughly; chill. Serve with pretzel sticks or Melba toast. Makes about 1½ cups.

## TWO-CHEESE DIP

1 package (8 ounces) blue cheese
1 package (8 ounces) cream cheese
½ cup undiluted evaporated milk
  Dash of garlic salt
¾ teaspoon celery seed
  Pimiento or green pepper, chopped

Combine cheeses, milk, and seasonings; beat together until fluffy. Chill in refrigerator. To serve, pile dip in serving dishes and garnish with pimiento or green pepper. Makes 2½ cups.

## CHILI DIP

1 cup dairy sour cream
1 tablespoon chopped fresh basil or 1 teaspoon crumbled dried basil
1 teaspoon paprika
½ teaspoon chili powder
  Salt to taste

Mix all ingredients well and chill. Serve with raw vegetable sticks. Makes 1 cup.

## EAST INDIAN DIP

½ cup orange marmalade
3 tablespoons cider vinegar
2 tablespoons granulated sugar
1 tablespoon brown sugar
½ teaspoon salt
¼ teaspoon curry powder
¼ teaspoon ground ginger
1½ teaspoons Worcestershire
⅓ cup dairy sour cream

Combine all ingredients except sour cream in saucepan. Bring to boil. Simmer, stirring constantly, until sauce is blended. Let cool. Mix with sour cream. This keeps very well in refrigerator, thickening somewhat as it stands. Makes about 1 cup.

## RÉMOULADE DIP FOR SCALLOPS OR SHRIMPS

2 cups mayonnaise
1 garlic clove, crushed
1 tablespoon prepared mustard
1 tablespoon chopped drained capers
1 tablespoon minced parsley
2 teaspoons minced chives

Blend all ingredients; chill. Serve in a bowl on a large plate surrounded by cooked and chilled scallops or shrimps, speared with toothpicks. Makes about 2 cups.

Cocktail Torte
Mile-a-Minute Appetizers

## MUSTARD DIP FOR RAW VEGETABLES

¼ cup mayonnaise
3 tablespoons heavy cream
2 tablespoons prepared mustard
1 teaspoon Worcestershire
2 teaspoons lemon juice
Salt and pepper
Dash of hot pepper sauce

Combine all ingredients and chill before serving. Makes about ⅔ cup.

## CREAMY LIVERWURST DIP

8 ounces liverwurst, coarsely chopped
1 cup dairy sour cream
2 tablespoons minced red or green onion
1 tablespoon chopped drained capers
¼ cup finely chopped water chestnuts
½ teaspoon seasoned salt
Finely chopped parsley

Beat liverwurst, then add sour cream and beat until well blended. Add next 4 ingredients and blend well. Pour into serving dish and garnish edge with parsley. Chill until serving time. Serve with corn chips, potato chips or crackers. Makes 2 cups.

## CRAB MEAT DIP

1 can (7½ ounces) crab meat, drained and flaked
1 cup mayonnaise
½ cup dairy sour cream
1 teaspoon lemon juice
1 tablespoon dry sherry
Salt and pepper to taste

Combine all ingredients and blend well. Chill and serve with chips or crackers. Makes about 2 cups.

## YOGURT-VEGETABLE DIP

½ cup creamed cottage cheese
1 tablespoon finely grated carrot
2 teaspoons finely grated onion
1 teaspoon finely grated green pepper
½ teaspoon salt
⅛ teaspoon garlic salt
Dash of white pepper
1 cup plain yogurt

With fork, beat cottage cheese in small bowl. Add remaining ingredients, except yogurt, and mix well. Fold in yogurt, cover and chill. Use as dip for raw vegetables or chips. Makes about 1 cup.

# HORS D'OEUVRES

## HERRING AND APPLES IN SOUR CREAM

1 jar (16 ounces) herring fillets
1 cup dairy sour cream
2 tablespoons lemon juice
1 medium onion, finely chopped
1 teaspoon salt
½ teaspoon pepper
2 medium unpeeled apples, cored and diced

Drain herring and cut into bite-size pieces if necessary. Whip sour cream until it stands in soft peaks. Blend sour cream with herring and remaining ingredients. Toss to blend well. Chill before serving. Serve on lettuce leaves if desired. Makes 6 to 8 servings.

## SCALLOPS AU GRATIN

½ pound sea scallops
2 tablespoons butter or margarine
⅓ cup condensed cream of mushroom soup, undiluted
Salt, pepper and hot pepper sauce
2 tablespoons grated Parmesan cheese
2 tablespoons fine dry bread crumbs

Cut scallops in small pieces and sauté gently in 1 tablespoon butter 1 to 2 minutes. Stir in soup, then season to taste with salt and pepper and add a dash of hot pepper sauce. Put in small baking shells. Mix cheese with crumbs and remaining 1 tablespoon butter, melted, and sprinkle over top. Broil a few inches from heat until lightly browned and hot. Makes about 8 servings.

## COCKTAIL TORTE

1 package (10 ounces) piecrust mix
1 egg yolk or white, slightly beaten
½ cup mayonnaise
½ cup dairy sour cream
2 teaspoons lemon juice
1 jar (3¾ ounces) black or red caviar
1 can (4½ ounces) shrimps, drained and rinsed (see Note)
Dill or parsley sprigs

Prepare piecrust mix as directed on label. Divide dough in half. Roll out one half on lightly floured surface and cut in 9-inch circle, using 9-inch pan or cardboard circle as guide. Put on ungreased baking sheet and prick with fork. Roll out remaining dough ⅛ inch thick. Cut out 9-inch circle, then put an 8-inch plate or cardboard evenly on circle and cut around it, forming a ring about 1 inch wide. Reroll center piece and any remaining scraps and cut in 7 strips ½ inch wide and 9 inches long. Weave strips loosely to form a lattice and put on ungreased baking sheet. Put ring over strips, covering ends. Trim ends even with ring. Brush lattice with egg and bake with circle in preheated very hot oven (450°F.) 8 minutes, or until golden brown. Loosen carefully with spatula and leave on sheet to cool. Just before serving, put circle on serving platter. Mix well mayonnaise, sour cream and lemon juice.

Spread on circle, cover with lattice and fill empty spaces with caviar. Top with shrimps and dill and serve in wedges to be eaten with fork. Makes 8 to 10 servings.

**Note:** Fresh or frozen shrimps, cooked, peeled and cleaned, can be substituted for the canned, if preferred.

## SALMON-STUFFED EGGS

    10  hard-cooked eggs
    ½  cup cooked or canned drained and boned salmon
    1  anchovy fillet
    ½  cup butter or margarine
    1  teaspoon Worcestershire
       Salt and pepper

Cut eggs into halves lengthwise. Take out yolks. Rub salmon, anchovy, and egg yolks through a sieve, or whirl in a blender. Cream butter. Add salmon mixture, Worcestershire, and seasonings to taste. Mix well. Stuff whites with mixture. Makes 20.

## CHEESE TARTLETS

    2  tablespoons butter
    2  tablespoons flour
    1  cup light cream
    1  cup grated Swiss or Parmesan cheese
       Dash of cayenne
    24  tiny tart shells, about 1½ inches across, baked

Melt butter. Blend in flour smoothly. Add cream and stir until thickened. Remove from heat. Add cheese and stir until melted. Add cayenne. Fill baked tart shells. Place under broiler 2 to 3 inches from heat until cheese is brown. Serve piping hot and bubbling brown. Makes 24.

## RUMAKI

    8  chicken livers
    8  water chestnuts
    8  slices of bacon
       Onion powder
    ½  cup soy sauce
    ¼  cup mirin (sweet saké) or sherry
    4  red chilies, ground
    1  garlic clove, mashed
    1  slice of green gingerroot, minced
    ½  teaspoon ground turmeric

Cut chicken livers, water chestnuts, and bacon slices into halves. Sprinkle each piece of chicken liver with onion powder and fold it around a slice of water chestnut. Wrap bundle in a half slice of bacon. Pierce with toothpick, being sure the pick goes through center of water chestnut. Mix soy sauce, mirin, and seasonings. Put bundles in mixture to marinate for at least 1 hour. Drain. Broil until bacon is crisp, turning to brown all sides. This recipe comes from the Orient. Makes 16.

## ENDIVE TEMPURA

Mix together lightly 1 cup all-purpose flour, 1 cup water, and 1 egg. The batter should be lumpy, like muffin batter. Add salt, if desired. Dip washed and dried leaves from

2 heads Belgian endive into batter and fry in hot deep fat (360°F. on a frying thermometer) until batter is golden brown, about 2 to 3 minutes. Drain and serve at once. Use soy sauce as a dip. Makes 3 to 4 servings.

## MUSHROOM BEIGNETS

    ½  cup water
    ¼  cup butter or margarine
       Dash of salt
    ½  cup sifted all-purpose flour
    2  eggs
       Mushroom Filling

Put water, butter, and salt in a small saucepan and bring to a boil. Add flour all at once. Stir hard, cooking until mixture leaves sides of pan and forms a ball. Beat in eggs, one at a time. Beat until mixture is thick and shiny. Using 2 teaspoons, shape little rounds of mixture (about 1 teaspoon each) and place 2 inches apart on ungreased baking sheet. Bake in preheated very hot oven (450°F.) for 15 minutes; lower heat to moderate (350°F.) and bake for 20 minutes longer. Cool. Slit puff shells on one side and fill with Mushroom Filling. Makes about 4 dozen.

### Mushroom Filling

    ½  pound fresh mushrooms
    1  tablespoon butter
    1  tablespoon flour
    ½  cup heavy cream
    ¼  teaspoon curry powder
       Salt and pepper

Remove stems from mushrooms. (Use stems in sauce or soup at another time.) Chop mushrooms fine. Sauté mushrooms in butter for about 5 minutes. Sprinkle flour evenly over the mushrooms and stir until smooth. Gradually stir in heavy cream. Stir over low heat until thickened. Add curry powder, and salt and pepper to taste. Makes enough filling for about 4 dozen beignets.

## SAVORY SANDWICH LOAF

    1  cup finely chopped cooked ham
    1  small dill pickle, minced
    1  teaspoon dry mustard
    2  tablespoons minced red or green onion
       Mayonnaise
    1  cucumber
       Salt and pepper
    2  hard-cooked eggs, finely chopped
    2  tablespoons chopped pimiento
       Few drops of hot pepper sauce
    1  loaf (1 pound) unsliced firm-type white bread
    1½  cups dairy sour cream
    2  teaspoons well-drained horseradish
       Paprika
       Chopped parsley
       Watercress or salad greens

Combine first 3 ingredients with 1 tablespoon onion and enough mayonnaise to make of spreading consistency.

Peel and halve cucumber. Remove seed and chop cucumber fine. Season with salt and pepper and let stand 15 to 20 minutes. Then squeeze out excess liquid. Combine cucumber and remaining 1 tablespoon onion. Mix eggs, pimiento and hot pepper sauce with mayonnaise to bind. Season with salt to taste. Trim crusts from bread; cut loaf in 8 lengthwise slices about ⅜ inch thick. Arrange 2 slices next to each other on 14-inch-long platter, board or foil-lined cardboard. Spread with ham mixture. Cover with 2 more slices of bread and spread with cucumber mixture. Top with 2 more slices. Then spread with egg mixture and cover with 2 remaining bread slices. Press slices down gently, cover tightly with plastic wrap or waxed paper and chill several hours. Mix sour cream with horseradish and use mixture to frost loaf completely. Sprinkle with paprika and parsley. Garnish with watercress; serve in 1-inch slices to be eaten with knife and fork. Makes 12 servings.

## CUBED COLD CUTS WITH TIERED FRUIT SALAD

Buy thick slices of olive loaf, liverwurst, bologna, salami, or other cold cuts; cut into cubes. Arrange slices of fresh pineapple on chicory or other salad greens and top each with pieces of fresh fruit (banana, plum, pear, nectarine, strawberries, etc.). Garnish with sprigs of mint, if desired. Insert cubed cold cuts on toothpicks in a whole Edam cheese or a grapefruit. Serve with Whipped-Cream Dressing: Combine equal parts of mayonnaise and whipped heavy cream.

## CORNUCOPIAS OF COLD CUTS WITH TWO-CHEESE MOLDS AND MIXED FRUIT

Soften 1 envelope unflavored gelatin in ¼ cup water. Dissolve over hot water. Beat well 1 pound creamed cottage cheese, ¼ cup crumbled blue cheese, ¼ teaspoon salt, ⅛ teaspoon paprika, dash of cayenne, and ½ cup milk or cream. Beat in dissolved gelatin. Put into 4 individual molds or one large mold. Refrigerate for several hours. Unmold and garnish with pimiento strips. Arrange on a bed of lettuce and watercress with cooked salami, pressed ham, or other cold cuts, rolled into cones. Serve with chilled mixed fruit. Makes 4 servings.

# NIBBLES

### ALMONDS

Salted, deviled, or fried almonds make excellent nibbles.

### CHEESE BOARD

Offer a board with several varieties of cheese to please all tastes; for example, a cheese board might contain a mild Cheddar, Swiss, Edam, Muenster, or any cheese which can be cubed and speared on toothpicks. Serve with simple crackers and cubes of fresh fruit.

## STUFFED CELERY

Fill trimmed celery stalks with highly seasoned cottage cheese; serve. Or two filled stalks can be pressed together, chilled, and cut into ½-inch slices.

## CUCUMBER SLICES

Slice cucumbers ¼ inch thick and spread with cottage cheese seasoned with a little anchovy paste.

## GARLIC RIPE OLIVES

1 can (7¼ ounces) large ripe olives
⅔ cup salad oil
⅓ cup cider vinegar
1 small garlic clove, minced

Drain olives. To olives, add mixture of remaining ingredients. Cover and chill. Save marinating liquid and use it for salad dressings.

## OLIVES IN CHEESE

1 package (3 ounces) cream cheese
½ teaspoon Worcestershire
   Cream
16 small stuffed olives, drained and dried
¼ pound salted almonds, finely chopped

Mix cheese and Worcestershire together with enough cream to make a thick smooth paste. Coat olives with mixture; roll in almonds. Chill. Makes 16.

## CLAM BITES

1 egg, separated
1 can (10½ ounces) minced clams
1 teaspoon melted butter
½ cup all-purpose flour
   Salt and pepper
   Fat for deep frying

Beat egg yolk until light. Drain clams, reserving liquid. Stir into egg yolk the butter, flour, ¼ teaspoon salt, and ¼ cup clam liquid. Add milk (if necessary) to make ¼ cup. Fold in stiffly beaten egg white. Add clams and let stand for at least 1 hour at room temperature. Drop by teaspoons into hot deep fat (375°F. on a frying thermometer) and fry until golden brown, 5 to 6 minutes. Drain on absorbent paper. Sprinkle with salt and pepper and serve hot on toothpicks. Fry these at the last minute before serving. Makes about 2 dozen.

## OLIVES, CALIFORNIA STYLE

1 can (7¼ ounces) ripe olives or
1 jar (10 ounces) green olives
3 lemon slices
2 garlic cloves, halved
½ cup olive oil

Discard brine from olives. Put olives in jar with remaining ingredients and cover tightly. Invert jar 2 or 3 times so olives will be coated with oil. Let stand for several hours. Chill slightly before serving.

## POTATOES MAYONNAISE

3 medium potatoes
2 tablespoons dairy sour cream
½ cup mayonnaise
Dash of curry
Salt and pepper to taste

Boil potatoes in jackets. Do not over-cook, as they must not be mushy. Cool potatoes. Peel and cut into small cubes. Mix remaining ingredients. Carefully coat cubes with mixture. Serve with toothpicks. Makes 3 to 4 dozen.

## PARTY SNACKS

6 tablespoons butter or margarine
1 teaspoon seasoned salt
2 teaspoons celery seed
1 teaspoon dry mustard
2 cups nuts
1 cup bite-size shredded rice
1 cup bite-size shredded corn
1 cup honeycombed whole-wheat chunks or other chunky wheat cereal

Melt butter in large shallow pan in preheated very slow (250°F.) oven. Add next 3 ingredients and mix well. Add next 3 ingredients and toast in oven, stirring occasionally, 15 minutes. Add wheat chunks and toast 15 minutes longer. Spread on paper towel to cool, then store in tightly covered container in cool place. Makes about 5 cups.

# RELISHES

## TOMATO APPETIZER

3 medium tomatoes, peeled and chopped
1 small green pepper, minced
⅓ cup diced celery
1 small onion, minced
1½ teaspoons salt
2 tablespoons cider vinegar
2 tablespoons sugar
½ cup cold water
⅛ teaspoon pepper

Mix all ingredients and chill. Makes 4 servings.

## BEET AND CUCUMBER RELISH

2 cups coarsely shredded cooked beets
¼ cup beet cooking liquid
¼ cup cider vinegar
1 cup diced peeled cucumber
1 small onion, grated
3 tablespoons sugar
¼ teaspoon salt
Dash of pepper
1 tablespoon chopped parsley or fresh dill

Thoroughly mix all ingredients except parsley. Cover, and store in refrigerator for several hours. Add parsley or dill just before serving. Makes 3½ cups.

## REFRIGERATOR SUMMER RELISH

4 cups peeled chopped ripe tomatoes, drained
1½ cups finely chopped celery
1 cup finely chopped onion
1 unpeeled apple, chopped
2 tablespoons prepared white horseradish
2 tablespoons salt
2 tablespoons mustard seed
⅓ cup firmly packed brown sugar
½ teaspoon ground cinnamon
¼ teaspoon each of ground cloves and mace
Dash of cayenne
1½ cups cider vinegar

Mix all ingredients thoroughly. Cover, and store in refrigerator. If relish is too juicy, drain off some liquid. This will keep for several weeks. Makes 1½ quarts.

## PENNSYLVANIA DUTCH CHOWCHOW

Salt
2 cups each of:
Sliced unpeeled cucumbers
Chopped sweet peppers
Chopped white cabbage
Sliced yellow onions
Chopped unpeeled green tomatoes
Lima beans
Cut green beans
Sliced carrots
Chopped celery
2 tablespoons celery seed
4 teaspoons mustard seed
4 cups cider vinegar
4 cups sugar
¼ cup ground turmeric

Using ¼ cup salt for each quart of water soak cucumbers, peppers, cabbage, onions, and tomatoes in salted water overnight. Cook Lima beans, green beans, carrots, and celery until barely tender. Drain *all* vegetables well. Mix soaked and cooked vegetables with remaining ingredients and 2 cups water. Bring to boil, lower heat, and simmer gently for 10 minutes. Place while hot in hot sterilized jars and seal at once. Makes 8 to 10 pints.

## CUCUMBER-ONION RELISH

3 large cucumbers
1½ teaspoons salt
1 onion, minced
½ teaspoon pepper
1 cup white vinegar
½ pimiento, chopped

Peel cucumbers, cut into halves lengthwise, and scoop out seeds with teaspoon. Discard seeds. Put cucumbers through food chopper, using coarse blade. Combine with salt. Let drain for 1 hour in colander or sieve. Add remaining ingredients. Cover and store in refrigerator. This will keep for several weeks. Stir every 2 or 3 days. Makes about 3 cups.

## PICKLED COOKED MUSHROOMS

Steam or boil 2 pounds mushrooms in salted water for 15 to 20 minutes, or until tender; drain and put in large jar. Add ½ lemon, sliced, 1 bay leaf, and 1 onion, sliced, if desired. While mushrooms are still hot, pour over them the following marinade:

        ½ cup mixed pickling spice
        2 cups white or wine vinegar
        1 teaspoon salt, or more to taste
        1 teaspoon sugar
        1½ cups oil (use part olive oil, if possible)
        1 garlic clove, halved

Mix pickling spice with vinegar. Add salt and sugar, bring to boil, and strain over mushrooms. Cool. Add oil and garlic. Keep in refrigerator. Shake jar well 2 or 3 times a day. Add more salt, if necessary, after 24 hours. Do not use for 2 or 3 days. These mushrooms will keep for 1 month in covered jar in refrigerator. Makes 8 servings.

# SPREADS

### WALNUT SPREAD

        ½ cup shelled walnuts
        2 garlic cloves, crushed
        2 slices of bread, crusts removed
        1½ teaspoons cider vinegar
        1 teaspoon olive oil
        Salt

Pound walnuts in a mortar or whirl in a blender. Add garlic and mix well. Soak bread in water. Squeeze out water and mix bread well with nuts and garlic, until you have formed a paste. Add vinegar and oil slowly, mixing well; season with salt. Serve with toast or crackers. Makes about ½ cup.

### LIPTAUER CHEESE

        2 packages (3 ounces each) cream cheese
        ½ cup unsalted butter
        2 tablespoons chopped drained capers
        1 teaspoon salt
        1 teaspoon anchovy paste
        ½ teaspoon minced onion
        1 teaspoon dry mustard
        1½ teaspoons paprika
        Dairy sour cream
        Whole drained capers
        Paprika

Cream cheese and butter together. Add other ingredients except last two. Mix well, using just enough sour cream to make mixture smooth and spreadable. Chill thoroughly. Serve in a mound decorated with whole capers and paprika. Surround with crisp crackers. Makes about 1 cup.

## PORK PÂTÉ

        1 pound pork liver
        1 pound lean pork
        1 tablespoon all-purpose flour
        1 egg
        1 onion, minced
        2 tablespoons minced parsley
        ¼ teaspoon dried thyme
        ¼ teaspoon dried sage
        1 teaspoon salt
        Pepper
        Dash each of ground nutmeg, mace, and cloves
        ½ pound fat salt pork, sliced very thin
        ¼ cup (2 ounces) brandy
        1 bay leaf

Grind liver and pork fine. Blend flour into mixture. Add egg, onion, parsley, herbs, seasonings, and spices; mix well. Line bottom and sides of pâté mold or deep casserole with slices of salt pork. Pour in half of pâté mixture. Put over it a layer of salt-pork slices. Fill with remaining pâté. Pour brandy over pâté. Cover top completely with salt-pork slices. Put bay leaf on top and put on cover. Seal edges of cover with a thick flour-and-water paste to prevent steam from escaping or wrap and seal casserole completely in foil. Place in pan of hot water and bake in preheated slow oven (300°F.) for 3½ hours. Remove from oven and let sealed pot stand until cold. Then remove seal and chill. Serve with toast points. Makes 8 to 10 servings.

### CORNED-BEEF AND MUSHROOM PÂTÉ

        1 small onion, finely chopped
        ½ pound fresh mushrooms, finely chopped
        2 tablespoons butter or margarine
        1 can (12 ounces) corned beef, coarsely chopped
        ½ cup dairy sour cream
        ½ teaspoon dry mustard
        ¼ teaspoon white pepper
        1 tablespoon drained horseradish
        Chopped parsley

Sauté first 2 ingredients in the butter until well browned; cool. Beat corned beef and sour cream until well mixed. Add mushroom mixture and next 3 ingredients and pack in oiled 2-cup mold. Chill several hours. Unmold and garnish with parsley. Makes about 2 cups.

### EGGPLANT CAVIAR

        1 eggplant
        1 large yellow onion
        1 garlic clove
        2 large tomatoes
        ½ cup olive oil
        1 teaspoon salt
        Pepper to taste
        ½ teaspoon sugar

Wash eggplant and bake in moderate oven (375°F.) until outside is black and inside soft, about 45 minutes. Run cold water over it. Peel carefully and dice. Peel onion, garlic, and tomatoes; chop well. Mix with eggplant. Add remaining ingredients; mix thoroughly. Chill well before serving with crackers or toast. Makes 6 to 8 servings.

## INDIA SPREAD

1 package (8 ounces) cream cheese
½ cup crumbled blue cheese
¼ cup finely cut dates
¼ cup finely chopped chutney
1 tablespoon lemon juice
¾ cup finely chopped pecans or walnuts

Beat creem cheese until fluffy. Add next 4 ingredients and mix thoroughly. Stir in ½ cup nuts. Put in serving dish, sprinkle with remaining ¼ cup nuts and chill. Serve with crackers. Makes about 2 cups.

## RED CAVIAR AND ZESTY CREAM CHEESE

Have 2 pounds cream cheese at room temperature. Beat until creamy. Beat in grated rind of 6 lemons. Mound on serving plate, making a hole in center about 1 inch deep. Refrigerate until serving time. At serving time, fill hole in cheese with 1 or 2 jars (4 ounces each) red caviar, letting a little run over top. Serve with melba toast.

# QUICKIES

**Cheese-Nut Appetizers** Mash together equal quantities of butter and Roquefort or blue cheese. Spread a little mixture between two walnut halves; chill.

**Swiss Dip** Add ½ to 1 cup finely grated Swiss cheese to ½ cup dairy sour cream. Add 5 or 6 pimiento-stuffed olives (chopped), 1 to 1½ teaspoons finely minced onion, 1 to 1½ teaspoons chopped pimiento. Add salt and pepper to taste. Put in serving dish and dust with paprika. Serve with crackers or melba toast.

**Garlic Black Olives** Rub bowl with cut clove of garlic and add about ¼ cup olive oil. Add 1 7¾ oz can of drained black olives and mix well. Let stand at room temperature 2 to 3 hours, then chill.

**Stuffed Tomatoes** Hollow out tiny tomatoes and fill with whipped cream cheese seasoned to taste with drained prepared horseradish, salt and pepper.

**Cheese-Fruit Appetizers** With cocktail stick, put a cube of sharp cheese and a grape, mandarin-orange section or pineapple chunk on a cocktail pick. Walnut or pecan halves are also good with cheese.

# APPLE COOKBOOK

**APPLE**—The fruit of any tree of the genus *Malus.*
Apples come in many varieties. The ancient Romans
knew twenty-two of them. At a banquet given by the
Grand Duke Cosmo III of Tuscany in the year 1670,
fifty-six different kinds of apples were served. Today,
there are a staggering 6,500 or more horticultural forms.

Since the days of the Garden of Eden, apples have
played their part in legend, science, art, and history.
Apples were raised in the gardens of the Phoenicians.
In Greek mythology, one of Hercules' labors was to obtain
the golden apples of the Hesperides which were extremely well guarded because they bestowed immortality
on those who had them.

Newton is said to have discovered the law of gravity
when an apple fell on his head. Countless painters have
used apples in their still lifes: Cézanne, Crivelli, and
Courbet, to name just three. And finally, apples figure in
the social history of our country. The first settlers included
apple seeds in their precious supplies and Peregrine
White, the first white child born in New England, planted
apple trees there. American apples were exported to
London before the American Revolution. Later, John
Chapman traveled the Ohio wilderness, preaching and
planting apple seeds, thus earning the affectionate nick-
name of Johnny Appleseed.

Who can describe an apple? It can be round or egg-
shaped. Its size can vary from two to six inches. The
flesh may be white, yellow, crisp, mellow, sweet, or tart.
The skin is thin and glossy and ranges in color from
bright or russet red to yellow to green. Apples fit into
every course in every meal and are munched between
meals too; they're found in a lunch box and in a fancy
torte. No wonder they are one of our favorite fruits.

## FRESH APPLES

*Availability*—See chart

*Purchasing Guide*—Fresh apples are sold by weight,
sometimes by unit or original container. All apples are
graded by U.S. standards for fresh fruit and vegetables.
These grades include Fancy or Extra No. 1, U.S. No. 1,
U.S. No. 2, U.S. No. 1 Cookers, U.S. Combinations; they
designate the maturity, appearance, quality, waste, and
use of the apple. The number count stamped on the
shipping box indicates the size of the apple: the lower
the number, the larger the apple.

> 1 pound = 3 medium apples
> ⅔ pound = 2 cups, sliced (about)
> 1⅓ pounds = 2 cups sauce (about)

The United States has developed a large number of
varieties of excellent apples suited to many different uses.
Whichever kind you choose, select firm well-shaped fruit
with good color. Avoid blemishes and soft spots.

*Storage*—Place small quantities in plastic bags in refrigerator to prevent shriveling and transfer of odors. Store
large quantities in a cool dark airy place. Long or improper
storage results in mealy apples with brown cores. Sort
occasionally to remove those with signs of spoilage.
Refrigerator shelf: 1 to 2 weeks, depending on variety
of apple
Refrigerator frozen-food compartment, prepared for
freezing: 2 months
Freezer, prepared for freezing: 1 year

*Nutritive Food Values*—Fresh apples, eaten raw, help
clean the teeth. The pectin in apples is an absorptive
cellulose fiber. Apples contain vitamins A and C, but not
enough to make them a good source of those nutrients.

> 1 medium, fresh = 70 calories
> Applesauce, unsweetened, ½ cup = 50 calories
> sweetened, with 1 tablespoon sugar,
> ½ cup = 100 calories
> Apple juice, 1 cup = 125 calories
> Apple butter, 1 tablespoon = 35 calories

## Basic Preparation

**To Serve, Raw**—Wash well. If cut apples must stand,
dip into or sprinkle with lemon, orange, or other fruit juice
to prevent darkening.

**To Cook**—To maintain shape, add sugar at start of
cooking. For sauces, add sugar after cooking. See recipes
for basic cooking methods.

**To Freeze, Whole**—Consult with County Home Agent
for best variety to freeze. Freeze only tree-ripened perfect
firm-fleshed apples.

**To Freeze, Slices in Syrup**—Peel, core, and slice
apples. Soak slices in a salt-water solution, ½ cup salt
to 1 gallon water. Drain. Spoon apple slices into freezer
containers, allowing 1-inch head-space. Cover with a
syrup of 3 cups sugar to 1 quart water. To avoid discoloration of fruit, add ½ teaspoon ascorbic acid to the above
amount of syrup. Or use a citric-acid compound (available
in grocery store dietetic departments) in amounts recommended on package. Place crumpled wax paper under
lid to keep fruit submerged in syrup.

**To Freeze, Dry Pack**—Peel, core, and slice apples.
Soak slices for 5 minutes (no longer or they will toughen)
in a solution of 1 teaspoon sodium bisulfite and 1 gallon
water mixed in a glass, enamel, or stainless-steel container. Drain and sprinkle with sugar, allowing 1 pound
sugar to 10 to 12 cups apple slices. Let stand to dissolve
sugar. Stir and pack as above.

**To Freeze, Applesauce**—Cook applesauce the usual
way. Sweeten to taste. Cool. Package with 1-inch
headspace.

**To Freeze, Baked Apples**—Chill, Pack in containers,
separating apples with freezer paper.

**To Freeze, Apple Juice**—Wash fruit and put through
the coarsest blade of a food chopper. Do not heat.
Squeeze juice out through 3 to 4 thicknesses of cheesecloth or muslin. Heat juice in the top part of a double
boiler or over direct heat to 190°F. Chill juice quickly. Fill
freezer containers, allowing 1-inch headspace.

## CANNED APPLES

*Availability*—All year round, also in combination with other fruits, as jelly, butter, baby food, and dietetic pack; sliced and whole, applesauce and unfermented juice.

*Storage*—Store cans and bottles at room temperature. Rotate use of cans.
Refrigerator shelf, opened and covered: 4 to 5 days
Kitchen shelf, unopened: 2 years.

*Nutritive Food Values*—See Fresh Apples

## FROZEN APPLES

Commercially frozen apples are used primarily by institutions and bakeries. Some consumer-size slices and sauce are also available, and frozen ready-to-bake apple pies, apple cobblers, turnovers, and strudels are plentiful.

## DRIED APPLES

Mature apples are peeled, cored, sliced, treated with sulfur dioxide, and dehydrated. They are marketed in 8-ounce packages which yield 4 cups when cooked. Once opened, the slices should be kept tightly covered, as mold forms rapidly from moisture. Available also in bulk or packed into dried-fruit mixtures.

*Storage*—Kitchen shelf: 2 to 5 months.

*Nutritive Food Value*—3½ ounces, dried = 291 calories

Apple Appetizer

# APPETIZERS

## APPLE APPETIZER

1 cup (8 ounces) creamed cottage cheese
1 small can (2¼ ounces) deviled ham
1 teaspoon grated onion
2 tablespoons chopped black olives
1 tablespoon minced pimiento
2 teaspoons dry sherry
3 unpeeled red eating apples, cut into wedges and sprinkled with lemon juice

Combine all ingredients, except apples, and mix well. Pile in small bowl and surround with apple wedges. Use apple wedges to dip into mixture. Makes about 1½ cups.

## APPLE SNACKS

Cut a cored eating apple into ¼-inch slices. Dip into lemon or pineapple juice; spread with peanut butter. Dip wedges of red-skinned apples, unpeeled, into lemon juice; sprinkle with curry powder or ground ginger.

# MAIN DISHES

## HAM SLICES WITH APPLE-RAISIN STUFFING

2 ready-to-eat ham slices about 8 x 5 x ½ inches thick
2 cups thinly sliced tart cooking apples
1 cup seedless raisins
3 tablespoons firmly packed brown sugar
⅔ cup apple cider

Lay 1 slice ham in greased shallow baking dish. Cover with apple slices and raisins and sprinkle with sugar. Top with remaining ham slice. Pour cider over all and bake in preheated hot oven (400°F.) about 35 minutes. Lift to platter, pour juice over all and serve. Makes 4 generous servings.

## APPLE-HAM CASSEROLE

¼ teaspoon ground cloves
½ teaspoon dry mustard
1 cup soft bread crumbs
3½ cups ground cooked smoked ham
1 tablespoon minced onion
1 egg, beaten
½ cup milk
Salt to taste
3 eating apples, peeled, cored, and sliced
¼ cup honey
2 tablespoons butter

Mix first 8 ingredients. Pack in greased shallow baking dish. Arrange apples on mixture. Sprinkle with honey and dot with butter. Bake in preheated moderate oven (375°F.) for about 40 minutes. Makes 4 to 6 servings.

## HAMBURGERS WITH APPLE RINGS

1½ pounds ground beef chuck
1 small onion, chopped
2 tablespoons minced parsley
1½ teaspons salt
⅛ teaspoon pepper
3 or 4 tart apples, peeled and cored
3 tablespoons butter or margarine

Mix lightly beef, onion, parsley, salt, and pepper. Shape into 8 patties. Broil to desired doneness. Keep warm. Cut eight ¾-inch apple rings. Sauté rings in butter in skillet. Cover and cook for 3 to 4 minutes. Put one ring on each patty and broil until just brown. Makes 4 servings.

## APPLE-SMOTHERED PORK CHOPS

6 center-cut loin pork chops, about ¾-inch thick
¼ teaspoon ground sage
¾ teaspoon salt
3 tart apples
3 tablespoons molasses
3 tablespoons all-purpose flour
2 cups hot water
1 tablespoon cider vinegar
⅓ cup golden raisins

Sprinkle chops with sage and ¼ teaspoon salt. Brown chops slowly in hot skillet. Reserve fat drippings in skillet. Put chops in large shallow baking dish. Peel and core apples and cut into ¼-inch slices; arrange on chops. Pour molasses over top. Stir flour into fat in skillet; cook until brown, stirring. Gradually stir in water and cook until mixture boils. Add vinegar, remaining ½ teaspoon salt, and raisins. Pour sauce over chops and apples. Cover and bake in preheated moderate oven (350°F.) for about 1 hour. Makes 6 servings.

## SPICED APPLES AND BEEF

2 pounds beef chuck or round, cut in 1-inch cubes
2 tablespoons vegetable oil
1½ cups water
¼ cup lemon or lime juice
2 cups sliced onion
1½ teaspoons curry powder
¼ teaspoon each ground cloves and cinnamon
1 teaspoon salt
3 cups peeled tart cooking apples in 1-inch wedges
¾ cup chopped watermelon pickle (optional)
Buttered hot cooked rice

Brown beef cubes in the oil in heavy kettle. Add 1 cup water, lemon juice, onion and seasonings. Bring to boil, cover and simmer 40 minutes. Add apple wedges and remaining ½ cup water, mixing gently. Cover and simmer 40 minutes, or until meat is tender. Gently mix in pickle, if used. Serve on rice. Makes 6 servings.

## APPLE MEAT LOAF

1½ pounds ground beef
1 cup soft stale-bread crumbs
1 medium onion, minced

2 eggs
½ cup finely diced apple
1½ teaspoons salt
¼ teaspoon pepper
1 teaspoon Worcestershire
1 unpeeled medium apple, cored and cut in eighths
3 tablespoons catsup
2 tablespoons light-brown sugar

Mix all ingredients, except last 3, and shape in loaf in baking pan. Insert apple wedges lengthwise on loaf. Dribble catsup over top and sprinkle with brown sugar. Bake in preheated moderate oven (350°F.) 50 to 60 minutes. Baste occasionally. Makes 6 servings.

## PORK CHOPS WITH APPLE-ONION SAUCE

4 center-cut pork chops, ¾ inch thick, about one pound
¼ cup water
Salt and pepper
2 tablespoons butter or margarine
2 cups diced apple
½ cup chopped onion
½ cup dairy sour cream
1 teaspoon lemon juice
½ teaspoon onion salt
Paprika
Chopped parsley

In heavy skillet, brown chops in own fat on both sides. Drain off fat, add ¼ cup water and season chops with salt and pepper. Cover and cook over low heat 45 minutes. Meanwhile melt butter and add apple and onion. Sauté over low heat 15 minutes, or until quite soft. Put chops on platter and keep warm. Add sour cream, lemon juice and onion salt to apple and onion and cook about 5 minutes. Spoon on chops and garnish with paprika and parsley. Makes 4 servings.

**Note** Sauce can also be served on pork-sausage patties.

## APPLE-PORK-VEGETABLE STEW

1 tablespoon margarine
1½ pounds boneless pork, cut in 1-inch cubes
10 small onions, peeled
2 teaspoons salt
Freshly ground pepper
¼ teaspoon paprika
½ teaspoon oregano
½ teaspoon crushed rosemary leaves
3 cups peeled raw potatoes in 1-inch dice
2 cups peeled apple wedges, ¾ inch thick
2 tablespoons all-purpose flour
1 can (12 ounces) vegetable juice
Chopped parsley

Melt margarine in heavy skillet or Dutch oven. Add meat and brown well. Add onions and seasonings. Bring to boil, cover and simmer while preparing potatoes and apples. Sprinkle meat and onions with flour. Add vegetable juice and bring to boil, stirring. Add potatoes, cover and simmer 15 minutes or until almost tender. Then add apple wedges and simmer a few minutes longer, or until potatoes are tender. Sprinkle with parsley. Makes 6 servings.

## APPLE SCRAPPLE

1 pound pork sausage meat
1 cup yellow cornmeal
1 cup cold water
1 cup boiling water
1 teaspoon salt
1 tablespoon parsley flakes
½ teaspoon dried oregano
1 cup canned applesauce
  Flour
  Bacon or salt-pork fat
  Sautéed apple slices (optional)

In heavy skillet, crumble sausage and cook until lightly browned. Drain off fat. Mix cornmeal with cold water. Pour into saucepan; add boiling water and seasonings. Cook, stirring, until thickened. Cover and simmer 10 minutes longer. Then fold in applesauce and sausage. Pour into greased 9 x 5 x 3-inch loaf pan; chill until firm. Unmold and cut in ½″ slices. Dip in flour and brown on both sides in hot fat. Serve with apple slices. Makes 6 servings.

## ROAST PORK LOIN WITH APPLE-GINGER SAUCE

2 teaspoons coarsely crushed fennel seed
1 teaspoon salt
¼ teaspoon each pepper and paprika
4 pounds pork loin
  Apple-Ginger Sauce

Mix spices and rub well on all sides of pork loin. Put on rack in shallow baking pan and roast in preheated slow oven (325°F.) 2½ hours, or until done. Serve with the sauce. Makes 6 servings.

### Apple-Ginger Sauce

2 cups canned applesauce
1 teaspoon grated orange rind
1 tablespoon minced crystallized ginger

Mix all ingredients in small saucepan and simmer 10 minutes. Serve hot or cold. Makes 2 cups.

## APPLE-MINT LAMB CHOP BROIL

4 shoulder lamb chops, ¾ inch thick
¼ cup lemon juice
2 tablespoons vegetable oil
1½ teaspoons salt
1 teaspoon each pepper and paprika
1 teaspoon chopped fresh mint or dried mint leaves
  Apple-Mint Sauce

Put chops in shallow baking dish. Mix remaining ingredients, except sauce, and pour over chops. Let stand, turning occasionally, at least 1 hour. Then broil chops about 6 inches from source of heat 6 minutes on each side, or until desired doneness. Put on hot platter and serve with the sauce. Makes 4 servings.

### Apple-Mint Sauce

Mix 1½ cups canned applesauce, ½ cup mint jelly, 1 teaspoon lemon juice and ½ teaspoon salt. Bring to boil and simmer 10 minutes.

## APPLESAUCE MEATBALLS AND SAUERKRAUT, DANISH STYLE

4 slices bacon
1½ pounds ground chuck
1 cup soft bread crumbs
1 medium onion, chopped
1 teaspoon salt
½ teaspoon pepper
½ teaspoon dried marjoram
1 egg
1¼ cups canned applesauce
1 can (27 ounces) sauerkraut
½ teaspoon caraway seed
1 tablespoon sugar
1 cup dairy sour cream (optional)

In large kettle or Dutch oven, cook bacon until crisp. Remove bacon reserving fat. Lightly mix beef, crumbs, half the onion, next 4 ingredients and ¼ cup applesauce. Shape in 12 to 14 balls. Brown about half at a time in hot bacon fat. Remove and set aside. Mix remaining half onion and remaining one cup applesauce, sauerkraut, seed and sugar. Put in Dutch oven and arrange meatballs on top. Cover and cook over low heat 30 to 40 minutes. Pour sour cream over top, if desired. Sprinkle with crumbled bacon. Makes 6 or 7 servings.

## APPLE BEEF STEW WITH VEGETABLES

3 pounds beef chuck, cut in 1½-inch cubes
½ cup all-purpose flour
2 teaspoons salt
½ teaspoon pepper
¼ cup shortening or margarine
1 bay leaf
1 can (8 ounces) tomato sauce
½ teaspoon chili powder
2 cups canned applesauce
2 cups water
1 cup diced celery
6 medium raw white potatoes, peeled and halved
6 medium onions
6 medium carrots

Toss beef cubes a few at a time in seasoned flour. Brown on all sides in hot shortening in large kettle or Dutch oven. Add next 5 ingredients. Bring to boil, cover and simmer 1½ to 2 hours. Add vegetables and simmer 1 hour longer, or until tender. Makes 6 to 8 servings.

## APPLE-FRANKFURTER CASSEROLE

2½ cups sliced peeled eating apples
3 large sweet potatoes, boiled, peeled, and sliced
1 pound frankfurters, split lengthwise and halved
¼ cup firmly packed light brown sugar
⅛ teaspoon ground cinnamon
¼ teaspoon salt
1 teaspoon fresh lemon juice
½ cup buttered soft bread crumbs

In shallow greased casserole alternate layers of apple, sweet potato, and frankfurter, until half are used. Mix next 3 ingredients and sprinkle half on contents of casserole. Add remaining apples, potatoes, and franks. Sprinkle with remaining sugar mixture and lemon juice. Top with crumbs. Cover and bake in preheated moderate oven (375°F.) for 45 minutes. Uncover and bake for 10 minutes. Makes 6 servings.

## APPLE-LAMB CURRY

    1 pound boneless stewing lamb
    1 onion, minced
    1 garlic clove, minced
    3 tablespoons fat or cooking oil
    3 teaspoons curry powder
    1 teaspoon paprika
    ½ teaspoon ground ginger
    ¼ teaspoon chili powder
    ¼ teaspoon sugar
    1 can (6 ounces) tomato paste
      Boiling water
    2 cups chopped peeled tart apples
      Hot cooked rice

Cut lamb into 1-inch cubes. Sauté onion and garlic in fat until golden brown. Add curry powder, paprika, ginger, chili powder, and sugar. Blend well. Add lamb and brown on all sides. Add tomato paste and enough boiling water to cover. Stir well. Cover; simmer for 30 minutes over low heat. Add apples; cook for 15 minutes longer. Serve with rice. Makes 4 servings.

## CURRIED APPLES

Cut 2 large cored unpeeled tart red apples into ½-inch slices. Blend 2 tablespoons molasses, 1 teaspoon curry powder, 3 tablespoons soft butter or margarine, and ⅛ teaspoon salt. Spread on one side of apple rings. Put on broiler pan, butter side up, and broil for 5 to 7 minutes. Mix ¼ cup each of toasted coconut and chopped almonds. Sprinkle apple slices with mixture. Serve hot with roast lamb, poultry, or ham. Makes 4 servings.

## SCALLOPED APPLES, PORK CHOPS, AND SWEET POTATOES

    2½ cups (1-pound, 4-ounce can) sliced apples, drained
    4 cooked peeled small sweet potatoes
    ⅓ cup seedless raisins
    ⅓ cup firmly packed light brown sugar
      Dash of ground nutmeg
    3 tablespoons currant jelly
    3 tablespoons prepared mustard
    4 center-cut rib pork chops, ¾-inch thick
      Salt and pepper

Put half of apple slices at each end of shallow baking dish. Cut sweet potatoes into thick slices and put in center of dish. Sprinkle with raisins, then with brown sugar and nutmeg. Trim excess fat from chops. Place chops over sweet potatoes and apples. Top with jelly mixed with mustard. Sprinkle with salt and pepper. Bake in preheated moderate oven (350°F.) for 1½ hours, or until chops are tender. Makes 4 servings.

## APPLE PANCAKES I

    2 cups buttermilk baking mix
    2 eggs
    ½ cup dry nonfat milk
    1 cup canned apple juice
    1 cup water
      Double-apple Sauce

Blend all ingredients, except Sauce. Using ⅓ cup batter for each cake, bake on hot greased griddle or in skillet until browned on both sides. Serve with sauce. Makes twelve 8-inch cakes.

# STUFFINGS

## SAVORY APPLE STUFFING

    ½ cup chopped celery and leaves
    1 yellow onion, chopped
    2 tablespoons minced parsley
    ¼ cup butter or margarine
    4 cups diced peeled tart apples
    ¼ cup firmly packed light brown sugar
    1 teaspoon salt
    ½ teaspoon each of ground sage, marjoram, and thyme
    ¼ teaspoon pepper
    2 cups toasted bread crumbs

Sauté celery, onion, and parsley in butter for 5 minutes. Add apples, sugar, and seasonings. Cook for 5 minutes longer. Add bread crumbs and mix well. Especially good with pork or duck. Makes about 4 cups.

## APPLE-PRUNE-RAISIN STUFFING

    2 cups chopped peeled tart apples
    ½ cup chopped cooked prunes
    ½ cup seedless raisins
    5 cups toasted bread cubes
    ¼ cup melted butter or margarine
    ¼ cup firmly packed light brown sugar
      Grated rind of 1 lemon
    ½ teaspoon paprika
    ½ teaspoon ground cinnamon
    1 teaspoon salt
    ¾ cup apple juice or cider

Mix all ingredients. Use as stuffing for chicken, duck, or pork shoulder. Makes about 8 cups.

# VEGETABLES & SALADS

## STEWED APPLES AND POTATOES

6 medium raw potatoes (1½ pounds), peeled
  Milk
2 medium cooking apples, cored, peeled and diced
  Salt
  White pepper
  Ginger
  Chopped parsley

Cut potatoes in ¼" slices, put in heavy skillet and add 1 cup milk. Bring to boil, cover and simmer until almost tender. Add apples, stir carefully and add more milk if necessary. (Milk should be almost absorbed when potatoes are soft.) Season with salt, pepper and ginger and sprinkle with parsley. Good with sausage or other pork. Makes 4 servings.

## SAUTEED APPLES, ONIONS, AND RAISINS

Heat ¼ cup bacon or sausage fat in skillet. Add 4 peeled and quartered medium yellow onions and 4 unpeeled cored red apples, cut into eighths. Sauté for about 5 minutes. Cover for 5 minutes; then add ⅓ cup golden raisins and cook slowly, uncovered, until apples and onions are tender, stirring occasionally. Serve hot with sausage, roast pork, or pork chops. Makes 4 servings.

## SPICY APPLES AND RED CABBAGE

2 yellow onions, minced
¼ cup butter or margarine
1 cup seedless raisins
3½ to 4 pounds red cabbage, cored and shredded
2 large apples, peeled, cored, and chopped
1 teaspoon mixed pickling spice
2 teaspoons salt
¼ teaspoon pepper
3 tablespoons sugar
¼ cup cider vinegar

Sauté onion in butter in large kettle until lightly browned. add raisins, cabbage, and apple. Tie pickling spice in wet piece of cheesecloth. Add to cabbage mixture. Season with salt and pepper. Cover and cook over low heat for about 45 minutes. Mix sugar and vinegar; stir into cabbage. Simmer for 5 minutes. Remove spice bag. Makes 6 to 8 servings.

## PARTY APPLE SALAD

4 large eating apples
  Orange, pineapple, lemon, or grapefruit juice
1 cup diced celery
1 large banana, diced
⅔ cup coarsely chopped pecans
  Mayonnaise
  Prepared mustard
  Endive or other salad greens

Core apples, leaving bottoms whole. Hollow out, leaving a ½-inch shell. Sprinkle cavities and apple pulp with fruit juice. Chop pulp; add celery, banana, and nuts. Moisten with mayonnaise and add mustard to taste. Mix well and fill apples, piling mixture up in center. Chill. Serve on greens. Makes 4 servings.

Party Apple Salad

## APPLE-CABBAGE SLAW

  Juice of 1 orange
  Juice of ½ lemon
2 medium red apples, cored and cut in ⅛-inch wedges
4 cups finely chopped white cabbage
½ cup mayonnaise
¼ cup applesauce
1 teaspoon horseradish
1 teaspoon prepared mustard
2 tablespoons each minced parsley and nuts

Pour fruit juices over apples. Add cabbage and mix lightly. Mix mayonnaise, applesauce, horseradish and mustard. Pour over apples and cabbage and mix carefully. Sprinkle top with parsley and nuts. Makes 6 to 8 servings.

## APPLE-ENDIVE SALAD WITH ORANGE-NUT DRESSING

3 medium eating apples, preferably red
2 medium Belgian endives, sliced ¼ inch thick
½ can (6-ounce size) frozen orange-juice concentrate
1 tablespoon sugar (optional)
¼ cup chopped filberts

Core apples and cut in thin wedges. Arrange in alternate layers with endive in glass bowl. Pour orange-juice concentrate on top, and sprinkle with sugar, if desired. Mix carefully and sprinkle with nuts. Good with pan-broiled meats. Makes 4 servings.

## JELLIED WALDORF SALAD

 3 medium-size red apples
   Lemon juice
 1 box (3 ounces) lemon-flavor gelatin dessert
 1 cup hot water
⅛ teaspoon salt
½ cup mayonnaise
 1 cup diced celery
½ cup chopped walnuts
½ cup heavy cream, whipped
   Salad greens
   Ripe olives

Core apples, but do not peel. Cut 1 into thin, even slices, and dice remaining 2. Sprinkle sliced and diced apple with a small amount of lemon juice. Arrange slices peel-side down, around bottom of an oiled 5-cup ring mold. Refrigerate all apples. Dissolve gelatin in the water. Chill until slightly thickened. Add salt, and blend in mayonnaise. Fold in diced apple, and remaining ingredients, except greens and olives. Turn carefully into prepared mold, and chill until firm. Unmold on greens, and garnish with olives. Makes 6 servings.

## CRANBERRY-APPLE SALAD

 1 cup cranberries
 2 seedless oranges (leave 1 unpeeled)
 2 apples, cored but unpeeled
   Sugar
 1 box raspberry-flavor gelatin dessert
 1 cup boiling water
   Salad greens

Force cranberries, oranges and apples through food chopper. Mix with ½ to 1 cup sugar and let stand 1 hour. Dissolve gelatin in 1 cup very hot water. Chill until slightly thickened. Then add fruit mixture. (Juice from fruit will make up extra liquid needed.) Pour into 8-inch square pan or gelatin mold and chill until firm. Cut in squares, or unmold. Serve with greens. Makes 6 to 8 servings.

Jellied Waldorf Salad

## CIDER GELATIN SALAD

 1 envelope unflavored gelatin
¼ cup sugar
   Dash of salt
1¾ cups apple cider
 2 tablespoons lemon juice
1½ cups diced unpeeled red apples
½ cup diced celery
   Salad greens
   Mayonnaise
   Chopped nuts

In saucepan mix gelatin, sugar, and salt. Add ½ cup cider. Let stand for 5 minutes. Heat, stirring, until gelatin is dissolved. Remove from heat and add remaining 1¼ cups cider and lemon juice. Chill until thickened to consistency of unbeaten egg white. Fold in apple and celery and pour into 6 lightly oiled individual molds or a 1-quart mold. Chill until firm. Unmold on greens, top with mayonnaise, and sprinkle with chopped nuts. Makes 4 to 6 servings.

# RELISHES & JELLIES

## APPLE-CRANBERRY-ALMOND RELISH

2½ cups canned applesauce
 1 can (8 ounces) whole-cranberry sauce
 1 tablespoon grated orange rind
¼ cup sugar
½ cup toasted slivered almonds

Mix all ingredients; refrigerate. Especially good with poultry. Makes 3½ cups.

## CONFETTI APPLE RELISH

 1 cup each chopped green pepper, celery and onion
¼ cup chopped canned pimiento
½ cup cider vinegar
½ cup sugar
 2 cups (1 pound can) applesauce
½ teaspoon each salt and ground allspice

Combine pepper, celery and onion in saucepan. Cover with boiling water and let stand 5 minutes; drain well. Add remaining ingredients and simmer, stirring occasionally, 30 minutes. Cool; refrigerate. Makes about 4 cups.

## APPLE-PINEAPPLE RELISH

½ cup finely diced celery
2½ cups canned applesauce
½ to ¾ teaspoon ground ginger
 1 can (13¼ ounces) pineapple tidbits, drained
 1 teaspoon grated orange rind

Cover celery with boiling water and let stand 5 minutes. Drain well. Combine with remaining ingredients and simmer 15 minutes. Cool; chill. Makes 4 cups.

## APPLE-MINCEMEAT RELISH

1 cup bouillon (1 cup water and 1 bouillon cube)
1 package (9 ounces) mincemeat, crumbled
2 cups (1 pound can) applesauce
1 teaspoon grated lemon rind

Bring bouillon to boil and add mincemeat. Simmer 5 minutes, or until mincemeat has absorbed all the liquid. Add applesauce and lemon rind and simmer 15 minutes. Cool, then refrigerate. Especially good with ham. Makes about 3 cups.

## GOLDEN CURRY RELISH

2½ cups canned applesauce
½ cup apple juice
2 teaspoons Worcestershire
½ teaspoon salt
3 tablespoons instant minced onion
½ teaspoon grated lemon rind
2 teaspoons curry powder
½ cup sweet-pickle relish, drained

Mix all ingredients, except relish, in saucepan. Simmer, stirring occasionally, 15 minutes. Remove from heat and stir in relish. Cool, then refrigerate. Especially good with lamb. Makes about 3½ cups.

## APPLE-HORSERADISH RELISH

2 cups (1 pound can) applesauce
½ cup finely minced celery
2 tablespoons prepared horseradish
2 tablespoons sugar
½ teaspoon lemon juice

Combine all ingredients and mix well. Refrigerate. Especially good with boiled beef. Makes about 2½ cups.

## APPLE-HERB JELLY

Select dry or liquid pectin, using manufacturer's directions as a guide. Measure amount of apple juice required to make apple jelly. Bring to boil and pour over dried un-crumbled herbs such as leaf marjoram, leaf sage, or basil; use 2 teaspoons herb for each cup juice. Add dash of salt and let stand for 10 minutes. Strain through fine sieve or cloth bag. Complete jelly-making, adding sugar as called for in pectin recipe. Pour into hot sterilized jelly glasses and seal at once with paraffin.

## WEST INDIES APPLE CHUTNEY

2½ cups (1 pound, 4 ounce can) sliced apples, un-drained
½ cup seedless raisins
¾ cup molasses
½ cup cider vinegar
½ teaspoon salt
1 teaspoon each of ground ginger and dry mustard
3 teaspoons curry powder

Mix all ingredients in saucepan. Bring to boil, stirring to blend ingredients. Simmer, uncovered, over low heat for 15 minutes, stirring occasionally. Makes 3 cups.

## APPLE JELLY

Remove stems and blossom ends from tart apples or crabapples. Quarter and add enough water to just cover. Simmer until soft. Strain through a jelly bag. Allow 1 cup sugar to each cup juice. Cook 4 cups juice at a time. Simmer juice and sugar until sheeting stage (220°-222°F.) has been reached. Pour hot jelly into dry hot sterilized jars. Seal with paraffin. Store in cool dry place. Four cups juice makes about 4 six-ounce glasses, depending on the pectin in the fruit, which is variable, and the length of time juice is cooked to reach the jelly stage.

## FESTIVAL RELISH

2 unpeeled oranges, quartered and seeded
2 unpeeled apples, quartered and cored
1 pound cranberries
2 cups sugar

Force oranges and apples through coarse blade of food chopper, reserving extra juice for other uses. Then grind cranberries and add with sugar to other fruits. Mix well and let stand several hours to ripen. Store covered in refrigerator. Good with roast turkey, chicken, duck, pork or fried liver. Makes about 4 cups.

# BREADS

## APPLE KUCHEN

- ¼ cup water*
- 1 package active dry yeast or 1 cake compressed yeast
- ¾ cup milk
  Butter or margarine
- ½ cup sugar
- 1 teaspoon salt
- 2 eggs, slightly beaten
- 2¾ cups sifted all-purpose flour (about)
- 5 cooking apples
- 2 tablespoons melted butter or margarine
- ½ teaspoon ground cinnamon
- 2 tablespoons raisins

*Use very warm water (105°F. to 115°F.) for dry yeast; use lukewarm (80°F. to 90°F.) for compressed. Sprinkle dry yeast or crumble cake into water. Let stand for a few minutes; then stir until dissolved. Scald milk; add ¼ cup butter, ¼ cup sugar, and salt, stirring until butter melts. Cool to lukewarm; stir in yeast and eggs. Beat in 1½ cups of the flour; cover and let rise in warm place until doubled in bulk, about 40 minutes. Stir in enough of the remaining flour to make an easy-to-handle dough. Knead lightly on a floured board. Cover and chill for 30 minutes. Roll out and fit into a greased baking dish, 9 x 13 x 2 inches.

Peel, quarter, and core apples; cut into eighths. Press closely together into dough. Brush apples and dough with melted butter. Combine remaining ¼ cup sugar, cinnamon, and raisins. Sprinkle over apples. Cover and let rise in warm place until dough springs back when touched lightly with finger. Bake in preheated moderate oven (350°F.) for 30 minutes, or until bread is done and apples are tender. Makes 8 to 10 servings.

## APPLE MUFFINS

- 1½ cups all-purpose flour
- ⅓ cup granulated sugar
- 2 teaspoons baking powder
- ½ teaspoon salt
- ½ cup dry nonfat milk
- 1 teaspoon ground cinnamon
- ¼ cup soft shortening
- 1 egg
  Water
- 1 cup finely chopped peeled apple
- ⅓ cup firmly packed brown sugar
- ⅓ cup finely chopped nuts

Mix first 5 ingredients and ½ teaspoon cinnamon in bowl. Add shortening, egg, ½ cup water and apple and mix quickly. Spoon batter into 12 greased 2¾-inch muffin cups. Mix remaining ½ teaspoon cinnamon, brown sugar and nuts and sprinkle on top. Bake in preheated moderate oven (375°F.) about 20 minutes.

## APPLE PANCAKES II

- 3 or 4 tart apples
  Melted butter or margarine (about ⅔ cup)
  Sugar (about ⅔ cup)
- ⅛ teaspoon ground nutmeg
- ¼ teaspoon ground cinnamon
- 2 eggs
- ½ cup milk
- ½ cup sifted all-purpose flour
- ¼ teaspoon salt

Peel and core apples. Slice thin and sauté in ⅓ cup butter for five minutes. Mix ⅓ cup sugar and spices and add to apples. Cover and cook for 10 minutes. Cool. Mix eggs, milk, flour, and salt. Beat with rotary beater for 2 minutes. Heat 1 tablespoon butter in 10-inch ovenproof skillet. Pour batter into pan. Bake in preheated very hot oven (450°F.) for 15 minutes. As soon as batter puffs up in center, puncture with fork, repeating as often as necessary. Lower heat to moderate (350°F.) and bake for 10 minutes. Remove from oven; spoon 2 tablespoons melted butter over surface. Sprinkle with 2 tablespoons sugar. Spread apple mixture over half the surface; fold over. Spoon 2 tablespoons melted butter over top; sprinkle with 2 tablespoons sugar. Makes 6 servings.

## AUTUMN APPLE BREAD

- ¼ cup shortening
- ⅔ cup sugar
- 2 eggs beaten
- 2 cups sifted all-purpose flour
- 1 teaspoon baking powder
- 1 teaspoon baking soda
- 1 teaspoon salt
- 2 cups coarsely grated, peeled, raw, tart apples
- 1 teaspoon grated lemon rind
- ⅔ cup chopped walnuts

Cream shortening and sugar until light and fluffy; beat in eggs. Sift next 4 ingredients. Add alternately with apple to egg mixture. Stir in lemon rind and nuts. Bake in greased and floured loaf pan (9 x 5 x 3 inches) in preheated moderate oven (350°F.) for 50 to 60 minutes. Cool before slicing. Makes 1 loaf.

## APPLESAUCE COFFEE CAKE

- 1⅓ cups buttermilk baking mix
- ¾ cup granulated sugar
- 3 tablespoons butter or margarine
- ¾ cup milk
- 1 egg
- 1 teaspoon vanilla extract
- ⅓ cup firmly packed brown sugar
- 1 teaspoon cinnamon
- ¼ cup chopped walnuts
- ½ cup applesauce
- ½ cup flaked coconut

Put biscuit mix and granulated sugar in small bowl of electric mixer. Cut in butter with pastry blender or 2 knives. Then add ¼ cup milk, egg and vanilla. Blend, then beat at medium speed 1 minute. Add remaining ½ cup milk and beat ½ minute longer. Spread in greased and floured 9-inch square pan or deep round 9-inch layercake pan. Bake in preheated moderate oven (350°F.) 35 to 40 minutes. Mix remaining ingredients and spread carefully on warm cake. Put under broiler 3 to 4 inches from heat and watch closely, 3 minutes, or until brown. Serve warm. Makes 6-8 servings.

# DESSERTS CAKES & COOKIES

## POACHED APPLES

¾ cup sugar
1½ cups water
1 slice of lemon
6 medium cooking apples (about 2 pounds)
Ground nutmeg

Cook sugar, water, and lemon for 5 minutes. Remove lemon. Peel, core, and slice apples; cook a few at a time until tender, adding a little more water when necessary. Pour syrup over cooked apples. Serve warm or chilled as a dessert, sprinkled with ground nutmeg. Makes 4 servings.

## APPLE OATMEAL COOKIES

½ cup butter or margarine
⅔ cup sugar
2 eggs
1 cup sifted all-purpose flour
1 teaspoon baking powder
1 teaspoon ground cinnamon
½ teaspoon each of ground nutmeg and salt
1 cup quick-cooking rolled oats
1 cup chopped well-drained canned apples
1 cup coarsely chopped walnuts

Cream butter and sugar until light. Add eggs, one at a time, beating well after each addition. Sift flour, baking powder, spices, and salt, and add to egg mixture. Stir in oats and apples and beat well. Fold in nuts. Drop by teaspoons onto greased cookie sheets. Bake in pre-heated moderate oven (350°F.) for about 15 minutes. Makes about 42.

## QUICK APPLE PEACH COMPOTE

1 can (1 pound, 6 ounces) apple-pie filling
1 package (12 ounces) frozen sliced peaches, thawed
½ cup cranberry-apple juice
Grated rind of 1 lemon

Mix all ingredients in saucepan. Bring to boil and simmer 6 to 8 minutes. Cool and serve as accompaniment for meat or as sauce for pancakes. Makes 4 cups.

## BAKED APPLES

8 Rome Beauty cooking apples
1 cup sugar
¼ teaspoon ground cinnamon or nutmeg
1 cup water

Wash and core apples. Starting at stem end, peel apples about ⅓ way down. Arrange in shallow baking pan. Mix sugar and spice; add water and boil for 5 minutes. Pour this syrup over apples and bake in preheated moderate oven (350°F.) for 45 to 60 minutes, basting frequently with syrup from pan and turning apples after 30 minutes. Makes 8 servings.

**To glaze**—Sprinkle peeled part of apples with ¼ cup sugar. Broil carefully under low heat, basting with syrup until glazed and lightly browned. Serve warm or cold.

Baked Apple

## BAKED APPLE DUMPLINGS

Pastry (2 cups flour recipe), unbaked
6 medium-tart cooking apples
1½ cups sugar
2 cups water
¼ cup butter or margarine
1¾ teaspoons ground cinnamon

Roll pastry about ⅛-inch thick and cut into six 7-inch squares. Peel and core apples. Bring to boil 1 cup sugar, the water, 3 tablespoons butter, and ¼ teaspoon cinnamon. Put an apple on each square of pastry. Mix remaining ½ cup sugar and 1½ teaspoons cinnamon; fill apple cavities. Dot with remaining 1 tablespoon butter. Bring opposite points of pastry up over apple. Overlap, moisten, and seal. Lift carefully and put a few inches apart in baking dish. Pour hot syrup around dumplings. Bake in preheated hot oven (425°F.) for 40 minutes, or until crust is well browned and apples are cooked through. Serve warm with cream or whipped cream. Makes 6 servings.

Baked Apple
Dumplings

## APPLE FLAN

1 cup all-purpose flour
  Sugar
⅛ teaspoon salt
  Butter or margarine
2 tablespoons cold water
2 large red-skinned apples, cored and cut in wedges
  ⅜ inch thick (3 to 4 cups)
  Juice of 1 lemon
1 teaspoon unflavored gelatin
½ cup apple juice

Combine flour, ½ cup sugar and salt in mixing bowl. Cut in 6 tablespoons butter. Sprinkle with water and form into ball. Chill while preparing apples. Put apples in mixing bowl. Add ¼ cup sugar, the lemon juice and 2 tablespoons melted butter; toss gently. Roll dough to a 14 x 8 inch rectangle, put on baking sheet and cut edges even. Arrange apple wedges, crosswise, slightly overlapping, leaving ½ inch margin. Turn edges over and press gently. Bake in preheated hot oven (400°F.) 20 to 25 minutes, or until apples are soft and pastry is browned. Loosen flan with spatula and let cool on sheet. Mix gelatin and 2 tablespoons sugar. Heat apple juice to a boil, add gelatin mixture and stir until dissolved. Chill until slightly thickened and spoon over apples. Serve in crosswise slices (use scissors if necessary). Makes 6 servings.

## APPLE BROWN BETTY

4 cups small bread cubes
½ cup melted butter or margarine
¾ teaspoon ground cinnamon
⅛ teaspoon salt
¾ cup firmly packed dark brown sugar
4 cups chopped peeled tart apples
1 cup medium cream
¼ teaspoon ground nutmeg

Mix first 5 ingredients and arrange in alternate layers with apples in 1½-quart greased baking dish. Bake in preheated moderate oven (375°F.) for 1 hour, or until apples are tender and top is brown. Serve warm with cream, flavored with nutmeg. Makes 4 to 6 servings.

Apple-Cranberry Shortcake

## APPLE-CRANBERRY SHORTCAKE

4 cups thinly sliced peeled eating apples
1 cup fresh cranberries
¼ cup water
⅔ cup firmly packed brown sugar
½ teaspoon ground cinnamon
  Dash of salt
  Shortcake mixture using 3 cups biscuit mix
  Whipped cream (optional)

Put apples, cranberries, water, sugar, cinnamon, and salt in saucepan. Bring to boil; cover and simmer until apples are tender. Bake shortcake in two 8-inch layers. Put hot apple mixture between layers and on top of hot shortcake. Cut into wedges and serve with whipped cream, if desired. Makes 6 to 8 servings.

## APPLE CRISP

2 pounds cooking apples, peeled and sliced (5½ cups)
¼ cup water
½ cup granulated sugar
½ cup firmly packed light brown sugar
½ teaspoon each of ground nutmeg and cinnamon
¼ teaspoon salt
¾ cup all-purpose flour
½ cup butter or margarine

Put apples in shallow greased 2-quart casserole; add water. Combine sugars, nutmeg, cinnamon, salt, and flour. Cut in butter with pastry blender. Spoon evenly over apples. Cover and bake in preheated moderate oven (350°F.) for 30 minutes. Uncover and bake for 30 minutes longer. Makes 6 servings.

## APPLE FRITTERS

3 large cooking apples
½ cup granulated sugar
2 tablespoons brandy
1 teaspoon each of grated lemon and orange rinds
1½ cups sifted all-purpose flour
¼ teaspoon salt
2 eggs, well beaten
1 teaspoon olive oil
⅓ cup beer
  Fat for deep frying
  Confectioners' sugar

Core and peel apples; cut into ½-inch rings. (Reserve ends for use in salad.) Mix ¼ cup granulated sugar, brandy, and grated rinds. Pour over apples and let stand for 2 hours. Mix remaining ¼ cup granulated sugar and other ingredients, except last 2. Let stand for 1 hour. Dip drained apples, one ring at a time, into the mixture. Fry in hot deep fat (375°F. on a frying thermometer) until brown on both sides. Drain on absorbent paper and sprinkle with confectioners' sugar. Serve warm. Makes 1 dozen.

## MACAROON-APPLE CAKE

3 medium-large tart apples, cored, peeled and cut in
   ¼″ wedges
   Light-brown sugar
2 tablespoons lemon juice
¼ cup butter or margarine, softened
1 egg, slightly beaten
1 teaspoon grated lemon rind
½ cup grated coconut
2 tablespoons all-purpose flour
¼ cup chopped nuts
   Chilled custard sauce, partly melted vanilla ice
   cream, or whipped cream

Layer apple slices in greased shallow 8-inch to 9-inch
round baking dish. Sprinkle with ⅓ cup firmly packed
brown sugar and the lemon juice and set aside. Cream
⅓ cup brown sugar with butter. Add next 5 ingredients
and mix well. Spread on top of apples. Bake in preheated
moderate oven (350°F.) 25 to 30 minutes, or until top
is delicately browned and apples are soft. Serve slightly
warm with custard sauce. Makes 4 to 6 servings.

## DUTCH APPLE CAKE

1 cup all-purpose flour
1½ teaspoons baking powder
¼ teaspoon salt
¼ cup seedless raisins
   Sugar
   Butter or margarine
1 egg, well beaten
¼ cup milk
3 cups peeled tart apple wedges, ¼″ thick
¼ teaspoon ground cinnamon
¼ teaspoon ground nutmeg

Mix first 4 ingredients and 2 tablespoons sugar. Cut in
⅓ cup butter. Add combined egg and milk and blend well.
Spread in greased 10 x 6 x 2-inch glass baking dish.
Arrange apple wedges in rows in batter. Brush with 2
tablespoons melted butter and sprinkle with mixture of
spices and 2 tablespoons sugar. Bake in preheated hot
oven (400°F.) 30 to 40 minutes. Cut in squares and serve
warm.

## APPLE MERINGUE CAKE

⅓ cup butter or margarine
   Sugar (about 1 cup)
2 egg yolks
¾ cup all-purpose flour
⅓ cup chopped blanched almonds
   Grated rind of ½ lemon
5 egg whites
4 to 6 medium apples, peeled, cored, and halved
   Juice of ½ lemon
⅓ cup raspberry jam
   Dash of salt

Cream butter; add 3 tablespoons sugar gradually, beating
until light and fluffy. Add egg yolks and mix well. Add

flour, almonds, and grated rind; mix just until flour is
evenly distributed. Press on bottom of 9-inch pie pan and
brush with 1 slightly beaten egg white. Bake in preheated
moderate oven (350°F.) for 15 minutes, or until crust is
browned. Combine apples, ⅓ cup sugar, and lemon juice
in large skillet; cover and cook over medium heat until
tender. Spread jam on crust in pie pan and arrange
drained apples on top. Beat 4 remaining egg whites with
salt until stiff, but not dry. Continue beating, adding ½
cup sugar, 1 tablespoon at a time (sugar granules must
be completely dissolved). Continue beating and feel the
meringue between the fingers until all gritty sugar particles dissolve. Pile lightly on apples. Bake in a preheated
moderate oven (350°F.) for about 18 minutes, or until
meringue is lightly browned. Makes 6 servings.

Apple Meringue Cake

## APPLE PANDOWDY

3 cups sliced peeled apples
⅓ cup firmly packed dark brown sugar
¼ teaspoon each of ground cinnamon and nutmeg
¼ cup butter or margarine
⅓ cup granulated sugar
1 egg
¾ cup sifted all-purpose flour
¾ teaspoon baking powder
¼ teaspoon salt
⅓ cup milk
   Cream

Put apples in buttered 1-quart baking dish. Sprinkle with
brown sugar and spices. Bake in a preheated moderate
oven (375°F.) for 30 minutes, or until apples are soft.
Cream butter; gradually add granulated sugar and beat
until fluffy. Add egg and beat well. Add sifted dry ingredients alternately with milk, beating until smooth. Spread
on cooked apples. Bake for 30 minutes. Serve warm with
cream. Makes 4 servings.

## APPLE STRUDEL
### Dough

1 egg, slightly beaten
½ teaspoon salt
  Cooking oil
1 cup all-purpose flour
1 tablespoon warm water
  Melted butter or margarine
  Sugar

### Filling

¼ cup seedless raisins
2 tablespoons water
6 to 8 apples, peeled and sliced
1 cup sugar
¾ cup fine dry bread crumbs
⅓ cup butter or margarine
½ cup chopped blanched almonds
1 teaspoon ground cinnamon

Mix egg, salt, 2 tablespoons oil, and the flour. Add warm water and mix to form a soft dough. Knead on lightly floured board for 10 to 15 minutes, or until dough is *very* smooth and *very* elastic. Brush top with more oil and cover with a warm bowl. Let stand for 30 minutes.

Meanwhile prepare ingredients for filling. Soak raisins in water. Peel and core apples and slice thin; sprinkle with ½ cup of sugar. Brown crumbs in butter; combine with raisins and liquid, almonds, cinnamon, and remaining ½ cup sugar.

When strudel dough is ready, roll out as thin as possible on a large lightly floured cloth about 36 inches square. Melt ½ cup butter and brush entire top of dough. With palms up, slip hands underneath dough and stretch it carefully to paper thinness, working from the center out. If edges remain thick, cut them off. Dough should almost cover the cloth. Brush again with more melted butter to keep pliable.

Pile apples in a row about 2 inches from one end of dough. Spread raisin mixture over remaining dough. Lift edges of cloth nearest the apples; continue to roll dough over and over with help of cloth. Put roll on ungreased cookie sheet. Make into U shape if roll is too long for sheet. Bake in preheated hot oven (400°F.) for 30 minutes. During baking, brush 2 or 3 times with melted butter. About 5 minutes before strudel is done, sprinkle thickly with sugar if desired. Makes 8 servings.

## NUT-STUFFED APPLE DUMPLINGS

  Pastry, (1-cup flour recipe), unbaked
6 medium-large cooking apples
  Sugar
2 tablespoons chopped nuts
2 tablespoons butter or margarine
½ teaspoon ground cinnamon
  Milk or beaten egg
  Sweetened whipped cream

Roll pastry to ⅛ inch thickness and cut in six 6-inch squares. Core and peel apples. Put an apple in center of each square of pastry. Mix 2 tablespoons sugar and next 3 ingredients. Divide mixture into apple cavities. Bring opposite points of pastry up over apple and seal in center. Put, a few inches apart, in shallow baking dish and brush with milk. Sprinkle with sugar and bake in preheated hot oven (425°F.) 30 to 40 minutes, or until crust is well browned and apples are soft. Serve slightly warm with whipped cream. Makes 6 servings.

## BAKED APPLE TAPIOCA

3 large tart cooking apples
  Juice of 1 lemon
3 cups water
1 cup firmly packed light brown sugar
½ cup quick-cooking tapioca
½ teaspoon salt
¼ teaspoon ground mace
2 tablespoons butter, melted

Peel and slice apples and put in greased shallow baking dish. Mix lemon juice and water and pour over apples. Cover, and bake in preheated moderate oven (375°F.) for about 45 minutes. Mix sugar, tapioca, salt, and mace. Stir into apples. Dot with butter. Cover, and bake for 10 minutes; stir. Bake, covered, for 5 minutes longer. Serve at once with cream. Makes 6 servings.

## OLD WORLD APPLE CAKE
### Filling

3 pounds cooking apples
⅓ cup sugar
½ cup water
2 slices of lemon

### Pastry

2 cups sifted all-purpose flour
  Sugar (about 1⅓ cups)
1½ teaspoons baking powder
  Butter or margarine, softened (about ⅔ cup)
2 egg yolks

Peel and slice apples. Cook with sugar, water, and lemon until tender but not mushy. Drain and cool. Remove lemon slices.

Mix flour, 1¼ cups sugar, and baking powder. Cut in ½ cup butter with pastry blender, or work in with fingers until mixture is crumbly. Mix in egg yolks. Reserve 1 cup flour mixture for top. Pat remainder on bottom and sides of greased 9-inch springform pan. Fill with apples; sprinkle with reserved topping; dot with 2 tablespoons butter; sprinkle with 1 tablespoon sugar. Bake in preheated moderate oven (350°F.) for 1 hour. Serve warm or cold. Makes 6 to 8 servings.

## ROSY GLAZED BAKED APPLES

Select large apples suitable for baking. Core and peel top half. Put in baking pan with about 1 inch of water. Cover, and bake in preheated hot oven (425°F.) for 30 minutes, or until apples are tender. Watch that apples do not get overdone. Uncover. If there is too much liquid in pan, remove some. Sprinkle each apple with 2 tablespoons sugar. Add a little grenadine to juice in pan. Continue baking until glazed, basting frequently with juice in pan. Sprinkle again with 2 tablespoons sugar a few minutes before serving. Allow 1 large apple per serving.

## APPLE DESSERT SOUP

1 can (20 ounces) pie-sliced apples
1 quart apple juice
1 can (1 pound) whole cranberry sauce
2″ piece vanilla bean or cinnamon stick
½ cup firmly packed light brown sugar
2 tablespoons cornstarch
¼ cup water
   Granulated sugar
   Whipped cream
   Nutmeg or cinnamon

Mix first 5 ingredients in saucepan. Bring to boil and simmer, covered, 10 minutes. Mix cornstarch with water. Add to fruit mixture. Bring to boil, stirring. Boil a few minutes, or until clear and slightly thickened. Remove vanilla bean, pour mixture into serving bowl and sprinkle top lightly with granulated sugar. Cool; top each serving with dab of whipped cream. Sprinkle with ground nutmeg or cinnamon. Makes 2 quarts.

Deep-Dish Apple Pie

# PIES

## APPLE PIE TIPS

For best results, eat apple pie when fresh. If leftovers must be kept a day or two, cover well and store on pantry shelf. Freshen by reheating a few minutes at 325°F. If refrigerated, let stand at room temperature 10 to 15 minutes before reheating.

Plain apple pies can be frozen baked or unbaked. Those frozen before baking have fresher flavor as well as crisper crust. However, baked pies keep longer. Either can be frozen in the metal, foil or oven-proof paper piepan in which pie was prepared. Put in contact with freezer surface and when solidly frozen, cover with second paper or foil piepan, wrap and label. Do not cut vents in top crust of unbaked pie before freezing. To bake, cut vents and bake in preheated hot oven (425°F.) 45 to 50 minutes. Defrost baked pie 45 minutes at room temperature or in preheated slow oven (300°F.) about 30 minutes. Unbaked pies can be stored in freezer 3 to 4 months and baked ones, 6 to 8.

For a fuller, more evenly filled pie, lay apple slices flat in bottom crust.

To test for doneness of apples, insert a toothpick through one of slits in top crust. If pick goes in easily, apples are cooked.

For variety, serve plain apple pie with one of the following toppings:
   Soft vanilla ice cream sprinkled with cinnamon or nutmeg
   Sharp Cheddar, Swiss, Gruyère or sage cheese
   Dairy sour cream or yogurt
   Hard sauce or shaved maple sugar
   Plain or whipped cream or dessert topping

## DEEP-DISH APPLE PIE

3 tablespoons quick-cooking tapioca
¾ cup granulated sugar
⅓ cup firmly packed dark brown sugar
¼ teaspoon salt
1 teaspoon ground cinnamon
½ teaspoon ground nutmeg
5 cups peeled, cored, and sliced tart apples
   Pastry (1 cup flour recipe), unbaked
   Whipped cream, flavored with nutmeg (optional)

Mix all ingredients except pastry and whipped cream. Pour into buttered deep 8-inch square baking dish. Roll out pastry ⅛ inch thick to fit top of dish. Cut several slits near the center and arrange pastry over apples. Bake in preheated hot oven (425°F.) for about 35 minutes. Serve with whipped cream. Makes 4 to 6 servings.

## RAISIN-APPLE PIE

Pastry for 2-crust 9 inch pie, unbaked
6 cups sliced peeled tart cooking apples (about 2½ pounds)
½ cup granulated sugar
¼ cup firmly packed light-brown sugar
2 tablespoons all-purpose flour
¼ teaspoon salt
⅛ teaspoon ground nutmeg
¼ teaspoon ground cinnamon
2 teaspoons lemon juice
⅓ cup raisins
2 tablespoons chopped citron
Glaze

Line 9 inch piepan with half the pastry. Combine apples with remaining ingredients, except glaze, and mix well. Fill pie shell. Roll out top crust and cut slits in several places. Moisten edges of bottom crust well with cold water and adjust top crust. With fingers or fork, pinch two crusts together to make a tight seal around pie. Bake in preheated very hot oven (450°F.) 15 minutes. Reduce heat to 350°F. and bake 45 minutes longer, or until crust is browned and apples are tender. Spread with Glaze while hot and serve pie warm. **Glaze** Mix ⅓ cup sifted confectioners' sugar, 2 to 3 teaspoons milk and 2 drops vanilla until smooth.

## SWEDISH APPLE PIE FOR A CROWD

3¾ cups all-purpose flour
Sugar
⅛ teaspoon salt
1½ cups margarine (not butter)
¼ cup cold water
8 medium apples, peeled and cored (about 8 cups)
3 teaspoons cinnamon
1 egg, slightly beaten

Combine flour, ¼ cup sugar and the salt in bowl. Cut in margarine with pastry blender, sprinkle with water and gather in a ball. Chill while preparing apples. Combine apples with 1½ cups sugar and the cinnamon; toss lightly. Divide chilled dough in 2 equal parts. Roll out one part on lightly floured board in a rectangle slightly larger than a 15½ x 10½ x 1 inch jellyroll pan. Loosely roll up dough or fold in quarters, transfer to pan and unroll or open out; fill with apples in an even layer. Roll out remaining dough to fit pan. Roll up, transfer to pan and unroll on apples. Flute edges and make slits in top for steam to escape. Brush with egg and sprinkle with sugar. Bake in preheated hot oven (425°F.) 25 minutes. Reduce heat to 350°F. and bake 15 minutes, or until well browned and done. Cool on rack and serve in squares while still slightly warm. Makes 12 to 15 servings.

## APPLE PIE IN A POKE

8 to 10 tart cooking apples
1 cup sugar
All-purpose flour
1 teaspoon ground nutmeg
Pastry for 1-crust 9″ pie, unbaked
1 tablespoon lemon juice
½ cup margarine

Peel, core and slice apples into eighths. Mix ½ cup sugar, 2½ tablespoons flour and nutmeg; toss with apples. Arrange apples in pastry-lined pie pan and sprinkle with lemon juice. Mix remaining ½ cup sugar and ½ cup flour. Cut in margarine until crumbly. Sprinkle on apples. Slide pie into large brown paper bag, fold open end under and fasten with paper clips. Set on cookie sheet and bake in preheated hot oven (425°F.) about 1 hour. Serve warm or cool.

## APPLE PIE

Pastry for 2-crust 9-inch pie, unbaked
¾ to 1 cup sugar
1 teaspoon ground cinnamon or nutmeg
6 to 7 cups peeled and sliced tart cooking apples
1½ tablespoons butter

Line 9-inch pie pan with pastry. Mix sugar and cinnamon. Add to apples and mix well. Heap in lined pan. Dot with butter. Adjust top crust and cut slits for steam to escape. Seal edges and flute. Bake in preheated hot oven (425°F.) for 50 minutes, or until crust is well browned and apples are cooked through. If necessary to keep edge from excessive browning, cover with strip of foil. Serve pie warm or cold, topped with cream, whipped cream, or ice cream, if desired. Makes 6 to 8 servings.

Apple Pie

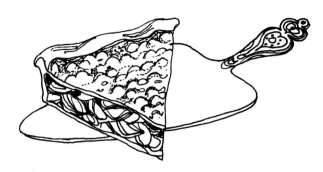

## APPLE CRUMB PIE

Crumb Topping
Pastry for 1-crust 9 inch pie, unbaked
6 cups sliced peeled tart cooking apples (about 2½ pounds)
⅓ to ½ cup sugar
2 tablespoons all-purpose flour
¼ teaspoon salt
⅛ teaspoon ground nutmeg
⅛ teaspoon grated lemon rind
2 teaspoons lemon juice

Prepare Crumb Topping and set aside. Line pie pan. Mix remaining ingredients and fill pie shell. Sprinkle with topping. Cover with foil, tucking under rim of pan. Bake in preheated hot oven (425°F.) 20 minutes, then uncover and bake 20 to 25 minutes longer, or until fruit is tender. Serve warm.

**Crumb Topping** Combine ½ cup firmly packed light-brown sugar, ¼ cup butter, ⅓ cup all-purpose flour and ¼ teaspoon cinnamon. Mix with fingertips until mixture resembles coarse crumbs.

## CHEESE-CRUMBLE APPLE PIE

1 package (10 ounces) piecrust mix
½ cup granulated sugar
¼ cup firmly packed light-brown sugar
½ teaspoon ground cinnamon
3 tablespoons butter or margarine
2 cups finely shredded sharp Cheddar cheese
2 tablespoons cold water
6 cups sliced peeled tart cooking apples (about 2½ pounds)
1 tablespoon all-purpose flour
Grated nutmeg

Measure 1 cup piecrust mix and mix with sugars and cinnamon. Work in butter with fingertips and set aside. Mix 1 cup cheese and remaining piecrust mix. Add enough water to hold dry ingredients together. Roll dough on floured board to fit 9 inch piepan and flute edges. Fill with apples and sprinkle flour evenly throughout slices. Sprinkle lightly with nutmeg. Cover with half the reserved crumb mixture. Sprinkle with remaining 1 cup cheese, then top with remaining crumb mixture. Bake in preheated moderate oven (375°F.) 45 minutes, or until apples are tender. Serve warm.

## APPLE CREAM PIE

5 large cooking apples, peeled and cut into eighths
½ cup sugar
½ cup water
Pastry for 1-crust 9-inch pie, unbaked
1 egg
½ cup heavy cream

Put apples in saucepan with sugar and water. Bring to boil, cover, and simmer for 10 to 20 minutes, or until apples are tender. Drain, reserving syrup. Cool apples slightly and put in 9-inch pie pan lined with pastry. beat egg and cream together and stir in reserved syrup. Pour over apples. Bake in preheated moderate oven (350°F.) for 30 minutes, or until firm. Cool. Makes 6 to 8 servings.

## UPSIDE-DOWN APPLE PIE

½ cup walnut halves
¼ cup butter or margarine, melted
⅓ cup firmly packed light brown sugar
Pastry (2-crust 9-inch pie), unbaked
½ cup granulated sugar
2½ cups (1-pound, 4-ounce can) apple slices, drained
2 tablespoons all-purpose flour
½ teaspoon ground cinnamon
¼ teaspoon salt
⅛ teaspoon ground nutmeg

Arrange nuts, flat sides up, in butter in deep 9-inch pie pan. Pat brown sugar over nuts and cover with round of pastry rolled ⅛ inch thick; trim edges. Mix remaining ingredients and spoon into pastry. Cover with top crust, seal edges, and cut a few slashes in top crust. Bake in preheated moderate oven (375°F.) for about 40 minutes. Cool for 5 minutes; turn out on plate. Serve warm, with whipped cream or ice cream. Makes 6 to 8 servings.

## CHEESE-CUSTARD APPLE PIE

3 cups thinly sliced peeled tart apples
Sugar
¼ teaspoon ground cinnamon
⅛ teaspoon ground nutmeg
Pastry for 1-crust 9 inch pie, unbaked
2 eggs
¼ teaspoon salt
¾ cup milk
¾ cup creamed small-curd cottage cheese
1 teaspoon vanilla extract
¼ cup seedless raisins

Mix apples, ¼ cup sugar and spices and put in pastry-lined pie pan. Bake in preheated hot oven (425°F.) 15 minutes. Combine ½ cup sugar and remaining ingredients, except raisins, and beat until thoroughly blended. Pour over apple mixture in pie and sprinkle wilth raisins. Reduce oven heat to 325°F. and bake 40 minutes longer, or until set. Let pie stand until it reaches room temperature before serving.

# APPLE SAUCES

## CIDER SAUCE FOR MEATS

To 1 cup dark brown sugar add 1 cup liquid. Use any meat liquid, ham or steak drippings, with bouillon cube and water to make desired amount. Boil mixture to reduce volume by one half. Reduce 1 cup cider to ⅓ cup. Add to first mixture with dash of cayenne, 1 teaspoon grated onion, and ¼ cup parboiled raisins, if desired. Heat and serve with baked ham or other smoked meat. Makes about 1 cup.

## DOUBLE-APPLE SAUCE

    1  cup applesauce
    1  cup apple juice
    ½  cup firmly packed light-brown sugar
       Dash of salt
    ½  teaspoon ground cinnamon
    ⅛  teaspoon ground cloves

Combine all ingredients and cook, stirring, over medium heat 10 minutes, or until thick and syrupy. Serve hot on pancakes. Makes about 2 cups.

## APPLE-SOUR-CREAM SAUCE

Chop 1 cored but unpeeled red apple. Add ¼ cup prepared white horseradish, ¾ teaspoon salt, ¼ teaspoon white pepper, and ¾ cup dairy sour cream. Serve cold on frankfurters, ham, or smoked meats. Makes 1¼ cups.

## APPLESAUCE 1 (Chunky)

Wash, peel, quarter, and core 6 medium cooking apples (about 2 pounds). Cook until soft in covered saucepan, using just enough water to keep them from scorching. Stir occasionally during cooking. Break up quarters a little

and sweeten to taste with granulated sugar or brown sugar. Vary by adding lemon juice, ground cinnamon, ground nutmeg, ground cloves, raisins, or nuts. Makes 4 servings.

## APPLESAUCE 2 (Smooth)

Wash and quarter 6 medium cooking apples (about 2 pounds). Do not peel or core. Cook until soft in covered saucepan, using just enough water to keep them from scorching. Stir occasionally during cooking. Force through a sieve or food mill and sweeten to taste. Vary as in Applesauce 1. Makes 4 servings.

## APPLE BUTTER

    4  pounds well-flavored apples, stemmed and quartered
    2  cups cider or water
       Sugar
    3  teaspoons ground cinnamon
    1½ teaspoons ground cloves
    ½  teaspoon ground allspice

Cook apples in cider or water until soft. Strain pulp. To each cup of pulp add ½ cup sugar. Stir in remaining ingredients. Cook over low heat, stirring constantly, until mixture sheets from spoon. Pour into hot sterilized jars. Store in cool dry place. Makes about 10 six-ounce glasses.

## BLENDER APPLESAUCE

Mix ½ cup light corn syrup, ⅛ teaspoon salt and ¼ cup lemon juice. Peel and core 6 eating apples and slice into mixture, stirring to keep apples coated. Whirl in electric blender until smooth. Chill. Makes 4 servings.

# MISCELLANEOUS

## APPLESAUCE FRENCH TOAST

Mix 2 cups (1-pound jar) applesauce, 1 tablespoon butter, and ½ teaspoon each of ground cinnamon and nutmeg; heat. Beat 2 eggs with 1 cup milk and dash of salt. Dip 8 slices of white bread into the mixture; brown on both sides in hot butter or margarine. Serve applesauce between 2 slices of toast and on top. Makes 4 servings.

## HOT APPLE-CHEESE SANDWICHES

Combine ½ cup applesauce with 2 tablespoons prepared mustard. Spread on 8 slices white bread and top with slices of cheese and more bread. Spread lightly with softened butter or margarine and toast on grill or in skillet.

## HALLOWEEN APPLES ON A STICK

12 small red eating apples
12 wooden skewers
3 cups sugar
¾ cup light corn syrup
1 cup water
Few drops oil of cloves
Red food coloring or 12 red cinnamon candies

Wash apples in hot water and dry. Insert a skewer in blossom end of each apple. In a saucepan mix sugar, corn syrup, and water. Cook over direct heat, stirring, until sugar dissolves. Add oil of cloves and a little coloring. Continue cooking, without stirring, until a small amount of mixture forms a hard piece that cracks when dropped into cold water (290°F. on candy thermometer). Set pan over boiling water. Dip each apple into syrup, remove, and whirl apple until syrup covers it smoothly. Stand apples, skewer side up, on tray or plate to cool and harden.

## APPLE CUP

4 cups apple juice
½ cup each lemon and orange juices
1 can (13½ ounces) crushed pineapple
1 bottle (28 ounces) ginger ale
Crushed ice

Mix fruit juices and pineapple and chill. At serving time, add ginger ale and serve over crushed ice. Makes about 2½ quarts.

## HOT MULLED APPLE JUICE

Combine 1 quart apple juice; 2-inch stick cinnamon, broken; 4 whole cloves and ¼ cup sugar. Bring to boil, cover and simmer 10 minutes. Strain. Serve hot. Makes 4 to 6 servings.

## APPLE-CRANBERRY FIZZ

Chill 2 cups apple juice with 1 cup cranberry juice cocktail. When ready to serve, add 1 cup carbonated water. Pour into glasses and garnish each with a slice of lime or lemon. Makes 4 cups.

**APRICOT** [*Prunus armeniaca*]—Oval-stoned fruit of a golden-yellow color which grows on a small tree belonging to the peach family. The apricot tree reaches a height of twenty to thirty feet and has ravishing pink flowers that come out before the leaves. Apricots hate frost and most varieties will grow only in warm temperate zones.

The tree is native to Asia, where it still grows wild. The Chinese cultivated apricots 2,000 years ago. From Asia, the tree came west to India, Persia, Armenia, and Egypt. It is said that Alexander the Great brought it from Persia to Greece, and from there it reached Italy. Apricots are grown extensively in the Middle East, in all of the Mediterranean countries from Turkey to Spain, in France, and to some extent, in espaliered form, in England. The first apricots in our country were probably those the Spanish missionaries brought to California in the 1770's. There it is still very much at home, both in private gardens and commercial orchards. Most commercial apricot shipments, fresh, canned, or dry, come from the Pacific Coast.

Apricots have been and are a staple food in many countries. The people of Hunza, a remote little kingdom in the high Himalayas, have attracted scientific attention because of their longevity and superb health; their chief food is apricots. In Persia, another country where apricots are widely eaten, poets have sung of the fruit and called it "the seed of the sun." The Chinese considered the apricot tree endowed with prophetic powers. Lao Tse, the famous Chinese philosopher, was born under one, and attributed his gifts to it. Confucius worked out his philosophy under an apricot tree. Syrians, Lebanese, Turks, Greeks, Romans, and Spaniards all doted and still dote on apricots, fresh, dried, raw, cooked, or made into ices. Few fruits are more delectable or more beautiful.

### FRESH APRICOTS

*Availability*—June through August. The crop comes from California, Washington, and Utah.

*Purchasing Guide*—Well-matured fruit, which has true apricot flavor, is plump, fairly firm, and a uniform golden to yellow-orange color. Because apricots are highly perishable and not a great many are grown, they are sometimes difficult to find in the market. Apricots are graded by the U.S. Department of Agriculture in the same grades and count as listed under Fresh Apples.
1 pound = 8 to 12 apricots

## APRICOT

*Storage*—Place ripe fruit in refrigerator in an uncovered container or perforated plastic bag. Green apricots should be allowed to ripen at room temperature, then stored in the refrigerator.
Refrigerator shelf: 3 to 5 days
Refrigerator frozen-food compartment, prepared for freezing: 2 months
Freezer, prepared for freezing: 1 year

*Nutritive Food Values*—Excellent source of vitamin A, high in natural sugars, 3 medium, about ¼ pound = 55 calories.

*Basic Preparation*—Wash, then strip off skin with a paring knife. If fruit is not ripe, it may be dipped into boiling water for 30 seconds, then into cold water, before peeling. Add a little lime or lemon juice to accent the flavor.

**To Freeze**—Cut ripe washed apricots into halves, peeled or unpeeled, remove pits, and pack in heavy syrup (5½ cups sugar to 5 cups water). To avoid discoloration of fruit, add ½ teaspoon ascorbic acid to every 5½ cups sugar, or use a citric-acid compound available in food store dietetic departments, in amounts recommended on package. Fill container ⅓ with syrup; add fruit to within 1 inch of the top. Fill with syrup. Top with crumpled wax paper to keep fruit submerged. Cover with lid.

Fresh apricots can also be frozen after steaming pitted halves for 4 minutes. Crush fruit and pack with sugar, allowing ½ cup sugar to 1 quart fruit. Ascorbic acid or citric-acid compound is not needed in this method of packing for freezing.

### CANNED APRICOTS

*Availability*—Peeled or unpeeled; packed in water, juice, or syrup; whole (pitted and unpitted), halves, or slices.

Apricots are also sold as strained and chopped infant food, in dietary packs, as preserves, and as juice, commonly called "nectar."

*Storage*—Store cans at room temperature. Rotate use of cans.
Kitchen shelf, unopened: 2½ years
Refrigerator shelf, opened and covered: 2 to 4 days

*Nutritive Food Values*—4 medium halves with 2 tablespoons syrup, about ½ cup, provide 2,255 International Units of vitamin A, less than 130 calories.

### DRIED APRICOTS

Dried fruits have a large percentage of the moisture removed. They are treated with sulfur dioxide to retain their color.

*Availability*—Sold only in halves, packed in bulk, in moisture-proof packages or plastic bags; also sold in dried-fruit mixtures.

*Purchasing Guide*
1 pound dried = 3¼ cups raw or 5 to 6 cups, cooked

*Storage*—Keep packages tightly sealed to keep fruit moist. Can be stored in carton, unopened, at room temperature for 2 to 5 months.

*Nutritive Food Values*
Dried apricots are a concentrated source of Vitamin A and natural sugars.
Uncooked, ¼ cup or 8 to 10 small halves = 98 calories
Cooked, unsweetened, fruit and liquid,
1 cup = 240 calories

*Basic Preparation*—Wash and cover dried apricots with water. Bring to a boil. Lower temperature, cover, and simmer for 15 to 20 minutes, or until tender, adding more water to keep up the level of the liquid. Sweeten to taste.

# DESSERTS

## APRICOT-OAT CRUMBLE

1 can (21 ounces) apricot pie filling
2 tablespoons lemon juice
¼ teaspoon ground ginger
Butter or margarine
⅓ cup firmly packed light-brown sugar
⅓ cup all-purpose flour
⅛ teaspoon salt
¼ teaspoon baking soda
⅔ cup quick-cooking rolled oats
½ teaspoon vanilla extract

Pour pie filling into buttered shallow 1-quart baking dish. Stir in lemon juice and ginger. Dot with 1 tablespoon butter. Mix together ¼ cup melted butter and remaining ingredients. Crumble with fingers and sprinkle over apricots. Bake in preheated moderate oven (350°F.) 45 minutes. Serve with cream, if desired. Makes 4 servings.

## APRICOT RICE PUDDING

⅔ cup dried apricots
½ cup raw rice (white or brown, not processed)
½ cup sugar
½ teaspoon salt
½ teaspoon ground nutmeg
2 quarts milk

Put apricots to soak in water to cover. Mix rice, sugar, salt, and nutmeg in shallow 2½-quart baking dish. Add 1 quart milk. Then, to prevent spilling, add second quart of milk after placing dish in oven. Bake in preheated slow oven (325°F.) for 2½ hours, stirring twice during first hour. Stir the brown crust into pudding several times during remainder of baking. Drain apricots and cut into strips. Add 30 minutes before pudding is done. Then allow crust to form again. Serve with cream, if desired. Makes 6 to 8 servings.

## APRICOT REFRIGERATOR CAKE

 1 pound dried apricots
2½ cups water
 1 cup butter
 2 cups sifted confectioners' sugar
 4 eggs, separated
   Grated rind and juice of 1 lemon
 ⅓ cup granulated sugar
 3 dozen ladyfingers, split
 ¾ cup heavy cream, whipped
   Canned apricot halves
   Fresh mint sprigs

Stew apricots in water until tender and liquid is absorbed. Put through ricer or sieve (there should be about 2⅓ cups thick pulp), and cool. Cream butter. Add confectioners' sugar and beat until light. Add egg yolks, one at a time, and beat well. Beat in apricot pulp, lemon rind, and juice. Beat egg whites until stiff, gradually add granulated sugar, beating until sugar is dissolved. Fold into apricot mixture. Line deep springform pan (9 inches) with split ladyfingers. Put in alternate layers of ⅓ of mixture and ⅓ of ladyfingers. Chill overnight, or a day or two. Remove sides of pan. Garnish with whipped cream and apricot halves. Decorate with mint sprigs. Makes 10 to 12 servings.

## APRICOT UPSIDE-DOWN CAKE

 ¾ cup butter or margarine
 ½ cup firmly packed brown sugar
 ½ teaspoon ground cinnamon
1½ cups (1 pound, 1 ounce can) unpeeled apricot halves, well drained
 ½ cup granulated sugar
 1 egg
1½ cups sifted all-purpose flour
 2 teaspoons baking powder
 ½ teaspoon salt
 ½ cup milk

Melt ¼ cup butter in square pan (9x9x2 inches). Sprinkle with brown sugar and cinnamon. Arrange apricot halves, rounded side down, in pan. Cream remaining ½ cup butter with granulated sugar until light. Beat in egg. Sift dry ingredients and add alternately with milk, beating until smooth. Spread on apricots. Bake in preheated moderate oven (375°F.) for about 30 minutes. Let stand for 10 minutes; turn out on serving plate and serve with whipped cream, if desired. Makes 6 large or 9 small servings.
**Note:** Halved, pitted, cooked prunes can be alternated with the apricots, for color contrast.

Apricot
Upside-Down
Cake

## JELLIED APRICOT DESSERT

Use 1 can (12 ounces) apricot nectar. Sprinkle 1 envelope unflavored gelatin into ½ cup apricot nectar. Let stand for 5 minutes. Heat over hot water or over low heat, stirring until gelatin is dissolved. Add remaining nectar and juice of 1 orange and 1 lemon. Pour into 8-inch square pan and chill until firm. Cut into cubes, pile in dessert dishes and serve with sweetened whipped cream or soft custard sauce. Makes 4 servings.

## APRICOT STRUDEL

 1 box (11 ounces) dried apricots
   Boiling water
 1 small orange, ground, including peel
 1 small lemon, ground, including peel
   Sugar (about 1⅔ cups)
 1 cup chopped nuts
1½ teaspoons ground cinnamon
 1 cup golden raisins
 1 cup fine plain-cake crumbs
 1 cup flaked coconut
   Melted butter or margarine
   Strudel Dough

Cover apricots with boiling water and soak for several hours or overnight. Drain. Chop apricots fine and add half of orange and lemon and ¾ cup sugar. Mix well. In another bowl, mix remaining half of orange and lemon, nuts, ¾ cup sugar, ½ teaspoon cinnamon, raisins, crumbs, coconut, and 1 tablespoon butter. Roll Strudel Dough as directed in recipe. Spread with nut mixture. Spoon a little butter evenly over top. Spread with apricot mixture and roll up. Slice into 1-inch pieces, but do not cut completely through. Sprinkle with a mixture of 2 tablespoons sugar and remaining cinnamon. Bake in preheated hot oven (400°F.) for about 1 hour. Remove from pan and complete slicing while still warm. Makes 8 servings.

## FROZEN APRICOT MOUSSE

 1 cup cooked dried apricots, sweetened to taste
 2 eggs
 ⅓ cup sugar
 ½ teaspoon vanilla extract
 ⅛ teaspoon salt
 1 cup heavy cream, whipped

Press apricots through a sieve or whirl in a blender. Beat eggs until fluffy. Gradually beat in sugar. Add apricots, vanilla, and salt. Fold in whipped cream. Turn into refrigerator tray and place in freezing compartment. Set control at coldest setting and freeze until firm. Makes about 1½ pints.

## APRICOT SOUFFLÉ

1 can (1 pound) apricot halves
3 tablespoons butter
3 tablespoons all-purpose flour
Granulated sugar
1 tablespoon lemon juice
Dash of salt
4 eggs, separated
Confectioners' sugar

Drain apricots, reserving syrup. Press apricots through sieve and add syrup to make 1¼ cups. Melt butter and blend in flour. Add apricot pulp and cook until thickened. Remove from heat. Stir in 2 tablespoons granulated sugar, lemon juice, and salt. Beat egg yolks and add to mixture. Beat egg whites until stiff and fold into batter. Butter a 1½-quart soufflé dish and sprinkle with granulated sugar. Pour in mixture. Bake in preheated moderate oven (375°F.) for 25 minutes. Sprinkle with confectioners' sugar and serve with cream, if desired. Makes 4 servings.

Apricot Soufflé

## APRICOT CRUMB PIE

2 tablespoons quick-cooking tapioca
¾ cup granulated sugar
⅛ teaspoon salt
2 pounds fresh apricots, halved and pitted
Juice of ½ lemon
Pastry for 1-crust 9-inch pie, unbaked
⅓ cup firmly packed light brown sugar
¼ cup all-purpose flour
½ teaspoon ground cinnamon
3 tablespoons butter or margarine

Mix tapioca, granulated sugar, and salt. Combine with apricots and lemon juice. Turn into 9-inch pie pan lined with pastry. Mix brown sugar, flour, and cinnamon; cut in butter to form crumbs. Sprinkle over apricots. Bake in preheated hot oven (425°F.) for 15 minutes; reduce heat to moderate (375°F.) and bake for 30 to 35 minutes longer, or until apricots are tender. Makes 6 to 8 servings.

## APRICOT CRISP

2 cans (30 ounces each) apricot halves, drained
2 tablespoons water
1 tablespoon lemon juice
½ cup firmly packed light-brown sugar
½ teaspoon each ground nutmeg and ground cinnamon
¼ teaspoon salt
¾ cup all-purpose flour
⅓ cup butter or margarine
Nutmeg cream

Put apricot halves in buttered shallow 1½-quart baking dish; pour over water and lemon juice. Combine sugar, spices, salt and flour. Cut in butter with pastry blender until finely blended; spoon evenly over apricots. Bake in preheated moderate oven (350°F.) about 40 minutes. Serve warm with Nutmeg Cream. Makes 6 servings.

**Nutmeg Cream.** Mix ¼ teaspoon ground nutmeg and 1 cup light or heavy cream.

## FRESH APRICOT RIPPLE ICE CREAM

1½ cups puréed or mashed fresh apricots
1 tablespoon lemon juice
¾ cup sugar
1 quart vanilla ice cream
½ cup heavy cream
¼ teaspoon almond extract

Mix apricot pulp with lemon juice and sugar. Chill for 30 minutes. Soften ice cream slightly. Whip cream and add flavoring. Mix apricot pulp, ice cream, and cream quickly, but not thoroughly. Freeze until firm. Serve with additional puréed fresh apricots if desired. Makes 8 servings.

## FRESH FRUIT COMPOTE

1 cup sugar
2 cups water
1 lemon, sliced
4 firm peaches, peeled, halved
4 pears, peeled, cored and halved
4 plums (see note)
8 apricots

Put first 3 ingredients in saucepan, bring to boil and simmer 5 minutes. Add peaches and pears, cover and simmer 5 minutes. Prick skins of plums and add with apricots to mixture. Cover and simmer 5 minutes, or until all fruit is tender. Cool, then chill. Makes 8 servings.

**Note** If purple plums are used, cook separately in a little syrup and add to compote just before serving.

## THE SIMPLEST APRICOT DESSERT

Served drained canned apricots with plenty of whipped cream that has been sweetened to taste and flavored with vanilla. Delicious.

## APRICOT-PRUNE PIE

1¼ cups drained cooked dried apricots, reserve ½ cup liquid
1¼ cups drained pitted cooked prunes
Pastry for 2-crust 9-inch pie, unbaked
1 tablespoon cornstarch
½ cup sugar
⅛ teaspoon salt
¼ teaspoon each of ground cinnamon and nutmeg
Juice of 1 lemon
1 tablespoon butter

Put fruit into 9-inch pan lined with pastry. Mix cornstarch, sugar, salt, and spices. Gradually stir in reserved liquid. Cook, stirring constantly, until slightly thickened. Stir in lemon juice and butter; pour over fruit. Cover with remaining pastry. Moisten edges of pastry with water and press together with tines of fork. Trim edges and cut slits in top to allow steam to escape. Bake in preheated hot oven (425°F.) for about 30 minutes. Serve either warm or cold. Makes 6 to 8 servings.

## APRICOT CRESCENTS

½ cup soft butter or margarine
2 packages (3 ounces each) cream cheese, softened
¾ cup sifted all-purpose flour
⅛ teaspoon salt
1 tablespoon cold water
Apricot preserves
Minced nuts
Confectioners' sugar

Cut butter and cheese into flour and salt. Add water and mix lightly with fork until blended. Chill until firm. Cut into 24 pieces. Keep dough chilled before rolling. Roll each piece very thin on floured board, to form 2½- to 3-inch squares. Spread each with apricot preserves and sprinkle with nuts. Roll up from one corner and bend ends in slightly to form crescents. Put folded side down on ungreased cookie sheets and bake in preheated very hot oven (450°F.) for about 10 minutes. Sift confectioners' sugar over cooled crescents. Makes 24.

Apricot
Crescents

## STEWED APRICOTS

Peel 12 large ripe fresh apricots. Cut into halves and discard pits, or leave whole. Bring to boil ¾ cup sugar, 1 cup water, and 4 whole cloves or a piece of cinnamon stick. Simmer for 5 minutes. Add apricots, cover, and simmer for 10 minutes, or until just tender. Chill. Replace ¼ cup of cooking water with ¼ cup white wine, if desired. Makes 4 to 6 servings.

## APRICOT PIE IN NUT CRUST

Nut Crust
1 cup dried apricots
¼ cup sugar
1¼ cups water
1 envelope unflavored gelatin
½ cup heavy cream, whipped
Chopped nuts

Prepare Nut Crust and cool. Put apricots, sugar and 1 cup water in saucepan. Bring to boil, cover and simmer 15 to 20 minutes, or until apricots are soft. Soften gelatin in remaining ¼ cup cold water. Add to hot apricots and force through sieve or food mill (there will be about 1 cup purée). Cool, then fold in whipped cream. Pour into crust and sprinkle with nuts. Chill until firm.
**Nut Crust** Mix 1 cup ground pecans or walnuts, 2 tablespoons sugar and 2 tablespoons softened butter. Press into 8-inch piepan; bake if desired in preheated moderate oven (350°F.) 15 to 20 minutes, or until edges are golden brown.

# MAIN DISHES

## APRICOTS WITH CURRIED PORK CHOPS

8 small center-cut rib pork chops
1 yellow onion, minced
¼ cup butter or margarine
¼ cup all-purpose flour
1 teaspoon salt
1 teaspoon (or more) curry powder
¼ teaspoon pepper
2 cups milk
½ pound fresh mushrooms, sliced
8 drained canned apricot halves

Brown chops quickly on both sides in skillet and put in casserole. Sauté onion in butter for 5 minutes. Blend in flour and seasonings. Gradually stir in milk and cook, stirring constantly, until thickened. Add mushrooms. Pour over chops. Cover and bake in preheated moderate oven (350°F.) for 1 hour, or until chops are tender. Top with apricot halves. Serve with rice and chutney. Makes 4 servings.

## APRICOT VEAL LOAF

    1   cup dried apricots
    ¾   cup diced celery
    3   tablespoons minced onion
    1   tablespoon minced parsley
    1   cup cooked rice
    1   teaspoon salt
    ⅛   teaspoon pepper
    ¼   teaspoon dried savory
    1   egg, slightly beaten
    1¼  pounds ground veal
    2   tablespoons honey
    4   slices bacon, slightly cooked and drained
        Sweet-Sour Sauce

Cover apricots with boiling water and let stand while preparing remaining ingredients. Then drain and cut in pieces with scissors. Mix well all ingredients, except honey, bacon and sauce. Put in 9 x 5 x 3-inch loaf pan and drizzle with honey. Arrange bacon slices on top. Bake in preheated moderate oven (350°F.) about 1 hour. Serve with the Sauce. Makes 6 to 8 servings.

## APRICOT-PORK SKILLET

    8   ounces dried apricots
    1½  cups boiling water
    2   pounds boneless pork, cut in 1½-inch cubes
        Butter or margarine
    2   tablespoons soy sauce
        Pepper to taste
    3   medium leeks, cut in 1½-inch pieces
        Hot seasoned cooked rice

Pour boiling water over apricots and let stand while preparing meat. Brown pork in small amount of butter in heated skillet over medium heat until well browned on all sides. Add soy sauce, pepper and ½ cup apricot liquid. Cover and simmer 45 minutes. Add leeks, apricots and more apricot liquid if necessary to prevent sticking. Simmer 10 more minutes, or until meat is tender. Serve over rice. Makes 6 servings.

## BROILED APRICOTS

Put drained canned apricot halves on rack in broiler pan. Brush with melted butter or margarine and sprinkle with lemon juice, sugar, and a little ground cinnamon, cloves, or nutmeg, if desired. Broil for about 8 minutes, 5 to 6 inches away from heat. Serve very hot with a mixed grill of lamb chops, kidneys, and sausages. Prepare 3 halves for each serving.

## APRICOT-PINEAPPLE JAM

    1   box (11 ounces) dried apricots
    4   cups water
    3½  cups (1 pound, 13 ounce can) pineapple chunks and
        juice
    6   cups sugar

In large saucepan mix all ingredients except sugar. Let stand for 1 hour. Then cook slowly until apricots are tender. Add sugar and cook slowly, stirring frequently, until thick and clear (220°F. on a candy-jelly thermometer). Pour at once into hot sterilized glasses and seal with paraffin. Cover with lids. Makes about 6 six-ounce glasses.

## APRICOT GLAZE

This simple glaze is much used in French home and professional cooking to give brilliance and glitter to any fruit tart, since the taste of apricot blends very well with that of other fruits. It can be used as a simple icing for cakes, cookies, and pies, or used inside a pastry shell to moistureproof it before the filling goes in.

Simply boil apricot preserves to between 225°F. and 228°F. Stir frequently. The preserve thus boiled will stiffen slightly as it cools and will not be sticky. Use a pastry brush in applying it.

Red currant jelly may be treated and used in the same way.

## APRICOT SAUCE

    1½  cups apricot jam
    ½   cup water
    1   tablespoon sugar
    1   teaspoon fresh lemon juice or 2 tablespoons brandy

Combine apricot jam, water, and sugar in a small heavy saucepan. Bring to a boil. Simmer for 5 minutes, stirring constantly. Remove from heat and stir in lemon juice. Serve hot or cold. Excellent for ice cream, puddings, and cake. Makes about 2 cups.

## APRICOT-CHEESE SALAD

    1   pound creamed cottage cheese
    2   teaspoons grated orange rind
    2   tablespoons chopped maraschino cherries
        Salad greens
    6   fresh apricots, halved and pitted
        Whole maraschino cherries
        Mint sprigs (optional)

Blend cheese, orange rind, and chopped cherries. Arrange salad greens on 4 salad plates and put 3 apricot halves in center of each. Put cheese mixture around fruit and garnish with whole cherries and mint sprigs. Makes 4 servings.

## ARAB INFLUENCE ON FOOD—We

owe much of our knowledge of such everyday foods as sugar, fruits, and spices to the Arab world. The Arabs, traders since antiquity, introduced many new foods to the West. Especially welcome was their trading with spices, since spices, which were costly and very desirable, played a most important role in making palatable the monotonous and often improperly preserved foods of the past.

Many Arab plants, crops, and foods were introduced to the West during the 11th, 12th, and 13th centuries, the time of the Crusades. The Crusaders, for instance, brought back sesame, rice, millet, melons, apricots, shallots, and scallions and, most important, sugar, which until then was almost completely unknown, all the sweetening having been done with honey and fruits. The very word "sugar" comes from the Arabic.

## AROMA—The word means a distinctive, agreeable

fragrance which is more penetrating and persuasive than a smell, and has none of the negative meaning sometimes associated with the words smell and odor. Though one speaks of the aroma of a cigar, the word is usually applied to foods. Thus we say the aroma of coffee, of spices, of herbs, of meat cooking, of fruits, etc.

The aroma of foods greatly affects our enjoyment of them since the connection between the senses of taste and smell is an extremely close one. Instinctively, one thinks that if the aroma of a food is pleasant, the taste will be too. This is true in most cases (think of the aroma of a dish of strawberries), but it can be otherwise. Test this by biting into a clove.

There is also a close connection between aroma and memory. Few things are as evocative as the aroma of a certain food or drink; it may recall experiences long forgotten.

## ARRACK—The name is given to two different

strong liquors. One is a liquor distilled from rice. It originated in the former Dutch East Indies (now Indonesia) where it was known as Batavia arrack. It is used mostly as a flavoring in confections, desserts, and punches.

Arrack is also the name of a liquor with a pronounced anise flavor which is distilled from local grains or grapes in the Middle East, Turkey, and Greece. It is known as *arrack* in Lebanon, *raki* in Turkey, and *ouzo* in Greece. Though a clear spirit in itself, it turns milky and opalescent when mixed with water. It is said that you have to be born to *arrack, raki,* or *ouzo,* but those who are, love it.

## ARROWROOT—The starch obtained from the

tubers of several kinds of tropical plants. The roots are peeled, washed, and pulped to produce a white fluid. This is made into a powder which is then milled into the form we know.

Arrowroot is an excellent thickening agent and can be used in lieu of flour or cornstarch. It is neutral in flavor and produces soups, sauces, pie fillings, and puddings that are clear and sparkling, with none of the heaviness of other starches. Arrowroot is easily digested and therefore suitable for invalid cookery.

Arrowroot is not much known in modern American home-cooking, although our grandmothers used it to make their famous delicate blancmange and other puddings. It is now mainly used commercially as a thickening agent for various desserts. Arrowroot is very popular in Great Britain, and was a great standby of Victorian cooking, with its puddings and jellied sweet dishes of all kinds, all of which arrowroot makes to perfection. Victorian cook books are full of arrowroot recipes to suit the delicate tastes and constitutions of the ladies of the time.

Arrowroot is usually found on the spice shelves of grocery stores.

**To Cook with Arrowroot**—The delicate texture of arrowroot allows it to cook at a lower temperature and for a shorter time than other starches. It is thus ideally suited for sauces and custards containing eggs, which must not boil or are heat sensitive.

To use arrowroot as a thickening agent substitute one half as much arrowroot as flour in the recipe. Cook mixture until just thickened, stirring as little as possible. High temperatures and excessive stirring will cause marked thinning.

### ARROWROOT BLANCMANGE

⅓ cup arrowroot
1 cup cold milk
2 cups milk, scalded
⅓ cup sugar
1 teaspoon vanilla extract
Dash of salt

Mix arrowroot with cold milk; gradually stir into scalded milk and cook over low heat, stirring constantly, until thickened. Add sugar, vanilla, and salt. Pour into 1-quart bowl and chill. Serve with stewed fruit or jam. Makes 5 to 6 servings.

## ARTICHOKE—Globe or common artichokes are

the leafy buds from a plant resembling the thistle. They have been widely cultivated as food in Europe for hundreds of years and cooked in a great many delicious ways. We know that they grew in the vicinity of Naples in the 15th century, and their popularity spread to other parts of Europe. In the 18th century French settlers brought them to Louisiana (they are sometimes called "French" artichokes). The Spanish brought artichokes to California, and they were also grown in Florida. Today they are cultivated in the United States where the climate is cool, foggy, and free of frost, mainly in the mid-coastal regions of California. Globe artichokes are not to be confused with Jerusalem artichokes, a completely different vegetable. Artichokes, like other vegetables, may be eaten in many ways. One way is to eat them with the fingers: pull off the leaves one at a time and dip them into a sauce which may be hot melted butter and lemon juice, hollandaise or mayonnaise, sour cream, or a French dressing. Eventually a core of thin, light-colored leaves is reached; this covers the choke and the heart. Eat the tender part of these leaves by drawing between teeth. Discard the remainder of the leaf. The fuzzy choke is scraped off with a knife or fork and discarded. The heart, also called "bottom," is eaten with a fork.

*Availability*—Fresh artichokes are available the year round; the main season is September to May, with the peak of production arriving toward spring.

Artichoke hearts or bottoms are available canned and ready for eating. Artichoke hearts are also available frozen and require a minimum of cooking.

*Purchasing Guide*—Look for uniformly solid heads with compact leaves. Loose, spreading, and discolored leaves indicate overmaturity or poor quality. Size has little to do with quality or flavor. Choose small, medium, or large, according to your preference or the way they are to be served. The small size is usually selected for pickling or baking with meat, the medium or large for salads, and the large for the hearts.

*Storage*—Use fresh artichokes as soon as possible. Hold in a covered container in the refrigerator. Keep cool and moist.
Fresh, refrigerator shelf: 4 days
Fresh, refrigerator frozen-food compartment, prepared for freezing: 1 month
Fresh, freezer, prepared for freezing: 1 year
Canned, kitchen shelf: 1 year
Canned, refrigerator shelf, opened and covered: 4 to 5 days

*Nutritive Food Values*—Artichokes contain small amounts of vitamins and minerals.
Fresh, 1 cooked = 50 to 60 calories, depending on size
About ½ cup, canned or frozen = about 40 calories; caloric values vary greatly.

*Basic Preparation—Important*—It must be remembered that artichokes discolor rapidly once they are cut. To prevent this, before starting to prepare the artichokes, have ready a bowl of water acidulated with vinegar or lemon juice, about 3 tablespoons to 1 quart water. Drop artichokes into this water as soon as they are prepared and keep them in the water until cooking time. This will keep them light.
**To Cook, Whole**—Wash, drain, and cut off artichoke stem to a 1- or ½-inch stub. Pull off and discard any coarse or misshapen leaves. With kitchen scissors, trim off the thorny tip of each leaf; then cook immediately. Cook in boiling salted water uncovered until tender, about 15 to 40 minutes, depending on size and variety. If you are preparing several artichokes, keep them in acidulated water as described above.

**To Cook, Hearts**—Slice off stem. Tear off tough outer leaves. Discard. Trim base piece smoothly with a sharp knife. Place artichoke on its side and cut off the pointed tips of the remaining leaves. Scoop out choke with a small spoon. Artichoke heart may be left whole or cut into halves or quarters. Drop into acidulated water. Drain. Cook in boiling salted water uncovered until tender, about 10 to 15 minutes, depending on size.
**To Cook, Sliced**—Trim as above. Slice off all leaves, leaving ½ inch of white leaf on base of artichoke. Dechoke as above. Slice firm base into ¼-inch slices and drop slices into acidulated water. The size of the artichoke slices will depend on the size of the original artichoke. Cook as above.
**To Freeze**—Prepare as for cooking whole. Scald whole artichokes in boiling water (use 3 tablespoons lemon juice for 3 quarts water) for 8 to 10 minutes. Artichoke hearts, slices, or bottoms should be scalded for 2 to 3 minutes. Cool for 15 minutes under cold or ice water. Drain and package.

## ARTICHOKE HALVES

Prepare artichokes as for eating whole. Stand upright in deep saucepan. Sprinkle with salt and put 2 teaspoons vegetable oil on each. Pour in about 1 inch of boiling water and add 1 or 2 minced garlic cloves and 1 sliced onion. Cover and simmer about 15 to 40 minutes, or until the bases are very tender. Add more water if necessary. Lift out the artichokes with 2 spoons or tongs. Drain upside down and chill. Before serving, split lengthwise and remove and discard chokes. Arrange artichoke halves around the edge of a shallow serving dish or large round platter. Serve with French dressing, or oil and lemon juice, or with a thinned well-seasoned mayonnaise. Garnish with greens, parsley sprigs, wedges of tomato.

## TWO SIMPLE WAYS TO COOK ARTICHOKES

Cut trimmed artichokes into thin slices. Sauté in a little hot butter or olive oil until tender. Shake pan to prevent sticking. Season with salt and pepper, and serve with a squeeze of lemon.

Cut trimmed artichokes into thin slices. Dip into seasoned flour and fry in hot olive or salad oil. Drain on paper towel. Serve very hot.

## ARTICHOKES WITH ROMAN PORK CHOPS

- 2 large or 4 medium artichokes, trimmed and sliced
- 3 tablespoons olive oil
- 6 pork chops, trimmed of excess fat
  Salt and pepper
- 1 garlic clove, minced
- ½ teaspoon rosemary, basil, or sage
- 2½ cups (1 pound, 4½ ounce can) Italian-style stewed tomatoes

Keep sliced artichokes in acidulated water until ready to use (see Basic Preparation). Heat olive oil in deep skillet or shallow casserole. Fry pork chops until browned on all sides. Pour off excess fat from skillet. Arrange artichoke slices around meat. Add seasonings and herbs; cover with tomatoes. Simmer, covered, for 1 hour, or until meat and artichokes are tender. If sauce is too thin, simmer, uncovered, until sufficiently reduced. Makes 4 to 6 servings.

## STUFFED ARTICHOKES, ITALIAN STYLE

- 4 medium artichokes
- 1½ cups soft stale bread crumbs
- ¾ cup grated Parmesan cheese
- 3 tablespoons chopped parsley
- 2 garlic cloves, minced
- ½ cup minced onion
- ½ teaspoon salt
- ¼ teaspoon pepper
- 4 tablespoons vegetable oil

Cut off stems of artichokes. Cut about 1 inch off tops and snip end of each leaf with scissors. Spread open with fingers, wash thoroughly and drain. Mix remaining ingredients, except oil, and fill artichokes with the mixture, being careful to put some stuffing in all the leaves. Set in deep heavy kettle with lid and add water to come halfway up sides of artichokes. Pour 1 tablespoon oil over each. Bring to boil and simmer, covered, 1 hour, or until tender and leaves are easily removed. Add more water if necessary. Makes 4 servings.

## ARTICHOKE HALVES, GREEK STYLE

- 6 large artichokes
  Water
- 3 lemons
- 1 tablespoon all-purpose flour
- 1 cup chopped onion
- 1 cup olive oil
  Salt and pepper

Cut stems off artichokes. Remove bottom leaves and with scissors trim off brown thorny tips of all remaining leaves. Cut off tops and halve each artichoke. Soak in 4 cups water and juice of 2 of lemons. Meanwhile, sprinkle flour over onion and sauté in olive oil until lightly browned. Arrange artichoke halves, cut side up, in roasting pan or large skillet. Add salt and pepper and juice of remaining lemon to onion and oil, and pour over artichokes. Add small amount of water, about ½ cup. Cover and simmer over low heat until artichokes are tender. Serve warm or cold. Makes 6 servings.

## ARTICHOKE AND SHRIMP SALAD

On individual plates arrange beds of finely shredded lettuce. Heap whole shrimp on lettuce and sprinkle with finely diced celery. Add mayonnaise to moisten if desired. Season with a few drops of fresh lemon juice and salt and pepper to taste. Press hard-cooked egg yolk through a sieve, sprinkle on shrimp. Surround with artichoke hearts. Garnish with pimiento. Chill. Two medium artichoke hearts make 1 serving for luncheon main dish.

## ARTICHOKE HEARTS PIQUANT

- 2 carrots, sliced
- ½ cup water
- 2 tablespoons salad oil
  Juice of 1 lemon
- 1 small bay leaf
- 1 teaspoon salt
  Dash of garlic salt
- 1 package (9 ounces) frozen artichoke hearts

Put all ingredients except artichokes in a saucepan. Bring to a boil and boil for about 5 minutes. Add artichokes and cook until tender, 5 to 10 minutes. Drain and serve. Makes 4 servings.

## ARTICHOKE OMELET

- 2 tablespoons butter
- 3 cooked artichoke hearts, diced
  Equal amount of diced cooked mushrooms
- 2 tablespoons tomato sauce
  Salt and pepper
  Dash of cayenne
- ½ garlic clove
- 8 eggs
- 1 small can flat anchovy fillets

In 1 tablespoon butter lightly sauté artichokes and mushrooms. Add tomato sauce and seasonings, mix well and set aside in warm place. Rub a bowl with garlic. Break eggs into bowl and beat with a fork. Cook omelet as usual in remaining 1 tablespoon butter. When omelet is cooked, top with artichoke mixture and fold over. Garnish with anchovies and serve at once. Makes 4 servings.

# ASPARAGUS

In Europe, asparagus is grown in a number of different varieties and ways. It is considered the most luxurious of vegetables, fit for a king. Great chefs have created some of their finest and most complicated dishes with asparagus; in aspics, for example, for which there are special molds tailored to the shape of the vegetable.

Especially prized is the variety of asparagus that yields very thick, white, fleshy stalks that are incredibly tender. These asparagus are grown in little individual mounds, and cut when only the green tip shows so that the stalks are still white. They are available at specialty markets or imported from Europe, canned in glass jars or metal cans.

Among the virtues of asparagus is that it not only tastes excellent with any kind of food, but it is equally good hot, lukewarm, or cold. Perhaps the most popular way of serving asparagus is boiled and hot, with either hot butter or hollandaise sauce, or cold, with a vinaigrette sauce, which is a simple French dressing.

**Availability**—The main market season for fresh asparagus may start as early as February with the southwestern (California) crop. The season continues until late June, when the northeastern (New Jersey) crop appears.

Canned and frozen asparagus is available in tips, spears, and cuts (pieces). Some white asparagus is canned.

**Purchasing Guide**—Tender asparagus has brittle, easily punctured, straight green stalks, and tips that are well formed and tightly closed. Spreading tips mean overmaturity, and very thin, wilted, or crooked stalks may be tough or stringy. Asparagus is sold mainly by weight, although it is often tied in bunches. Bunches are frequently standardized to weigh 2½ pounds.
1 pound = 16 to 20 stalks

**Storage**—Keep stalks in the refrigerator in a covered container or plastic bag until ready to use. If stalks seem a little limp, cut a thin slice from ends and stand in cold water for a short time before storing. Do not wash before storing. Cook as soon as possible.
Fresh, refrigerator shelf or vegetable compartment: 4 days
Fresh, refrigerator frozen-food compartment, prepared for freezing: 1 month
Fresh, freezer, prepared for freezing: 1 year
Canned, kitchen shelf, unopened: 1 year
Canned, refrigerator shelf, opened and covered: 4 days

**Nutritive Food Values**—A good source of vitamin A, fair for vitamin C, the B vitamins, calcium, and iron.
Spears, ½-inch diameter at base, cooked, drained, 4 spears = 10 calories
Pieces, 1 cup, drained, cooked, = 30 calories
1 cup canned, solids and liquids = 45 calories

**Basic Preparation**—When ready to cook, wash in cold running water and lift from water to eliminate any sand or grit. Do not soak. Break or cut off the stalks as far down as they will snap easily. Usually the white portion is tough. Shear off heavy scales with a vegetable parer or sharp knife. Rinse stalks again, hold tips up. If you

**ASPARAGUS**—This vegetable, the fifth most popular in the United States, is a member of the lily-of-the-valley family. The name comes from a Greek word meaning "stalk" or "shoot." It is thought to be native to the eastern Mediterranean lands and Asia Minor, where it still grows wild. It spread to Europe; as early as 200 B.C. the Romans wrote down directions for growing and drying the vegetable. Later, the English developed a fondness for eating it raw. Undoubtedly some of our earliest settlers brought roots with them from Europe. We know that Thomas Jefferson grew asparagus in the greenhouses of his beautiful Monticello. As pioneers traveled west, they took it with them, developing colloquial names for it. One was "sparrow grass," and even today, asparagus is known as "grass" in the vegetable trade. Yet asparagus, with its crisp stalks and tightly closed, tender tips, maintains a special place among vegetables, almost a symbol of pleasant eating. Not all of it is green. In some areas blanched, or white asparagus, somewhat milder in flavor, is available.

wish lots of stalk, strip the peeling from the ends with a vegetable parer. Stalks may be left whole, cut into 1½-inch pieces, or sliced diagonally. Tips may be used separately. Asparagus tastes best when cooked until just tender. (A fork will pierce the tough ends easily.) It may be cooked by steam-boiling or boiling.

**To Steam-boil**—Divide stalks into serving-size bunches; tie each loosely with a string; or tie in 1 bunch, if amount is not large. Stand each bunch upright in a deep pan, such as the bottom of a double boiler. Add enough boiling water to cover bottom of stalks about 1 inch. Salt or not, as desired. Cover with inverted top part of double boiler. Cook for about 15 minutes. (The tougher ends of stalks cook in water, the tender tips in steam.) Special pans and tongs to be used in cooking asparagus are available. Remove from pan by using tongs. Drain, remove string, arrange on serving plate, and season.

**To Boil**—Arrange prepared stalks in a skillet or wide-bottomed pan; pour in about ½ inch of boiling water. Sprinkle with salt if you wish. Cover pan. Bring quickly to boil, then lower heat to medium or low. Cook for 10 to 12 minutes, or until stalks are just tender. Lift from pan with tongs or 2 forks. Drain and serve at once with melted butter.

When asparagus is prepared in pieces, prepare as above, omitting tips. Cook, covered, for 2 minutes. Add tips and cook, covered, for an additional 6 to 8 minutes.

**Skillet Method**—Put asparagus in large skillet; add 1½ teaspoons salt and 1″ boiling water. Bring to boil, cover and simmer 10 to 12 minutes, or until stalks are barely tender.

**To Pan-cook Slices**—For a tender crisp vegetable in the Chinese manner, slice asparagus stalks slantwise about ¼ inch thick; leave tips whole. Melt enough butter to cover bottom of a skillet. Heat until butter is hot and bubbly but not brown. Add slices; sprinkle with salt (and pepper if desired). Cover pan; bring to steam, then lower heat and cook until barely tender, 3 to 5 minutes. Serve.

**To Cook Ends and Peelings**—Cut coarse ends in quarters lengthwise and add to peelings with a quartered onion. Cover with boiling water and cook, covered, about 30 minutes. Cool and strain through sieve or food mill, forcing some of pulp through. Store in covered jar in refrigerator and use as basis for cream soup.

**Note**—If not to be used at once, liquid can be frozen in ice-cube trays, removed and kept frozen in plastic bags. Use in soups, stews, creamed dishes, etc.

**To Freeze**—Use young crisp stalks with compact tips. Clean and scale and remove woody portion of the stalk. Wash in cold water. Scald whole stalks for 3 to 4 minutes in boiling water, using 1 gallon of water to each pint of asparagus. Scald cut asparagus for 2 to 3 minutes. Drain and chill quickly in cold running water or ice water. Drain, place in freezer container, allowing ½-inch headspace, and freeze.

## CHEESE-BROILED ASPARAGUS

Put cooked asparagus spears in greased shallow baking dish or pie pan. Sprinkle generously with grated Romano cheese. Put under broiler until heated.

## ASPARAGI ALL' UOVO

- 1 bunch asparagus (2½ pounds)
- 6 tablespoons olive oil
  Salt and pepper
- ⅓ cup grated Parmesan cheese
- 1 garlic clove
- 8 eggs
  Paprika

Cook asparagus in boiling salted water until just tender; drain well. Put whole asparagus spears in shallow baking pan. Pour 3 tablespoons oil over asparagus and sprinkle with salt, pepper, and cheese. Halve garlic and cook slowly in remaining 3 tablespoons oil for about 5 minutes; do not brown. Remove garlic. Put asparagus under broiler and brown lightly under medium heat. While asparagus is browning, drop eggs into oil; cover and cook slowly for 3 minutes. Serve 2 eggs on each portion of asparagus. Sprinkle with paprika. Makes 4 generous servings.

Asparagi All'Uovo

## BREADED ASPARAGUS

Dip cooked asparagus spears in beaten egg. Then roll in fine dry bread crumbs or cracker meal and sauté in butter or margarine until well browned.

## ASPARAGUS CRISPS

1½ pounds fresh asparagus
   Salt
3 tablespoons butter or margarine, melted
1 tablespoon lemon juice

Wash asparagus; cut in wafer-thin diagonal slices, the longer the better. Put in cooking basket or strainer and submerge in boiling salted water 2 minutes. Serve hot or cold with butter and lemon juice, mixed. Makes 4 to 6 servings.

## ASPARAGUS CHINOISE

36 spears asparagus
¼ cup butter or margarine
3 tablespoons soy sauce
⅛ teaspoon salt

Cut the asparagus diagonally in ¼-inch slices. Sauté in the butter until tender, about 6 minutes. About 2 minutes before the asparagus is done, add soy sauce and salt. Makes 6 servings.

## ASPARAGUS AND MUSHROOMS IN CREAM

1 pound fresh asparagus
3 tablespoons salad oil
¼ cup water or mushroom liquid
1 small onion, minced
½ cup (3- or 4-ounce can) sliced mushrooms, drained
½ teaspoon salt
⅛ teaspoon pepper
¼ cup cream

Wash asparagus and slice diagonally into 1½-inch pieces. Put oil and water in large skillet and bring to boil. Add asparagus, onion, mushrooms, salt, and pepper. Cook, covered, for 8 to 10 minutes, shaking skillet occasionally. Add cream. Reheat slightly, but do not boil. Makes 3 to 4 servings.

## BAKED ASPARAGUS WITH ALMOND-CHEESE SAUCE

1½ pounds asparagus
   Salt
¼ cup butter or margarine
½ cup small soft bread cubes
2 tablespoons all-purpose flour
1 cup milk
1 cup shredded sharp Cheddar cheese
½ cup toasted slivered almonds
   Pepper

Wash and trim asparagus and cook in boiling salted water until tender. Drain; arrange in 9-inch piepan or other greased small shallow baking dish. Melt butter in saucepan and add 2 tablespoons to bread cubes, mixing well to coat. Blend flour into remainder. Add milk and cook, stirring, until smooth and thickened. Stir in cheese, almonds, and salt and pepper to taste. Pour over asparagus and sprinkle with bread cubes. Bake in preheated moderate oven (350°F.) about 20 minutes. Makes 4 servings.

## ASPARAGUS VINAIGRETTE

2 pounds asparagus
   Salt
⅛ teaspoon pepper
   Dash of cayenne
¼ teaspoon paprika
3 tablespoons tarragon vinegar
½ cup olive or vegetable oil
1 tablespoon minced green pepper
1 tablespoon chopped sweet pickle
1 tablespoon minced parsley
2 teaspoons chopped chives or green onion
   Lettuce (optional)

Wash and trim asparagus. Cook in boiling salted water until tender. Drain and chill. Mix 1 teaspoon salt and remaining ingredients, except lettuce; chill. When ready to serve, arrange asparagus on serving platter (on lettuce, if desired). Pour remaining ingredients over asparagus or serve separately, if desired. Makes 6 servings.

## ASPARAGUS PIQUANT

⅓ cup soft bread crumbs
2 tablespoons butter or margarine
3 slices bacon, diced
1 small garlic clove
1½ pounds asparagus
   Salt
3 tablespoons wine vinegar

In small skillet, brown crumbs in the butter; set aside. In same skillet, cook bacon with garlic until crisp and browned. At same time, cook asparagus in boiling salted water by any preferred method, drain and put in hot serving dish. Remove garlic from skillet, add vinegar heat and pour over asparagus. Sprinkle with reserved crumbs. Makes 4 servings.

## ASPARAGUS WITH BLUE CHEESE

1½ pounds asparagus
   Salt
⅓ cup crumbled blue cheese
½ cup small croutons
1 tablespoon butter or margarine

Wash and trim asparagus and cook in boiling salted water until tender. Drain thoroughly and put in greased small shallow baking dish or 9-inch piepan. Sprinkle with cheese, then with croutons. Dot with butter and bake in preheated moderate oven (375°F.) about 20 minutes. Makes 4 servings.

## ASPARAGUS CHIFFONADE

1½ pounds asparagus
   Salt
¼ cup well-seasoned French dressing
1 hard-cooked egg, minced
1 pimiento, minced
1 tablespoon minced parsley

Wash and trim asparagus. Cook in boiling salted water until tender. Drain, put in hot serving dish and keep warm. Heat dressing, add remaining ingredients and pour over asparagus. Serve at once. Makes 4 or 5 servings.

## CURRIED ASPARAGUS

  1 pound asparagus
    Salt
⅓ cup butter or margarine
½ cup soft bread crumbs
  3 tablespoons all-purpose flour
½ to 1 teaspoon curry powder
⅛ teaspoon pepper
1½ cups milk
  1 teaspoon instant minced onion

Wash and trim asparagus and cook in boiling salted water until almost tender. Drain and put in greased small shallow baking dish or 9-inch piepan. Melt butter in saucepan. Add 2 tablespoons to crumbs, mix well and set aside. Blend ½ teaspoon salt and next 3 ingredients into remaining butter. Add milk and cook, stirring, until thickened. Add onion, pour over asparagus and sprinkle with the crumbs. Bake in preheated 425°F. oven about 15 minutes. Makes 3 to 4 servings.

## ASPARAGUS WITH LEEKS

  2 pounds asparagus
  2 leeks, cleaned, trimmed and thinly sliced
  1 can (10½ ounces) condensed chicken broth
¼ cup butter or margarine
¼ cup all-purpose flour
½ teaspoon paprika
⅛ teaspoon pepper
¼ cup cream

Wash and trim asparagus and put in saucepan with leeks. Add broth and cook until asparagus is tender. In another saucepan, melt butter and blend in next 3 ingredients. Remove from heat. Drain liquid from vegetables and add to butter mixture. Cook, stirring, until thickened; add cream. Put vegetables in hot serving dish and pour sauce over them. Makes 6 servings.

## ASPARAGUS AND GREEN ONIONS WITH SOUR CREAM

  2 pounds asparagus
    Salt
  2 bunches green onions, cut to length of asparagus
¾ cup dairy sour cream
  1 tablespoon lemon juice
    Freshly ground black pepper to taste

Cook asparagus in boiling salted water by any preferred method. Drain and put on hot platter. Cook onions in boiling salted water 3 to 5 minutes. Arrange on platter with asparagus. Heat remaining ingredients slightly and pour over vegetables. Makes 6 servings.

## ASPARAGUS RATATOUILLE

  1 medium onion, sliced
  2 tablespoons olive or vegetable oil
  1 clove garlic, crushed (optional)
  1 medium green pepper, cut in strips
  1 bay leaf
½ teaspoon salt
¼ teaspoon pepper
  1 can (1 pound) tomatoes
  1 medium zucchini
  1 pound asparagus, cut in ¾ inch pieces
½ cup fresh or frozen peas

Sauté onion lightly in the oil in large skillet. Add next 6 ingredients and simmer, uncovered, 10 minutes. Cut zucchini in half lengthwise, then cut in ¼ inch slices. Add to mixture with remaining ingredients and simmer about 15 minutes. Serve on rice, toast points or pasta. Makes 6 servings.

## ASPARAGUS HAM ROLLS

16 asparagus stalks, cooked
  4 thin slices of boiled ham
½ cup grated sharp Cheddar cheese
  1 cup medium white sauce (2 tablespoons butter, 2 tablespoons flour, 1 cup milk, salt and pepper)
    Toast points

Put 4 asparagus stalks on each ham slice; roll up. Fasten with toothpick. Broil for 5 minutes on each side. Add cheese to heated sauce. Stir until cheese is melted; pour over ham rolls. Broil to golden brown. Garnish with toast. Makes 4 servings.

Asparagus Ham Rolls

## DEVILED ASPARAGUS-CHEESE SANDWICHES

Softened butter or margarine
6 slices firm-type bread
2 cans (4½ ounces each) deviled ham
24 cooked asparagus spears
6 slices process pimiento cheese

Butter one side of each bread slice and arrange slices, buttered side down, on jelly-roll pan. Spread with deviled ham. Top each with 4 asparagus spears and cover with a cheese slice. Bake in preheated moderate oven (400°F.) about 10 minutes. Makes 6 servings.

# SAUCES FOR ASPARAGUS

### HOLLANDAISE

½ cup butter, softened
¼ cup hot water
¼ teaspoon salt
⅛ teaspoon pepper
4 egg yolks, slightly beaten
2 tablespoons lemon juice

Combine butter, hot water, salt, and pepper in top part of double boiler. Blend small amount of butter mixture, about 2 teaspoons, into beaten egg yolks. Gradually beat into remaining butter. Place over hot, not boiling, water. Beat with rotary beater or wire whip until thick and smooth. Blend in lemon juice. If sauce curdles, add 1 teaspoon hot water and blend well. Makes about 1 cup.

### POLONAISE

¼ cup butter
½ cup fresh bread crumbs
1 hard-cooked egg, finely chopped
1 tablespoon chopped parsley

Heat butter; brown bread crumbs. Add hard-cooked egg and heat through. Sprinkle with parsley. Spoon over hot drained cooked asparagus. Makes about ¾ cup.

### SALSA VERDE

3 tablespoons cider vinegar
½ cup olive oil
¾ teaspoon prepared mustard
3 tablespoons mixed finely chopped parsley, raw spinach, and watercress
1 medium onion, minced

Combine all ingredients and blend thoroughly. Makes about ¾ cup sauce.

**Note**—This Italian sauce is also good for other vegetables served cold, for seafood and salads.

# QUICK SAUCES FOR ASAPARAGUS

**Pimiento Butter**—Melt ¼ cup butter; add 1 pimiento, finely chopped, and 1 teaspoon lemon juice.

**Black Butter**—Heat ¼ cup butter until browned. Slowly add juice of ½ lemon and dash of pepper.

**Variations**—Sprinkle hot, buttered asparagus with grated Parmesan or Romano cheese; toasted almonds; capers; crumbled blue cheese; bits of crisp bacon; sautéed, chopped mushrooms; or chopped anchovies or hard-cooked eggs. Or serve asparagus, hot or cold, with French dressing or mayonnaise.

## ASPARAGUS SOUFFLÉ

3 tablespoons butter or margarine
3 tablespoons all-purpose flour
¾ teaspoon salt
⅛ teaspoon pepper
1 cup milk
6 eggs, separated
1 cup (1-inch pieces) drained canned asparagus
1 tablespoon instant minced onion
1 pimiento, chopped

Melt butter and blend in flour, salt, and pepper. Gradually stir in milk and cook, stirring constantly, until thickened. Cool. Beat egg whites until stiff. Then beat yolks until thick and lemon-colored. Stir first mixture gradually into yolks. Fold in whites and asparagus, onion, and pimiento. Pour into greased 2-quart casserole and set in pan of hot water. Bake in preheated moderate oven (350°F.) for 45 minutes, or until tip of knife inserted in center comes out clean. Serve at once. Makes 4 to 6 servings.

Asparagus Soufflé

## ASPARAGUS-CUCUMBER SALAD

1 pound asparagus, cooked and chilled
½ cucumber, peeled, halved lengthwise and thinly sliced
3 green onions, shredded lengthwise in 3-inch strips
1 jar (2 ounces) sliced pimiento, drained
¾ cup French dressing
1 tablespoon chopped green onion

Arrange asparagus in shallow serving dish. Arrange next 3 ingredients on asparagus. Mix dressing and chopped onion and pour over top. Chill 30 minutes. Makes 3 to 4 servings.

## ASPARAGUS-EGG SALAD

1½ pounds fresh asparagus
Salt
Shredded lettuce
6 eggs, hard-cooked
Creamy Dressing

Cook asparagus in boiling salted water by any preferred method. Drain, chill, then arrange on lettuce on platter. Slice eggs and arrange around asparagus. Serve with the Dressing. Makes 4 servings.

### Creamy Dressing

Beat 1 package (3 ounces) softened cream cheese and ¼ cup mayonnaise in electric mixer until blended. Add 1 tablespoon cider vinegar, ½ teaspoon prepared mustard, ¼ teaspoon paprika, dash of cayenne, and salt to taste; mix well. Makes about ⅔ cup.

## ASPARAGUS WITH HERB BUTTER

Cook 1 package (10 ounces) frozen asparagus spears until tender. Cream ¼ cup soft butter, dash each of cayenne and paprika, and a pinch each of dried rosemary and thyme. Blend in juice of ½ lemon. Serve on drained hot asparagus. Makes 2 or 3 servings.

## SESAME ASPARAGUS SALAD

1 package (10 ounces) frozen cut asparagus
1 head romaine, broken in pieces
2 pimientos, diced
1 green onion, chopped
¼ cup sesame seed, toasted
¼ teaspoon cracked pepper
¼ teaspoon herb seasoning
2 tablespoons each lemon juice and salad oil
Salt to taste

Cook, drain, and chill asparagus. Add to next 3 ingredients. Mix with remaining ingredients. Toss with asparagus. Makes 4 servings.

Sesame Asparagus Salad

# ASPIC—By Helen Evans Brown.

A clear, savory, nonsweet jelly used to decorate or to mold entrées, salads, and canapés of meat, fish, poultry, eggs, and the like. The origin of the word is French, meaning "lavender" as well as aspic, the food, and it may well be that the original aspic was a lavender-flavored jelly. In French culinary use, aspic refers not to the jelly, but to the whole decorated dish. The jelly itself is called "gelée."

A crystal-clear shimmering aspic is a beautiful and impressive sight and one that any reasonably careful cook can make as perfectly as a trained chef. Aspics have three uses: the first, and best known, is for making molds in which various meats, poultry, seafoods, or vegetables are encased; a second use is for glazing and decorating previously cooked and chilled foods; the third use is for garnishing, the jelly being either chopped or cut into shapes for decorative purposes. In each case the aspic must be crystal clear, but this is easily accomplished as you'll learn below. Although a quick aspic can be made from canned bouillon, many dedicated cooks will prefer to make it from scratch. You'll have to start the day before you need it, but it's worth the trouble.

**Equipment**—Most kitchens have everything needed for a perfect aspic: a large pot (one with a capacity of 10 quarts), a large strainer or colander, a piece of closely woven cloth (sheeting, a dish towel, or a napkin, somewhat larger than the colander). A long-handled wire whip and a set of tiny cutters (usually called truffle cutters) are optional.

**Ingredients**—For 2 quarts of regular aspic:

    2 pounds beef shank (meat and bones)
    2 pounds veal knuckle (meat and bones)
    1 small stewing hen (or ½ large hen, or 3 pounds
      chicken backs and necks)
    1 calf's foot
    1 gallon cold water
    1 peeled split onion
    4 whole cloves
    1 tablespoon salt
    1 large carrot, sliced
    2 large celery stalks, sliced
    4 sprigs parsley
    1 bay leaf
    ¼ teaspoon black peppercorns, crushed
    1 cup port or Madeira or sherry (optional)
    1 tablespoon minced parsley
    ½ teaspoon each of dried tarragon and basil
    3 egg whites

Tomato Aspic

1. Have meat and chicken chopped into pieces. (If you are able to find a calf's foot, have it skinned and split. The calf's foot is used for its strong gelatin content; plain gelatin may be used instead; see step 6.)

2. Put meats all together in the 10-quart pot and add water, onion, cloves, and salt. Bring slowly to a boil, skimming off the grayish scum as it forms on top.

3. When boiling, add carrot, celery, parsley, bay leaf, and peppercorns. Turn heat down until the stock is simmering slowly, cover and cook for 5 or 6 hours, or until meat has fallen from bones and liquid has reduced one half.

4. Strain stock, discard the vegetables, seasonings, and tasteless meat and bones.

5. Cool the strained stock. Put into the refrigerator overnight.

6. Next day, remove the cake of fat that has formed on top of the jellied stock. If you have used the calf's foot, you should have a stiff enough jelly for any purpose (as stiff as a commercial gelatin dessert). Otherwise you'll have to add plain gelatin. If the jelly is fairly stiff, 1 envelope gelatin softened in ¼ cup cold water should do. Heat the stock and add the softened gelatin, stirring until dissolved. Pour a little in a cup and put in the refrigerator. If it doesn't set stiffly enough, add more gelatin, but you'll soon be able to judge how much. Sometimes the aspic is too stiff, in which case add boiling water, starting with a cupful and testing as above.

7. The next step is to flavor and clear the aspic. Melt the jellied stock. If you are using wine, simmer the wine until it has almost evaporated and add to the stock, along with the parsley, tarragon, and basil.

8. Beat the egg whites slightly, pour into the melted stock and bring the mixture to a boil, stirring constantly, preferably with a wire whip or slotted spoon. When the mixture comes to a boil, it should separate in spots so that you can see the clear liquid.

9. Turn off heat and let settle for a few minutes, then skim the top.

10. Wring the cloth out in cold water and line the colander with it, then strain the stock through it. Don't let the cloth slip, because even a few drops of the unstrained liquid will cloud your masterpiece.

11. Taste and add salt if it's needed.

## CHICKEN ASPIC

Make this the same way as the regular aspic, but use 2 small stewing hens or 6 pounds chicken backs and necks, and omit the beef and veal. If possible, include calf's foot, otherwise you will need to add commercial gelatin. The wine may be omitted or 3 tablespoons of Cognac can be substituted for it.

## FISH ASPIC

Make this the same way as the regular aspic, but use 2 small stewing hens or 6 pounds chicken backs and necks, and omit the beef and veal. If possible, include calf's foot, otherwise you will need to add commercial gelatin. The wine may be omitted or 3 tablespoons of Cognac can be substituted for it.

## TOMATO ASPIC

3½ cups tomato juice
1 celery stalk, cut up
1 onion, chopped
½ lemon, sliced
1 teaspoon ground basil
1 teaspoon sugar
1 teaspoon salt
 Dash of cayenne
2 envelopes unflavored gelatin
¼ cup cider vinegar

Combine tomato juice with vegetables and seasonings. Cover and simmer over low heat for 20 minutes. Strain. Add gelatin softened in vinegar and stir until dissolved. Pour into mold and refrigerate until firm. If vegetables, fish, or meat are to be added, chill until aspic is of the consistency of unbeaten egg white; fold in vegetables, fish, or meat and pour into a lightly oiled mold. Chill until firm. Makes 6 servings.

## QUICK ASPIC

Soften 1 envelope plain gelatin in ¼ cup cold water. Heat the contents of 2 cans (10 ounces each) condensed beef bouillon or consommé and add the gelatin, 2 tablespoons port, sherry, or Madeira (optional) and the slightly beaten white of 1 egg. Proceed as for regular aspic.
**To Decorate and Fill Aspic molds—**
1. Pimientos, hard-cooked-egg whites, green peppers, black truffles or ripe olives, carrots, or any colorful food can be used for decoration. Slice them as thin as possible, then cut into fancy shapes with truffle cutters, or into squares, diamonds, or julienne pieces with a sharp knife. Thinly sliced stuffed olives or hard-cooked eggs, chives, or leaves of fresh tarragon can also be used.
2. Measure mold you are using and have corresponding amount of aspic, or less if large pieces of meats or other foods are to be jellied.

3. Cool melted aspic until it has the consistency of raw egg white by putting the bowl of aspic in a pan of ice and stirring with a metal spoon until the aspic reaches the proper consistency.

4. Have decorations ready and mold well chilled. If you want decorations on the sides as well as the bottom of the mold, have ready a pan larger than the mold, filled with cracked ice. Pour a small amount of the aspic in the ice-cold mold; and tip and turn the mold so that the aspic glazes the entire inside. Put at once in the pan of ice. (If you wish to decorate only the bottom of the mold, as in a loaf pan, pour a thin layer in the mold, then refrigerate until set.) If you want a thicker coating of aspic, repeat this process.

5. Dip decorations in the syrupy aspic and arrange in the desired design on the sides and bottom of the mold. They will stick in place if the mold is cold enough. Return to ice to set, then add another layer of aspic by again pouring in a small amount and turning until the decorations are covered. Again return to ice.

6. When set, add chicken, fish, tongue, shellfish or vegetables, either sliced or cut into pieces, and fill to the top of the mold with the remaining aspic. Put in the refrigerator until completely set before unmolding.

**To Unmold Aspic**—Loosen the aspic by pressing gently all around the edge of the mold or by running a small pointed knife around the inside. Dip the mold into warm water, making sure that none spills over the edge. Do this quickly; it should not stand in the water. Put a plate over the top of the mold and reverse the mold quickly. Hold both plate and mold with both hands, on the table, and slide and shake mold back and forth a couple of times. Lift mold off carefully. (If aspic doesn't unmold, repeat process.)

**To Serve Aspics in the Mold**—This is an easier version of aspic, since food is served from the dish or dishes in which it is molded. It's often used for eggs in aspic, for instance. Arrange the cold food in an attractive serving dish or, in the case of eggs *mollet*, in individual oval-shaped dishes. Cover the food with aspic and allow to set, then decorate as above. When decorations have set, pour another thin film of aspic over them and allow to set before serving in the dish.

**To Glaze Food with Aspic**—The food to be glazed with aspic should be cooked and very cold. Favorite foods for coating are breast of chicken, neatly trimmed, whole trout with the skin removed between head and tail, pieces of salmon steak, trimmed poached eggs, eggs *mollet* (cooked 5 minutes, then cooled and shelled immediately), decorative canapés, or even a whole salmon or chicken. Arrange food on a cake rack placed over a cookie sheet. Chill thoroughly. Have aspic at the raw-egg-white consistency as above. Spoon aspic over the food, using the side of a large metal spoon. (The excess will drop onto the pan and can be used again.) Chill, decorate as for molds, chill again, then add one more layer of aspic. When set, arrange on a cold platter and garnish with greens or with cut or chopped aspic.

**To Garnish with Aspic**—Pour ½ inch of aspic into a baking pan (an 8- x 8-inch glass one is good) and allow to set. Using small cookie cutters, cut into shapes and use as a garnish, or turn out on a board covered with wax paper and chop the aspic into glittering pieces, then pile around the food on the platter. If you have chopped more than you need, slide aspic from paper into pan, melt and reset.

**Jellied Soups**—If you want a particularly delicious jellied meat, fish, or chicken consommé, make any of the aspics as above, but add enough boiling water so that the aspic sets into a quivering jelly, one not quite as stiff as the usual canned jellied soups. Garnish with a slice of lemon, or with minced chives, or sour cream and red caviar, or with chopped fresh herbs.

## EGGS IN ASPIC À LA FRANÇAISE

1 envelope unflavored gelatin
2 cups well-seasoned chicken bouillon
1 teaspoon instant minced onion
½ teaspoon monosodium glutamate
4 hard-cooked eggs, halved lengthwise
2 pimientos, cut into strips
  Chopped parsley and chives
  Salad greens
  Mayonnaise

Soften gelatin in ½ cup of bouillon for 5 minutes. Dissolve gelatin while stirring over hot water or low heat. Add to remaining bouillon with onion and monosodium glutamate. Pour half into an oiled pan (10 x 6 x 2 inches). Chill until firm. Chill remaining half until thickened to the consistency of unbeaten egg whites. Arrange eggs, cut side down, on firm mixture. Make a cross of pimiento on each. Sprinkle with herbs. Spoon remaining thickened mixture over eggs. Chill until firm. Cut into squares and serve on greens on individual plates with mayonnaise. Makes 4 servings.

## JELLIED TONGUE RING

1 envelope unflavored gelatin
¼ cup cold tongue stock
1 beef bouillon cube
1½ cups hot tongue stock
¼ cup cider vinegar
1 tablespoon sugar
½ teaspoon Worcestershire
¼ cup chopped sweet pickle
¼ cup chopped green pepper
½ cup chopped celery
2 hard-cooked eggs, sliced
1¼ cups cold diced tongue

Sprinkle gelatin over cold stock. Let stand for 5 minutes. Dissolve bouillon cube in hot tongue stock. Add gelatin and stir until dissolved. Add vinegar, sugar, and Worcestershire. Chill until jelled to the consistency of unbeaten egg whites. Fold in remaining ingredients. Pour into a lightly oiled 5-cup mold. Chill until firm. Unmold on salad greens. If desired, serve with dairy sour cream or mayonnaise, seasoned with prepared mustard. Makes 4 servings.

**Note:** Make this the day before you plan to serve it.

**ATTELET**—This French word is derived from the Latin *hasta*, meaning "rod." An *attelet* is a kitchen accessory in the shape of a long pin or a little skewer, with a top in the shape of an ornament that might be an eagle, a flower, a harp, a design of scrolls, or arabesques, etc. *Attelets* are used only for decorating hot or cold dishes in the elaborate grand manner which is becoming rarer and rarer. To do so, bits of food such as truffles, shrimps, cocks' combs, or olives are threaded on the *attelets*, and sometimes separated by paper ruffles for greater effect. The *attelets* are then stuck into other foods or around them, giving the effect of a crown.

**AU (plural, aux)**—A French word which means in culinary usage "with," and is used in naming dishes. It is usually followed by an ingredient of the dish, as in *au gratin*, with cheese; *au lait*, with milk; *aux marrons*, with chestnuts; roast beef *au jus*, with natural gravy.

**AU GRATIN**—A cooking process done in a hot oven or under the broiler which produces dishes with a crisp, golden-brown crust. This is achieved by sprinkling the food with fresh or toasted bread crumbs, or with grated cheese especially Parmesan, sprinkled with melted butter. But *au gratin* also applies to dishes that will crust of their own accord.

Foods to be finished *au gratin* may be raw or cooked, and they may or may not be blended with a sauce. The most frequently used sauce in foods served *au gratin* is white sauce.

To make a dish *au gratin* is to add taste, texture, and eye appeal, since the bubbly golden surface looks tempting. It is also an excellent way of utilizing leftovers of meat, fish, vegetables, cereals, and other foods, either singly or in combinations.

To gratin a dish, sprinkle top of food with 1 to 2 cups plain or buttered coarse bread crumbs, or with ¼ to ¾ cup grated cheese, depending on quantity of food. Drizzle with a little melted butter. Brown under a preheated broiler, or bake uncovered in a preheated moderate oven (375°F.) until food is heated through and golden brown on top. If necessary to prevent overcooking, raise oven temperature to hot (400° to 425°F.) for 3 to 6 minutes, or until slightly browned.

## FISH FILLETS AU GRATIN

1 pound fish fillets
⅔ cup canned condensed soup such as celery, mushroom, or asparagus
2 tablespoons milk
1 cup coarse bread crumbs or ¼ cup grated cheese
2 tablespoons melted butter

Arrange fish fillets in buttered baking dish. Combine soup and milk and heat. Pour over fish. Sprinkle with bread crumbs. Drizzle with melted butter. Bake, uncovered, in preheated moderate oven (375°F.) for 10 to 15 minutes, or until golden on top. Makes 2 to 3 servings.

## ARTICHOKE HEARTS AU GRATIN

2 packages (9 ounces each) frozen artichoke hearts
¼ cup butter or margarine
¾ teaspoon salt
Dash of pepper
1 teaspoon onion salt
¼ teaspoon dry mustard
⅓ cup all-purpose flour
1½ cups milk
1 egg, slightly beaten
½ cup grated Swiss cheese
1 tablespoon fine dry bread crumbs
Paprika

Cook artichokes as directed on package. Drain; reserve ½ cup liquid. Melt butter in saucepan. Stir in seasonings and flour. Gradually stir in artichoke liquid and milk. Cook over low heat, stirring constantly, until thickened. Remove from heat. Stir hot sauce gradually into egg and half of cheese. Blend well. Put artichokes in a layer in greased shallow baking dish. Cover with sauce. Sprinkle with remaining cheese, crumbs, and paprika. Bake in preheated very hot oven (450°F.) about 15 minutes. Makes 6 servings.

## ASPARAGUS AU GRATIN

1½ pounds asparagus, trimmed and cooked, reserve ½ cup liquid
3 tablespoons butter or margarine
2 tablespoons all-purpose flour
½ cup asparagus cooking water
¼ cup heavy cream
Salt and pepper
¼ cup grated Parmesan cheese
2 tablespoons fine dry bread crumbs

Arrange asparagus in greased small shallow broiler-proof baking dish. Melt butter in small saucepan and blend in flour. Add reserved liquid and cream. Cook, stirring, until thickened. Season to taste with salt and pepper and pour over asparagus. Sprinkle with cheese, then with crumbs. Put under broiler about 8 inches from heat and watch closely until golden brown. Makes 4 servings.

**AU JUS**—A French term that describes meat served with its own natural juices, not with a gravy.

**AU LAIT**—A French term that describes a beverage, such as coffee, made or served with milk.

**AU NATUREL**—In culinary French, this term describes food prepared or cooked to resemble its natural state as much as possible, or in other words, food plainly done.

# AUSTRIAN COOKERY

What makes Austrian food different from that of Central European countries is its variety and liveliness. Austrian cooking has been influenced by the cooking of neighboring countries, some of which were once part of the Austrian Empire. They contributed dishes, seasonings, and ways of cooking to this charming country of luminous mountains, cool rivers and lakes, and picture-book towns.

From Hungary came the paprika dishes, and from Germany all kinds of dumplings. Italy sent pasta, tomato cookery, and the ubiquitous schnitzel, which started out as a Milanese veal cutlet. Serbia, Croatia, Bulgaria, and the rest of the Balkans contributed mutton, rice, vegetables, spices. To Poland, we trace an affection for sour cream, carp, and pike; to Czechoslovakia, fondness for goose, smoked pork, and noble yeast pastries. To the Turks, who besieged Vienna twice, goes the credit for Austria's heavenly coffee which is served in the country's innumerable coffeehouses in a dozen shades that range from black to white, each with its own name. Whatever the dish, in Austria's kitchens it became smoothed over, refined, expanded, richer, and generally improved to assume an expansive character of its own which is uniquely Austrian.

In Austria, women were rated on their ability to cook, and although no Austrian ever closed his eyes at the sight of a pretty face or a trim ankle, these were not first considerations in the choice of a lifetime mate. Or, as the Austrian writer Adolf Glassbrenner has said: "Do not believe to be already in paradise when you see an apple tree."

From Austrian kitchens came the nourishing soups that are a cornerstone of all Austrian eating. The women were thrifty, making much of dumplings, pancakes, and cereal puddings, both savory and sweet. They cooked pot roasts slowly, almost in their own juices to bring out every smidgen of the meat's flavor. They were canny, combining vegetables, putting them into soufflés to make them more interesting. They were imaginative, devising dozens of ways to cook cabbage and potatoes.

When it came to desserts and cakes, Austrian women were temptresses out to capture kings. It would take a major poet to do justice to the infinite variety of Austrian torten rich with nuts, caramel, and chocolate, redolent with rum, and gussied up with billows of whipped cream reminiscent of the frills on imperial ball gowns. The most elaborate of these are served for dessert. And, if for nothing else, Austrian cooks must be praised for having introduced the use of a tart jam, such as red currant or apricot, as a filling for cakes, to provide an unexpected and delicious flavor contrast.

The Austrians not only eat well, they also eat often. The day begins with coffee and milk and the rolls that we know and love as "Vienna rolls." To sustain life until lunch, which is really dinner and the main meal of the day, a Gabelfrühstück, fork breakfast, takes place in the middle of the morning in a restaurant or coffeehouse.

Kleinigkeiten, that is, trifles, are served here—such as a small plate of goulash, or a sausage, or an egg dish, for, as the Austrians say, it is not healthy to come to the lunch table with an empty stomach.

The big meal is soup, meat, vegetables and potatoes, and dessert. Much entertaining is done at the midday main meal, which might then be increased to include a fish from the Danube or the much-prized venison of the Austrian Alps. Then comes the Jause, pronounced "yow-zeh," a gossipy interlude in the late afternoon, over coffee and two or three devastatingly tempting cakes, with whipped cream on the side. Supper is light, and it might be a soup, an omelet, or dumplings sweet or savory, with a salad or a compote. And if one feels weak during the day or night, there are sausage stands with very good sausages on crisp rolls with a dollop of spicy mustard!

So much excellent and rather rich food as well as the joyous Austrian wines have had the sunniest influence on the Austrian character. They infused it with a warmth, a charm, and a wit that found its expression in Johann Strauss' waltzes. The food, like the music, can be enjoyed in any country.

## GERSTENSUPPE [Barley Soup]

    3 tablespoons butter or margarine
    ½ cup medium barley
    1 celery stalk, minced
    1 medium onion, minced
    1 tablespoon flour
    6 cups hot vegetable or chicken broth
      Salt and pepper
    ½ cup heavy cream

Heat butter in heavy saucepan. Sauté barley, celery, and onion in it. Sprinkle with flour. Gradually stir in hot broth. Season with salt and pepper. Simmer, covered, for about 1 hour, stirring occasionally, until barley is very tender. Remove from heat and add cream. Makes 4 to 6 servings. **Note:** This soup can be prepared in advance without the addition of the cream. At serving time, add cream.

## KÜCHERLKRAUT [Beef and Sauerkraut]

    4 to 5 pounds short ribs of beef, cut into cubes
    2 pounds fresh sauerkraut
    1½ teaspoons salt
    4 large onions, sliced
    ½ cup lard or shortening
    ⅓ cup all-purpose flour

In a Dutch oven combine meat cubes, sauerkraut, salt and 1 onion, sliced. Mix well. Add enough hot water to make ¾ inch of water in pan. Cover and cook over low heat for 2 hours. When meat is almost done, melt lard in a saucepan and brown remaining 2 sliced onions lightly. Add flour and brown well over low heat. Drain liquid from meat and gradually stir into flour mixture. Cook, stirring constantly, over low heat until thick and smooth. Add sauce to meat and sauerkraut. Blend well. Cook, covered, for 30 minutes longer, stirring occasionally to prevent scorching. Serve with mashed potatoes or noodles. Makes 8 servings.

## PICHELSTEINER FLEISCH
### [Pichelsteiner Casserole]

1 pound beef stew meat, cut into ¾-inch cubes
1 pound veal stew meat, cut into ¾-inch cubes
1 pound lean pork stew meat, cut into ¾-inch cubes
1 teaspoon salt
1 medium leek, white and green, cut into pieces
8 celery stalks, no leaves, cut into pieces
8 large raw potatoes, peeled and cubed
2 large onions, chopped
4 large carrots, diced
1 parsnip, diced
6 parsley sprigs, chopped
½ cup butter or margarine

Mix all meat cubes and sprinkle them with salt. Combine vegetables. In a casserole with tight-fitting lid, or a Dutch oven, spread a thin layer of vegetables, then a layer of meat. Dot each layer with butter. Continue in this way until all ingredients are used. Cover and bake in a preheated moderate oven (350°F.) for about 2 hours. Shake the pot often but do not remove the cover. Makes 8 servings.

## PARMESANSCHLEGEL
### [Leg of Veal with Cheese]

½ pound sharp Cheddar or Parmesan cheese, in one piece
One 4- to 5-pound boneless roast of veal
1 teaspoon salt
½ cup melted butter
¼ cup water or dry white wine

Cut cheese into strips 2 inches long and the thickness of a pencil. Punch holes in meat with a thick knitting needle or a knife. Push cheese into these holes. Sprinkle meat with salt. Place roast on rack in roasting pan, and pour melted butter and water over it. Roast in preheated slow oven (325°F.) for about 2 hours, or until meat thermometer registers 170°F. Baste frequently with pan juices. If necessary, add a little more butter and water, about ¼ cup each. Slice and serve hot with potatoes and a green vegetable, or cold with a tossed green or vegetable salad. Makes 6 servings.

**Note:** In Austria they use Parmesan, but a sharp Cheddar gives excellent results. The cheese will melt during the roasting.

## KALBSGULASCH [Veal Goulash]

2 pounds boneless veal, cut into 1½-inch squares
Salt and pepper
¼ cup butter or margarine
2 medium onions, sliced
2 large tomatoes, peeled and quartered
1½ tablespoons all-purpose flour
⅔ cup dry white wine or beef bouillon
2 teaspoons caraway seeds
2 teaspoons paprika
Juice of ½ lemon
¼ cup hot beef bouillon

Trim all fat and gristle from meat. Season with salt and pepper. Heat butter and brown meat in it, but only lightly. Add onions and tomatoes. Cook, uncovered, stirring constantly, until pan juices have cooked down. Sprinkle flour over meat and brown for 1 minute. Add wine, caraway seeds, paprika, lemon juice, and hot bouillon. Simmer, covered, for 45 minutes to 1 hour, or until meat is tender. Check at intervals; if too dry, add a little more hot bouillon. Serve with buttered rice or noodles. Makes 4 servings.

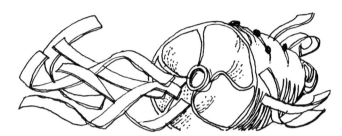

## SCHINKENFLECKERLN
### [Noodles with Ham]

⅓ cup butter or margarine
1 medium onion, minced
3 cups cubed, cooked ham
4 cups (8 ounces) medium egg noodles, cooked
½ teaspoon salt
¼ teaspoon pepper
1 teaspoon caraway seeds

Heat butter or margarine in large skillet. Sauté onion in it until soft and golden. Add ham and cook over low heat for 10 minutes, stirring occasionally. Add remaining ingredients and toss together. Cook for 5 minutes, or until thoroughly heated through, stirring frequently. Makes 4 servings.

**Note:** The Austrians use noodles in the shape of little squares for this dish. If you wish to be completely authentic, you can break your raw noodles into ¾-inch pieces, then cook them until tender.

## BACKHENDL [Fried Chicken]

2 broiling chickens (2½ to 3 pounds each), quartered
Seasoned all-purpose flour
2 eggs, beaten
2 tablespoons water
Fine dry bread crumbs
Fat or lard for frying

Wash chickens and pat dry. Tuck wing tips back under second wing joint. With sharp knife cut leg tendon at the joint of drumstick and thigh. Dip pieces into seasoned flour, then into eggs beaten with water. Roll in bread crumbs. Fry in 3 inches of fat heated to 375°F. for 15 to 20 minutes. When chicken is browned on one side, turn and brown on the other side. Use tongs or a pancake turner to turn chicken, to keep from piercing skin. Place cooked chicken pieces on absorbent paper and put in preheated very slow oven (250°F.) to keep warm. Dip liver, gizzard, and heart into flour, egg mixture, and bread crumbs. Fry until brown. Serve with green salad, stewed fruit, or green peas. Makes 6 servings.

## KOPFSALAT MIT ERBSEN
### Romaine Lettuce with Peas

1 large head romaine lettuce, coarsely shredded
1 package (10-ounce) frozen peas
¼ cup chopped parsley
2 teaspoons sugar
1 teaspoon salt
1 cup water
1 small onion, minced
2 tablespoons butter
2 tablespoons flour
   Salt and pepper

Combine lettuce, peas, parsley, sugar, salt, and water. Cook over low heat until peas are just tender. Drain; reserve vegetables and 1 cup of the liquid. Sauté onion in butter until soft. Sprinkle onion with flour. Stir in reserved vegetable liquid. Blend thoroughly to prevent flour from lumping. Add drained vegetables. Season to taste with salt and pepper. Simmer, covered, until thoroughly heated, 3 to 5 minutes. Makes 4 generous servings.

## GURKENSALAT
### Cucumber Salad

3 medium cucumbers
1 large sweet onion
   Salt
   Ice water
¼ cup salad oil
¼ cup cider vinegar
1 cup dairy sour cream
   Pepper
   Chopped parsley
   Paprika

Peel cucumbers. Score with a fork. Thinly slice cucumbers and onion. Arrange alternate layers of cucumber and onion in a bowl, sprinkling each layer heavily with salt. Cover with ice water. Refrigerate for several hours. Drain and wash with running water. Drain well. Blend oil with vinegar. Pour mixture over cucumbers and onion, and marinate for several hours. Drain. Stir in sour cream and pepper to taste. Top with parsley and paprika. Prepare several hours ahead of serving. Makes 6 to 8 servings.

## KAISERSCHMARRN
### The Emperor's Omelet

4 eggs, separated
2 tablespoons sugar
1 cup sifted all-purpose flour
⅛ teaspoon salt
2 cups milk
2 tablespoons raisins
2 tablespoons butter

Beat egg yolks with sugar until light and pale. Combine flour and salt. Add to egg mixture alternately with milk, beating well after each addition. The batter should be smooth. Add raisins. Beat egg whites until stiff and gently fold into batter. Butter two 8-inch skillets with 1 tablespoon butter each. Heat. Pour half the mixture into one skillet. When one side is brown, turn pancake into second heated skillet. Repeat for second half of batter. Cook pancake until brown on both sides. Shred coarsely with 2 forks. Serve warm, with additional sugar and a sprinkling of cinnamon, or a fruit compote. Makes 6 servings.

**Note:** A cross between a pancake and an omelet. Easy to make because it is shredded.

## SALZBURGER NOCKERLN
### Dessert Puffs

¼ cup butter or margarine
4 egg yolks
¼ cup all-purpose flour
⅛ teaspoon salt
4 egg whites
1 cup milk
1 teaspoon vanilla extract
1 teaspoon granulated sugar
   Confectioners' sugar

Cream butter until fluffy. Gradually beat in egg yolks. Beat in flour and salt. Beat egg whites until stiff but not dry. Fold egg whites into mixture. In a 9-inch iron skillet, mix milk, vanilla and granulated sugar, heat to a boil. Remove from heat, stir egg mixture into milk. Bake in preheated moderate oven (350°F.) until golden brown, about 15 to 20 minutes. Cut into wedges, lift out in pieces with a pancake turner or spatula. Sprinkle with confectioners' sugar. Serve at once. Makes 6 servings.

## KANARI MILCH
### Canary's Milk

1 egg yolk
1 cup milk
¼ cup sugar
   One 1-inch piece vanilla bean or ½ teaspoon vanilla extract

Combine egg yolk, milk, sugar, and vanilla bean in top part of double boiler. Over hot, not boiling, water beat together until mixture rises slightly and is quite foamy. Remove vanilla bean before serving. Or, add vanilla extract. Serve hot or cold on strudels, apple desserts, pancakes, etc. Makes 3 to 4 servings.

## WIENER EISKAFFEE
## [Viennese Iced Coffee]

1 scoop rich vanilla ice cream, softened
1 cup cold strong black coffee
Whipped cream
Powdered sugar

Place ice cream in parfait glass. Pour coffee over it. Top with whipped cream and sprinkle with sugar. Stir as you drink. Makes 1 serving.

## KUGELHUPF
## [Coffee Cake]

½ cup water*
2 packages dry yeast or 2 cakes compressed yeast
4 cups sifted all-purpose flour
1 cup butter or margarine
1 cup granulated sugar
½ teaspoon salt
Grated rind of 1 lemon
4 eggs
¼ cup blanched almonds
½ cup each of diced citron, golden raisins, and dry currants
Confectioners' sugar

*Use very warm water (105°F. to 115°F.) for dry yeast; use lukewarm (80°F. to 90°F.) for compressed. Sprinkle dry yeast or crumble cake into water. Let stand for a few minutes; then stir until dissolved. Add 1½ cups of sifted flour; beat until smooth. This is a sponge. Cover and let rise in warm place for 1 hour.

In an electric mixer, cream butter and beat in sugar; add salt and grated lemon rind. Add eggs, one at a time, beating well after each addition. Add sponge and remaining 2½ cups flour. Beat for 10 minutes. Butter a 9-inch Turk's-head pan (a fluted pan with tube), and decorate bottom and sides with blanched almond halves. Pour in half the dough; sprinkle over the citron, raisins, and currants; cover with remaining dough; this should half fill the pan. Cover and let rise in warm place until dough just reaches top of pan. Cake will be coarse and dry if allowed to rise too long. Bake in preheated moderate oven (350°F.) for 45 to 55 minutes. Cool in pan for 5 minutes, then carefully remove to cake rack. Serve sprinkled with confectioners' sugar. Makes 6 to 8 servings.

## DOBOSTORTE
## Hungarian Seven-Layer Cake

6 eggs, separated
¾ cup sugar
1 cup sifted all-purpose flour

Beat egg yolks with electric beater until very thick. Gradually add sugar, beating well after each addition. Eggs should be beaten for about 8 to 10 minutes altogether. Sift flour over batter and fold in. Then fold in egg whites, beaten until stiff but not dry. Spread as evenly as possible a few tablespoons in each of two or three 8-inch layer-cake pans, greased and lined on the bottom with wax paper. Batter should reach edge of pan evenly. Bake on lower rack of preheated moderate oven (350°F.) for 8 to 10 minutes, or until golden. Cool for about 3 minutes before removing from pans. Cool completely on rack. Peel off paper. Repeat baking process until 7 layers are made.

### Chocolate Filling

1½ cups semisweet chocolate pieces
⅓ cup coffee
⅓ cup sugar
6 egg yolks
¾ cup butter, cut into small pieces and softened to room temperature

Melt chocolate pieces, coffee, and sugar together in top part of double boiler over hot water. Stir until completely smooth. Remove from heat. Beat in egg yolks, one at a time. Return to heat and cook until thickened. Cool to lukewarm. Beat butter into chocolate mixture until blended and satiny. Cool to spreading consistency.

### Caramel Topping

Melt ¾ cup sugar in a skillet, stirring until caramel is smooth and brown. Put 1 layer of cake over inverted 8-inch layer-cake pan and pour boiling caramel syrup over it. Immediately, before caramel hardens, mark with long buttered knife into 12 wedges. Trim excess caramel from edges of cake.

**To assemble**—Spread layers (except caramel-topped layer) with chocolate filling and stack. Use about half of filling. Place caramel layer on top. Frost sides of cake with remaining filling. Sprinkle with one cup shredded filberts.

**To serve**—Place knife over previously marked lines and tap gently with another knife to crack caramel. Makes 12 servings.

## NUSSKIPFERLIN
## [Nut Crescents]

1 cup finely ground walnuts or pecans
1 cup butter (must be butter)
¾ cup sugar
2½ cups sifted all-purpose flour
1½ teaspoons vanilla extract
Vanilla Sugar

Combine all ingredients, and with the fingers work quickly to a smooth dough. Shape 1 teaspoon of dough at a time into small crescents, about 1½ inches long. Bake on ungreased cookie sheets in preheated moderate oven (350°F.) until slightly browned, about 15 to 17 minutes. Cool for 1 minute. While still warm, roll cookies in Vanilla Sugar. Cool completely and roll again in Vanilla Sugar. Makes about 70.

### Vanilla Sugar

Break 2 to 3 vanilla beans into inch-long pieces. Place in a jar with 1 pound sifted confectioners' sugar. Let stand for 3 days. The longer the sugar stands, the more fragrant it becomes.

# THE SAVORY SCHNITZELS OF AUSTRIA

**by MARCIA COLMAN MORTON**

Ask an Austrian what his country's proudest exports are, and he'll answer "The waltz, Freud, and schnitzel." But if it's an American he's talking to, chances are he'll only get two nods out of three: Yes, even our dancing teenagers call for *The Blue Danube* at their proms, and every three-year-old knows he must relate to the group, but schnitzel? Let's see. Isn't that some kind of breaded meat?

This is not only slander, it's a self-deprivation. Not to know the rich range of schnitzelkind: the delectably creamed *Champignon Schnitzel,* the hot savor of a *Paprika Schnitzel!*

The very sound of the word, schnitzel, is chewy, mouth-watering. Literally it means "little cut" of meat, like the English cutlet. But in Austria if you want a slice of, say, pork, you must specify *Schweinsschnitzel.* Schnitzel, without a prefix, always means veal: veal chosen with care, pounded into tenderness, dipped into the just-right this, fried or sautéed with the just-right that, done to a golden brown. And not merely breaded! A schnitzel can be smothered in vegetables, covered with melted cheese, simmered with curry. Each is a different dish, yet all have

in common the gusto of Austrian cooking and the fine toothsomeness of veal.

*Wiener Schnitzel,* the runaway national favorite, is named for Vienna (spelled *Wien* in German). But you can bet your *schillings* that wherever the Austrian flag flies, beneath it a *Wiener Schnitzel* is sending up redolent fumes. Rules amounting to a mystique surround the dish. It must be deep-fried, not in oil, not in lard, but in a mixture of the two for a perfect taste and texture. Ideally it's eaten in a portion large enough to overlap your plate, with a side dish of mealy boiled potatoes and a salad of peeled translucent-thin cucumber slices marinated in equal parts of water, vinegar, and olive oil with plenty of salt and pepper. For some reason the mystique forbids eating hot vegetables, except potatoes, with a *Wiener Schnitzel.*

Because the breading is so important, a *Wiener Schnitzel* must be eaten immediately, out of the frying pan, onto your plate, no warming over, or the succulent coat of crumbs will be hard and tasteless. Even in the humblest Austrian restaurant the menu is divided into Freshly Made and Ready dishes, and the *Wiener Schnitzel* is always in the first list.

## WIENER SCHNITZEL

To prepare the meat for this and every other schnitzel: Choose mild-fed veal, top quality, fine grained, and a soft bright pink in color. Use ¼-inch slices from the center of the rump, allowing approximately a 4-ounce slice per person. Trim all fat. Pound each slice as thin as possible (about ⅛ inch), or have the butcher do it for you. Make small vertical cuts all around the edges of the veal. Salt each veal slice. Dip first into a soup plate containing flour, and shake off excess; next into a soup plate of beaten egg (one egg will cover two 4-ounce slices, or you can stretch by beating egg with a little milk); finally into a soup plate containing fine, dry bread crumbs, pressing crumbs well in with the palm of your hand, then shaking off excess. Fry for 2 or 3 minutes on each side in deep fat, half olive oil, half melted lard, so hot that it smokes, (380-390°F. on a frying thermometer). Heat is right when the breading ripples golden brown. You'll know your skillet as it fries; you'll know your schnitzel is done and tender when a fork goes right through the meat. Drain. Serve garnished with lemon wedges.

Austria is a nation of sports lovers who breathe happiest in the appetite-whetting mountain air that tingles through two-thirds of their country. Every Saturday, spring and fall, half the citizens get our their alpenstocks and knapsacks and head for the nearest hiking trail. At night they want to eat! Summer means Carinthia, the southern province barely discovered yet by Americans, whose two hundred mountain-ringed lakes are filled with sailing, swimming, water-skiing Austrians working up to a hearty lunch. In winter everyone heads for an Alpine ski town to swoop his days away and sit down to deservedly bountiful meals.

In a country where people get so hungry, eating is serious. Nobody blinks an eye at the hiker or skier who starts lunch with a brimming bowl of thick pea soup laced with frankfurter chunks; who goes on to a plump little trout; who has as a main dish a *Cordon Bleu;* and who finishes with a sigh and *Zwetschknödel,* the fist-sized potato-dough dumpling, stuffed with a whole plum, crusted with sugared buttered bread crumbs! To take only one course (and that's all you *can* take if you haven't just scaled a mountain peak), the *Cordon Bleu* is the only other breaded schnitzel.

## CORDON BLEU

Salt each veal slice. Over veal, lay a boiled ham slice large enough to cover. Over ham, lay a Swiss cheese slice large enough to cover. Double the whole thing over, and fasten with wooden toothpicks. Dip in flour, beaten egg, bread crumbs, exactly as with *Wiener Schnitzel* (above). Fry for 2 to 3 minutes on each side in smoking hot deep fat, half olive oil and half melted lard (385° to 390° on a frying thermometer) or until golden brown. Drain, remove toothpicks. Serve with buttered peas or green beans.

Schnitzels can be light, too. In the city of Salzburg they often have to be. Every July and August, when the Salzburg Music Festival turns the lovely baroque town into a giant Mozartean music box, the calorie-counting international set crowds in for *Everyman* acted against a cathedral façade, and for chamber music played in old palaces. And Salzburg restaurants feature the *Pariser Schnitzel* (named for the French capital), lighter than the *Wiener* and easier on the waistline. To heighten the *Pariser Schnitzel's* diet-worthiness, you can go so far as to skip the everloving Austrian potatoes, and hold yourself to a salad of sliced tomatoes and chopped onions in the salted, peppered marinade of vinegar, oil, and water.

## PARISER SCHNITZEL

Salt each veal slice. Dip only in flour, then in beaten egg. Deep-fry in smoking-hot half olive oil, half melted lard, for 2 to 3 minutes on each side, or until golden brown. (385°-390°F. on a frying thermometer) Drain and serve.

If you want to make a real gesture of abstention, there's the still sparer *Natur* ("natural," in other words, untampered with) *Schnitzel.* Since this leaves out the egg as well as the bread crumbs, the veal with its subtle texture and flavor has no batter to absorb the robust oil and lard. So a *Natur Schnitzel* is sautéed delicately in purest butter.

## NATUR SCHNITZEL

Salt, and pepper just a little, each veal slice. Dip one side only into flour; shake off excess. Sauté in butter, floured side first, for 2 to 3 minutes on each side, or until golden brown. Serve floured side up (for its attractive color). Pour the butter gravy from skillet over schnitzel. Serve with shredded endive in oil-water-vinegar.

The *Natur Schnitzel* is so dainty a tidbit by Austrian standards that it's the standard dish for convalescents. Diners in the bloom of health add an anchovy here, a peach there, and feast on the sumptuous *Schnitzel à la Holstein,* named for a north German province, but undoubtedly invented there by an itinerant Austrian.

## SCHNITZEL À LA HOLSTEIN

Prepare *Natur Schnitzel* as above. Garnish with an egg fried in butter. Crisscross egg with flat anchovies. Around egg, sprinkle capers and chopped onions. For still more elaborate effect, add caviar, sardines, strips of smoked salmon. Garnish with wedges of lemon and cucumber. Serve flanked by a bowl of tossed salad and a bowl of stewed fruit (peaches, apricots, plums).

Lying between Germany and Italy, Austria (the Austrians like to say) is a happy blend of the two. Solid comfort they get from the North. The lilt in life wafts up from the South. In Tirol provinces, for example, the towns of Innsbruck and Lienz run day buses across the border to, respectively, Cortina and Venice. In their wake the buses leave such Latin touches as tapered-cut ski trousers, espresso coffee bars, and Neapolitan records for Tirolean jukeboxes. Lienz restaurants serve the homey lentil and bean soups of Austria, and the tangy Italian cheese soups as well, the *pavese* and the egg-flecked *stracciatella.* And the schnitzel you get is often Latinized into a *piccata.*

## SCHNITZEL PICCATA

Salt each veal slice. Dip first into flour, shaking off excess; next into egg beaten with grated Parmesan cheese (1 egg to 1 teaspoon cheese). Deep-fry in smoking-hot half olive oil, half melted lard, for 2 to 3 minutes on each side, or until golden brown (380°-390°F. on a frying thermometer). Serve with rice and a salad of lettuce dressed in oil and vinegar.

But the most striking foreign accent in any Austrian province is the Balkan tint over the Burgenland on Hungary's border. Here the Alps are forgotten in vistas of steppelike plains; fir trees and the mountains' white water give way to rustling reeds around the huge, glassy Neusiedler Lake. Villages turn thatch-roofed and gray-steepled, with flocks of geese of flat, melancholy town commons. The men wear boots, breeches, and drooping mustaches. The women go babushkaed. You're this side of the Iron Curtain but just barely.

The Burgenland actually belonged to Hungary once, and so, in a restaurant, as gypsy violinists in satin blouses bend over you with czardas, you eat (what else?) *Paprika Schnitzel.* The Austrian recipe retains all the old Magyar savor, but tames things a little by using sweet paprika. The cook with a Hungarian soul can try the sharp variety. But cautiously. When Hungarians say "sharp," they mean it. And even sweet paprika grows fiercer if you cook it longer or use more of it.

## PAPRIKA SCHNITZEL

Salt each veal slice. Dip one side only in flour, shaking off excess. Fry in deep, smoking-hot lard (the traditional Hungarian cooking fat) (385°-390°F. on a frying thermometer) for 2 to 3 minutes on each side, floured side first, or until golden brown. Put 2 tablespoons of same lard in skillet; fry small onion, chopped, until soft; add veal; sprinkle with ½ teaspoon Hungarian sweet paprika (or more if desired) and 1 teaspoon all-purpose flour. Keep turning veal, blending paprika and flour with lard and onions, for 3 minutes (longer for spicier schnitzel). Add to skillet ½ cup or more heavy cream and about 1 tablespoon beef bouillon or soup stock (enough to give sauce the consistency you prefer). Keep mixing until sauce is hot and all ingredients are well blended. Serve schnitzel, smothered in sauce, with broad noodles.

For an even more Hungarian platter, garnish with strips of fiery red pepper and you have *Debrecziner Schnitzel,* named for a town in Hungary.

## SCHNITZEL FLORENTINE

Cover a mound of freshly cooked spinach with *Natur Schnitzel.* Over schnitzel, pour hollandaise sauce into which grated Parmesan cheese has been blended. Oven-brown the whole thing.

To set the stage, you must know that in Vienna, if a Hapsburg prince once wined and dined his mistress in a certain restaurant, the place was crested with chic forevermore. The more famous the romance, the more brilliant the dining room that beheld it. Imagine, then, the hallowed elegance of the Kerzenstuberl. Its red-damask walls, silk-tapestry chairs, and cyrstal chandeliers have framed the midnight suppers of Crown Prince Rudolph and Countess Marie Vetsera, the legendary lovers who killed themselves at Mayerling.

The restaurant determined to match its menu to its pedigree, to banish the homely, native schnitzel in favor of a purely international cuisine. The edict lasted one week. Outraged Viennese set up such a clamor that the exiles were back before you could say Kerzenstuberl.

That is, a compromise was effected. The menu still doesn't list schnitzels openly, but there's a discreet little note, "Our chefs are ready at any time to execute your culinary wishes," that most Austrians take to mean "your schnitzel wishes." In a bow to the gourmet atmosphere, however, they order such stylish variations as the *Champignon Schnitzel.*

## CHAMPIGNON SCHNITZEL

Prepare *Natur Schnitzel.* Remove veal from skillet. Add butter and sauté fresh mushrooms, finely sliced lengthwise. Add ¼ cup heavy cream, blend well. Heat veal in sauce for 1 to 2 minutes. Serve with white rice and peas.

As I say, the menu doesn't list a single schnitzel. But there is something called *Piccata à la Kerzenstuberl* and What would *you* say it is?

## PICCATA À LA KERZENSTUBERL

Prepare *Champignon Schnitzel,* but mushrooms are diced (instead of sliced) and sautéed with an equal amount of diced boiled ham. Serve, smothered in mushroom-ham-cream sauce, with Austrian *Risibisi*—boiled white rice mixed with cooked green peas.

Again not on the printed menu, but ready to fulfill the culinary wish of any Maharajah who wanders in, is the chef's supreme exotic triumph, the *Curry Schnitzel.*

## CURRY SCHNITZEL

Prepare *Natur Schnitzel.* Remove veal from skillet. Add butter and sauté ½ onion, chopped, until soft. Replace veal; sprinkle with ¼ teaspoon curry powder (or more if desired) and 1 teaspoon all-purpose flour. Keep turning veal, blending curry and flour with butter and onion for about 3 minutes. Add ½ cup or more heavy cream and about 1 tablespoon beef bouillon or soup stock (enough to give sauce consistency you prefer). Keep mixing until sauce is hot and well blended. Serve schnitzel, smothered in sauce, topped with sautéed chopped almonds, with side dishes of chutney and sautéed sliced bananas.

# AVOCADO (Alligator pear)—This fruit is native

to Central or South America and references to it have been found in records kept by Spanish explorers as far back as 1519. The word is said to come from the Central American Indian word *ahuacatl*, which was modified by the Spanish explorers into *aguacate*. More and more North Americans have become enchanted by the delicately nutty flavor and buttery texture. Today avocado orchards flourish along our southern coast from California to Florida, especially in the Rio Grande Valley. The fruit may vary from the small round ball variety, shiny green, to the huge pear-shaped, slightly russet-coated fruit; the fruit may weigh from five to six ounces to two to three pounds. Avocados have a coarse shell-like skin or a smooth thin skin, depending on the variety. They are yellowish-green with a fairly firm flesh and a single large seed, round or conical. If you enjoy cultivating house plants, you'll use the seed to add to your indoor garden. With three toothpicks, prop it pointed end up on the rim of a glass of water until roots form. Then plant it in soil, stand in a warm sunny spot, and water it frequently. The result: a beautiful, lush, leafy plant.

*Availability*—The peak period is from December to April, with smaller amounts available the remainder of the year. Florida and California produce most of the crop.

*Purchasing Guide*—Select fruit that is heavy and fairly firm or just beginning to soften. The skin should be uniform in color and without cracks, bruises, or punctures. When touched, the avocado skin should yield to light pressure. They are sold by the pound or by the unit.

*Storage*—If firm to hard, keep at room temperature for two to three days until soft to the touch. An hour or two before using, put in your refrigerator, but away from the cooling unit. Never put avocados in the refrigerator unless they are ripe.

Room temperature: 1 to 2 days after they are ripe
Refrigerator shelf, whole: 2 to 4 weeks
Refrigerator shelf, cut and covered: 1 to 2 days
Refrigerator frozen-food compartment, prepared for freezing: 2 months
Freezer, prepared for freezing: 1 year

*Nutritive Food Values*—Avocados offer fair amounts of thiamine, riboflavin, and vitamin C. Unlike most fruits, they have a high fat content which varies from less than 5 per cent to more than 20 per cent.
1 avocado, 3⅛-inch diameter = 370 calories

*Basic Preparation*—Cut in half lengthwise, using a stainless-steel knife. (Always use stainless-steel utensils when cutting or mashing avocados, to keep them from darkening.) Twist halves slightly to get them apart, and remove seed. If you are removing the skin, place the shell cut side down on a counter. Cut off the skin with a paring knife or pry it off, using a teaspoon with the back of the spoon under the skin. Avocados are usually used raw

or baked. Halves can be sliced, diced, mashed, or sieved. Since avocados discolor quickly, sprinkle immediately with lemon juice, weak cider vinegar, or one of the commercial fruit-darkening preventatives.

*To Freeze*—Use ripe avocados free of dark blemishes. Cut in half, peel and remove seed. Mash well and blend with ⅛ teaspoon ascorbic acid to 1 quart mashed avocado. Package with 1-inch headspace and freeze.

# APPETIZERS

## GUACAMOLE

1 large ripe avocado
2 teaspoons fresh lemon juice
1 teaspoon chili powder
1 garlic clove, crushed
2 tablespoons mayonnaise
Salt

Peel avocado and remove seed. Mash pulp completely. Add lemon juice and mix well. Add chili powder, garlic, and mayonnaise. Season. Serve with king-size corn chips. Makes about 1½ cups.

## AVOCADO DIP

1 large ripe avocado
¼ teaspoon onion juice
Dash each of pepper, curry powder, and cayenne
1 tablespoon white wine vinegar
¼ teaspoon salt

Peel avocado and remove seed. Mash to smooth pulp and mix with remaining ingredients. Use as dip for potato chips, cauliflowerets, diagonally cut carrot slices, or tiny cheese crackers. For variety, use horseradish or Worcestershire in place of curry powder. Makes 1 cup.

# SOUP

## CHILLED AVOCADO SOUP

1 large ripe avocado
2 cans clear consommé madrilène
1 cup dairy sour cream
Salt, chili powder, and cayenne to taste
Grated onion
Minced fresh dill or crushed dillseed

Peel avocado and remove seed. Whirl until smooth in electric blender or force through sieve or food mill. Mix with consommé and sour cream. Season with salt, chili powder, cayenne, and onion. Chill until mixture jells. Serve in cups; garnish with dill. Makes 4 servings.

# SALADS

## AVOCADO CRAB MEAT SALAD À LA RITZ

½ cup diced cooked lobster
1 cup flaked cooked crab meat
1 tablespoon chopped peeled fresh tomato
½ teaspoon chopped chives or green onion tops
¼ teaspoon dried tarragon
½ teaspoon salt
3 tablespoons mayonnaise
¼ teaspoon chili powder
1 large ripe avocado, halved and seeded
4 strips pimiento
lettuce

Combine first 8 ingredients and toss gently to mix. Spoon mixture into avocado halves. Top each with 2 crossed strips of pimiento. Serve on lettuce. Makes 2 servings.

## AVOCADOS WITH HAM SALAD

1 cup diced boiled ham
4 radishes, thinly sliced
⅓ cup thinly sliced water chestnuts
6 or 7 small fresh mushrooms, sliced
⅓ cup mayonnaise
3 ripe medium avocados
Lemon juice
Shredded salad greens (optional)

Mix first 5 ingredients. Peel avocados, cut in half and pour a little lemon juice over each. Fill with ham mixture, and serve on salad greens, if desired. Makes 6 servings.

## PUERTO RICAN AVOCADO SHRIMP BOATS

2 large ripe avocados
Lemon juice
2 medium tomatoes
1 teaspoon sugar
½ teaspoon salt
Pepper
⅛ teaspoon ground turmeric
1 teaspoon chopped parsley
2 green onions, minced
Sprig of fresh mint, chopped fine
½ tablespoon cider vinegar
½ tablespoon water
Dash cayenne
2 tablespoons French dressing
1 cup cooked shrimps
Watercress

Halve avocados and remove seed. Scoop out pulp and dice. Rub shells with lemon juice and set aside. Peel and chop tomatoes. Mix all remaining ingredients except shrimps and watercress. Pour over tomatoes and avocado pieces. Mix carefully. Fold in shrimps. Pile mixture in avocado shells. Top with watercress sprigs. Chill. Makes 4 servings.

Chilled Avocado Soup

Puerto Rican Avocado Shrimp Boats

## CHICKEN AVOCADO SALAD

2 cups finely chopped cold cooked chicken
½ cup finely chopped celery
Salt and pepper
1 tablespoon fresh lemon juice
Dash of hot pepper sauce
½ cup mayonnaise
2 large ripe avocados
2 hard-cooked eggs, sliced

Combine all ingredients except avocados and eggs. Halve avocados and remove seeds. Scoop out pulp and reserve avocado shells. Dice pulp and add to chicken mixture. Fill shells with mixture. Top with egg slices. Makes 4 servings.

## AVOCADO GELATIN SALAD

2 envelopes unflavored gelatin
¼ cup cold water
1 cup boiling water
Juice of 1 lemon
Dash of hot pepper sauce
1 teaspoon salt
⅛ teaspoon pepper
1 teaspoon onion juice
2½ cups mashed avocado pulp (2 or 3 avocados)
1 cup dairy sour cream
1 cup mayonnaise or salad dressing

Soften gelatin in cold water for 5 minutes. Dissolve gelatin in boiling water. Add lemon juice, hot pepper sauce, salt, pepper, and onion juice. Cool. Stir in mashed avocado, sour cream, and mayonnaise. Beat to blend. Pour into 1½-quart mold. Chill until firm. Unmold and serve on greens. Makes 8 servings.

Avocado Lime Pie

## CRABMEAT STUFFED AVOCADOS

Stuff avocado halves with canned or thawed frozen crabmeat. Squeeze a little fresh lime juice over top. Put a dollop of mayonnaise on top of each, and sprinkle with shredded hard-cooked egg yolk. Serve with cooked green beans marinated in a little French dressing. Garnish with ripe olives, and serve with additional French dressing, if desired. Makes 6 servings.

# DESSERTS

## AVOCADO CITRUS DESSERT

Halve unpeeled avocados and remove seeds. Sprinkle avocados with lemon juice and fill cavity with grapefruit or orange segments. Add honey to taste and garnish with fresh mint. This can be served as a salad, too.

## AVOCADO CREAM

2 ripe avocados
Juice of 1 lemon
¼ cup sugar

Halve avocados and remove seeds. Peel avocados and slice into blender containing lemon juice. Add sugar. Whirl until smooth. Fill punch cups or dessert dishes. Chill thoroughly. Makes 4 servings.

## AVOCADO LIME PIE

1 large ripe avocado
1 can (14 ounces) sweetened condensed milk
Grated rind of 1 lime
½ cup fresh lime juice
2 egg yolks
Dash of salt
1 baked 9-inch pie shell
Avocado prepared for garnish
Chopped nuts

Mash avocado well (there should be about 1¼ cups). Combine sweetened condensed milk, lime rind, lime juice, well beaten egg yolks, and salt. Stir until mixture is thickened. Fold in avocado. Turn into baked pastry shell and chill for several hours. Garnish with avocado balls. (Cut avocado in half and scoop out balls with melon cutter. Cover with fresh lemon juice.) Sprinkle with chopped nuts. Makes 6 to 8 servings.

# 50 Well-balanced Meals

It's no small job to balance a menu—juggling color, texture, flavor, and nutrition until you have just the right mix for both maximum appeal and food value. It's no small job, but it's a mighty important one for you and your family. In planning these menus for you, we realized the many variables involved—the contents of different brands of the same or similar packaged foods, the way you cook and season certain foods, the way foods can be doctored up at the table, the size of servings, and so forth. So our menus are at best basic guidelines. You'll know to add milk for children or to substitute low-fat or diet foods for anyone with special needs. We've planned breakfasts and brunches, luncheons and suppers, and dinners. They're not meant to go together; each is a properly balanced meal in itself; and, as a note of economy, all the meals are not necessarily based on meat.

## BREAKFASTS AND BRUNCHES

| | | | | |
|---|---|---|---|---|
| Fruit Cup<br>Sautéed Canadian Bacon<br>or Pork Roll<br>Corn Fritters<br>Toasted Cheese Bread<br>Currant Jelly | Fresh Pineapple Cubes<br>Ham Croquettes<br>Creamed Eggs<br>Toasted Wheat-Germ Bread | Tangerine Juice<br>Poached Eggs on Toast<br>with Cheese Sauce<br>Extra Toast | Sliced Oranges with<br>Whole-Cranberry Sauce<br>Hot Whole-Wheat Cereal<br>Milk<br>French Omelet With<br>Mushroom Sauce<br>Toasted English Muffins | Grapefruit Sections<br>with Grape Juice<br>Eggs Benedict Mock Hollandaise<br>Coffee Cake |
| Pear Slices with<br>Fresh or Frozen Strawberries<br>Western Sandwiches<br>Lettuce Wedges<br>Thousand Island Dressing | Sliced Bananas with<br>Thawed Frozen Raspberries<br>Cheese Soufflé<br>Bran Muffins | Vegetable Juice<br>Chicken Livers and<br>Scrambled Eggs<br>Whole-Wheat Toast<br>Marmalade | Crisp Bacon<br>Creamed Celery and Mushrooms<br>Broiled Tomato Halves<br>Toasted Oatmeal Bread<br>Apricot Preserves | Sliced Oranges<br>Honeyed Stewed Prunes<br>on Oatmeal with<br>Skim Milk<br>(An easy, low-cholesterol menu) |

## LUNCHES AND SUPPERS

| | | | | |
|---|---|---|---|---|
| Tamale Pie<br>Broccoli<br>Lettuce Wedges<br>Russian Dressing<br>Frozen Peaches<br>Vanilla Cookies | Scalloped Corned Beef<br>and Potatoes<br>Parsley Carrots<br>Coleslaw<br>Honeyed Stewed Prunes | New England Style<br>Fish Chowder<br>Assorted Crackers<br>Mixed Green Salad with<br>Cheese Cubes<br>Hot Corn Bread<br>Baked Caramel Custard | Sliced Ham and Gruyere Cheese<br>on Rye Bread<br>Mustard Butter<br>Carrot, Celery Sticks<br>Apple-Cream Pudding | Thermos of Hot<br>Chile con Carne with Beans<br>Large Corn Chips<br>Vegetable Cottage Cheese<br>Banana<br>Molasses Macaroons |
| Thermos of Hot<br>Vegetable Soup<br>Crisp Whole-Wheat Crackers<br>Cold Chicken<br>Fresh Apple<br>Plain Yogurt<br>Sesame Candy Bar | Baked Sausage Patties<br>Baked Yams<br>Brussel Sprouts<br>Sautéed Apple Rings<br>Cream Puffs | Thermos of Clam Chowder<br>Cheese Cubes Rolled<br>in Chopped Chives<br>Peanut Butter, Bacon, and<br>Lettuce Sandwiches on<br>Pumpernickel<br>Small Can of Fruit<br>Small Box of Raisins | Sliced Liverwurst and Salami<br>Baked Macaroni and Cheese<br>Celery Hearts, Olives,<br>and Radishes<br>Sherbet with Grape | Sliced Turkey and Gravy on<br>Hot Whole-Wheat Biscuits<br>Mixed Green Salad<br>Baked Fresh Pears |
| Hot Tomato Juice<br>Curried Chicken Salad<br>Watercress<br>Hot Crescent Rolls<br>Orange Soufflé | Mulligatawny Soup<br>Pear-Peanut Salad<br>Whole-Wheat French or<br>Italian Bread<br>Fudge Sundae | Chicken and Rice Soup<br>Chef's Salad: Corned<br>Beef, Swiss Cheese, Tongue,<br>and Eggs<br>Assorted Olives<br>Crisp Rye Crackers and<br>Whole-Wheat Melba Toast<br>Cherry Cobbler | Chile Con Carne on<br>Corn Bread Squares<br>Shredded Lettuce, Sliced Egg<br>Green Pepper, and<br>Pimiento Salad<br>Diced Fresh Pineapple<br>Coconut Cookies | Split Pea Soup<br>Shrimp Salad, Watercress<br>and Other Greens<br>Hot French-Style<br>Croissant Rolls<br>Cheesecake |
| Corn Chowder with<br>Oyster Crackers<br>Hamburgers with French-Fried<br>Onion Rings on Toasted<br>Rye Bread<br>Carrot Curls, Radishes<br>Orange Ambrosia | Clear Tomato Soup<br>Fluffy Bacon-Cheese Omelet<br>Hashed Brown Potatoes<br>Green Peas<br>Canned Pears<br>Coconut Cookies | Cream of Spinach Soup<br>Garlic Croutons<br>Tuna-Celery Salad on<br>Sprouted Rye Bread<br>Olives<br>Apple Crisp | Spaghetti and Meatballs<br>Grated Cheese<br>Romaine Hearts<br>Brown-and-Serve<br>Sesame Italian Bread<br>Peach Gelatin | Vegetable Soup<br>Tuna Fish Salad<br>Corn-Molasses Bread<br>Jellied Fruit, Whipped Cream |

# BUFFETS

Hot Individual Ham Loaves
Apple Chutney
Corn Pudding
Buttered Cabbage
Artichoke Hearts on Greens,
French Dressing
Orange Shortcake

Shrimp Curry
Brown Rice with Raisins
Condiments: Cashews,
Chopped Green Peppers,
Fruit Chutney
Cold Marinated Broccoli
Spears with Pimiento
Indian Breads or Breadsticks
Fruit Plate: Sliced Fresh
Pineapple, Strawberries, and
Canned Apricots or Peaches
Lemon Sherbet

Beef Stroganoff
Buttered Green (Spinach)
Noodles with Poppy Seeds
Baked Hubbard Squash
Endive Salad,
Garlic Dressing
Meringues with Ice Cream
and Canned Cherry Pie
Filling

Antipasto Plate: Tuna,
Hard Salami, Pimientos
Celery Hearts
Chicken Marengo
Noodles Italian Style
Spiced Peaches and Pears
Toasted, Garlic-Buttered,
Whole-Wheat Italian Bread
Spumoni or Tortoni
Ladyfingers

Poached Salmon Steaks with
Dill Mayonnaise
Parsley Potatoes
Buttered Spinach
Watercress and
Raw Mushroom Salad
Pineapple Upside-Down Cake

# DINNERS

Roast Beef
Glazed Carrots
Creamed Broccoli
Lettuce Wedges,
Russian Dressing
Whole-Wheat French Bread
Lemon Chiffon Pie

Baked Chicken and
Sweet Potatoes
Wax Beans
Cranberry-Orange Relish
Applesauce
Gingersnaps

Roast Duckling
Sauerkraut
Parsnips Cooked in
Orange Juice
Olives, Celery Hearts
Tapioca Cream with
Frozen Strawberries

Roast Lamb Shoulder
with Herbs
Pan-Browned Potatoes
Broccoli
Waldorf Salad
Vanilla Ice Cream
Butterscotch Sauce

Grilled Ham Slice
Pineapple Chutney
Mashed Potatoes
Green Beans and Mushrooms
Avocado-Watercress Salad
Cream Puffs with Ice Cream
and Butterscotch Sauce

Simmered, Smoked
or Corned Tongue
Mashed Hubbard Squash
Curried Brussels Sprouts and
Cauliflower Casserole
Black Olives, Celery Hearts
Hot Whole-Wheat Biscuits
Lemon Pudding with
Mandarin Orange Segments

Ground Beef-Potato Casserole
Steamed Cabbage Wedges
Celery Stuffed with
Pimiento Cheese
Deep Dish Blueberry Pie

Boiled Beef with
Horseradish Sauce
Mashed Potatoes
Glazed Carrots
Cabbage-Pepper Slaw
Chocolate Layer Cake

Creamed Salt Cod
Baked Potatoes
Chopped Spinach
Orange-Celery Salad
Raspberry Gelatin

Simmered Smoked Pork
Shoulder or Boneless Butt
Parsley Potatoes
Sliced Cauliflower and Peas
Jellied Cranberry Salad
Pound Cake

# PARTY REFRESHMENTS

## Evening Buffet

Fresh Pineapple Cubes and
Strawberries on
Cocktail Picks in Ice Bowl
Canned Eggplant Caponata
Roast Fillet of Beef
Fusilli (Corkscrew Noodles)
with Mornay Sauce
Sautéed Mushrooms
Chocolate Ice Cream Roll

## Refreshments for Small Informal Group

Cheese Fondue
Endive-Lettuce Salad
Chunks of French or
Italian Bread
Fresh Fruit Cup
Sugar Cookies

## Late Supper

Cold Seafood Platter
Cocktail Sauce
Hot Pea Soup with Sausages
Raw Relish Plate
Caraway Rye Toast
Tiny Hot Biscuits
Chocolate-Almond Sundae

## After Theater Supper

Quiche Lorraine
Jellied Tomato-Celery-Radish
Salad, Greens
Marinated Asparagus Spears
Fresh Berries with Sour
Cream and Brown Sugar
Butter Cookies

## Teenage Bash

Frankfurter Chunks in
Barbecue Sauce on
Toasted Whole-Wheat Buns
Frozen, Crinkle Cut French-Fried Potatoes
Cabbage-Pepper Slaw
Peanut-Marshmallow Sundae
Apples

# Table of Equivalents

few grains = less than 1/8 teaspoon (tsp.)

3 tsp. = 1 Tablespoon (Tb.)

4 Tb. = ¼ cup

8 Tb. = ½ cup

5 Tb. plus 1 tsp. = ⅓ cup

16 Tb. = 1 cup

1 cup = ½ pint (pt.)

2 cups = 1 pt.

4 cups = 1 quart (qt.)

4 qts. = 1 gallon

16 ounces (oz.) = 1 pound (dry weight)

16 oz. = 1 pt. (liquid measure)